PILOT'S HANDBOOK
of
Aeronautical Knowledge

Revised 1997

U.S. DEPARTMENT OF TRANSPORTATION
FEDERAL AVIATION ADMINISTRATION
Flight Standards Service

PREFACE

The Pilot's Handbook of Aeronautical Knowledge provids basic knowledge that is essential for pilots. This handbook introduces pilots to the broad spectrum of knowledge that will be needed as they progress in their pilot training. Except for the Code of Federal Regulations pertinent to civil aviation, most of the knowledge areas applicable to pilot certification are presented. This handbook is useful to beginning pilots, as well as those pursuing more advanced pilot certificates.

This advisory circular supersedes AC 61-23B, Pilot's Handbook of Aeronautical Knowledge, dated 1980.

Comments regarding this handbook should be sent to U.S. Department of Transportation, Federal Aviation Administration, Airman Testing Standards Branch, AFS-630, P.O. Box 25082, Oklahoma City, OK 73125.

This publication may be purchased from the Superintendent of Documents, P.O. Box 371954, Pittsburgh, PA 15250-7954, or from U.S. Government Printing Office bookstores located in major cities throughout the United States.

AC 00-2, Advisory Circular Checklist, transmits the current status of FAA advisory circulars and other flight information and publications. This checklist is free of charge and may be obtained by sending a request to U.S. Department of Transportation, Subsequent Distribution Office, SVC-121.23, Ardmore East Business Center, 3341 Q 75th Avenue, Landover, MD 20785. The checklist is also available on the Internet at http://www.faa.gov/abc/ac-chklst/actoc.htm

CONTENTS

CHAPTER 1—PRINCIPLES OF FLIGHT

INTRODUCTION 1-1

FORCES ACTING ON THE AIRPLANE IN FLIGHT 1-1
  Terms and Definitions 1-2
  Lift 1-3
  Gravity (Weight) 1-4
  Thrust 1-5
  Drag 1-5
      Induced Drag 1-5
      Parasite Drag 1-5
  Relationship Between Angle of Attack and Lift 1-6
  Relationship of Thrust and Drag in Straight-and-Level Flight 1-7
  Relationship Between Lift and Weight in Straight-and-Level Flight 1-7
  Factors Affecting Lift and Drag 1-7
      Effect of Wing Area on Lift and Drag 1-7
      Effect of Airfoil Shape on Lift and Drag 1-7
      Effect of Wing Design on Stall 1-8
      Effect of Airspeed on Lift and Drag 1-8
      Effect of Air Density on Lift and Drag 1-8

TURNING TENDENCY (TORQUE EFFECT) 1-9
  Torque Reaction 1-10
  Spiraling Slipstream 1-10
  Gyroscopic Precession 1-10
  Asymmetric Propeller Loading ("P" Factor) 1-10
  Corrections for Turning Tendency or Torque During Flight 1-11

AIRPLANE STABILITY 1-11
  Positive Stability 1-11
  Neutral Stability 1-11
  Negative Stability 1-12
  Longitudinal Stability about the Lateral Axis 1-13
  Longitudinal Control (Pitch) about the Lateral Axis 1-14
  Lateral Stability about the Longitudinal Axis 1-15
      Dihedral   1-15
      Sweepback 1-15
      Keel Effect 1-15
  Lateral Control about the Longitudinal Axis 1-16
  Lateral Stability or Instability in Turns 1-16
  Directional Stability about the Vertical Axis (YAW) 1-16
  Directional Control about the Vertical Axis (YAW) 1-17

LOADS AND LOAD FACTORS 1-17
  Load Factors and Airplane Design 1-18
  Effect of Turns on Load Factor 1-18
  Effect of Load Factor on Stalling Speed 1-19
  Effect of Speed on Load Factor 1-20
  Effect of Flight Maneuvers on Load Factor 1-20

Effect of Turbulence on Load Factor 1-21
Determining Load Factors in Flight 1-21
Forces Acting on the Airplane when at Airspeeds Slower than Cruise 1-22
Forces in a Climb 1-22
Forces in a Glide 1-23
Turns During Flight 1-24

CHAPTER 2—AIRPLANES AND ENGINES

INTRODUCTION 2-1

AIRPLANE STRUCTURE 2-1

FLIGHT CONTROL SYSTEMS 2-1
Wing Flaps 2-2
Landing Gear 2-2
Conventional Landing Gear 2-2
Tricycle Landing Gear 2-2

ELECTRICAL SYSTEM 2-3

ENGINE OPERATION 2-5
How an Engine Operates 2-6
Cooling System 2-7
Ignition System 2-8
Fuel System 2-9
Fuel Tanks, Selectors, Strainers, and Drains 2-9
Fuel Primer 2-9
Fuel Pressure Gauge 2-9
Induction, Carburetion, and Injection Systems 2-9
Carburetor System 2-9
Mixture Control 2-10
Carburetor Icing 2-10
Conditions Conducive to Carburetor Icing 2-10
Indications of Carburetor Icing 2-11
Use of Carburetor Heat 2-11
Carburetor Air Temperature Gauge 2-11
Outside Air Temperature Gauge 2-12
Fuel Injection System 2-12
Proper Fuel is Essential 2-12
Fuel Contamination 2-13
Refueling Procedures 2-13
Oil System 2-14

PROPELLER 2-14
Fixed-Pitch Propeller 2-15
Controllable-Pitch Propellers 2-16

STARTING THE ENGINE 2-17
Engines Equipped with a Starter 2-17
Engines Not Equipped with a Starter 2-17
Idling the Engine During Flight 2-18

Exhaust gas temperature gauge 2-18

Aircraft documents, maintenance, and inspections 2-18
    Aircraft Owner Responsibilities 2-18
    Certificate of Aircraft Registration 2-19
    Airworthiness Certificate 2-19
    Aircraft Maintenance 2-20
    Inspections 2-21
        Annual Inspection 2-21
        100-Hour Inspection 2-21
        Other Inspection Programs 2-21
        Preflight Inspection 2-21
    Preventive Maintenance 2-21
    Repairs and Alterations 2-22
    Deferred Repair 2-22
    Special Flight Permits 2-22
    Airworthiness Directives 2-22

CHAPTER 3—FLIGHT INSTRUMENTS

Introduction 3-1

The pitot-static system and associated instruments 3-1
    Impact Pressure Chamber and Lines 3-1
    Static Pressure Chamber and Lines 3-1
    Altimeter 3-2
        Principle of Operation 3-2
        Effect of Nonstandard Pressure and Temperature 3-2
        Setting the Altimeter 3-3
    Types of Altitude 3-4
    Vertical Speed Indicator 3-4
        Principle of Operation 3-4
    Airspeed Indicator 3-5
    Kinds of Airspeed 3-5
        Indicated Airspeed 3-5
        Calibrated Airspeed 3-5
        True Airspeed 3-5
        Airspeed Indicator Markings 3-6
        Other Airspeed Limitations 3-6

Gyroscopic flight instruments 3-6
    Sources of Power for Gyroscopic Operation 3-7
        Vacuum or Pressure System 3-7
        Engine-Driven Vacuum Pump 3-7
    Gyroscopic Principles 3-7
    Turn Coordinator 3-8
    The Heading Indicator 3-8
    The Attitude Indicator 3-9

MAGNETIC COMPASS 3-10
    Compass Errors 3-11
        Variation 3-11
        Deviation 3-11
    Using the Magnetic Compass 3-12

CHAPTER 4—WEIGHT AND BALANCE AND AIRPLANE PERFORMANCE

INTRODUCTION 4-1

WEIGHT CONTROL 4-1
    Effects of Weight 4-1
    Weight Changes 4-2

BALANCE, STABILITY, AND CENTER OF GRAVITY 4-2
    Effects of Adverse Balance 4-2
    Management of Weight and Balance Control 4-3
    Terms and Definitions 4-3
    Control of Loading—General Aviation Airplanes 4-4
    Basic Principles of Weight and Balance Computations 4-4
    Weight and Balance Restrictions 4-5

DETERMINING LOADED WEIGHT AND CENTER OF GRAVITY 4-6
    Computational Method 4-6
    Graph Method 4-6
    Table Method 4-8
    Shifting, Adding, and Removing Weight 4-8
        Weight Shifting 4-8
        Weight Addition or Removal 4-9

AIRPLANE PERFORMANCE 4-10
    Density Altitude 4-10
        Effect of Density Altitude on Engine Power and Propeller Efficiency 4-10
    Humidity 4-11
    Effect of Wind on Airplane Performance 4-11
    Runway Surface Condition and Gradient 4-11
    Ground Effect 4-11
    Use of Performance Charts 4-11
    Interpolation 4-12
    Performance Charts 4-13
    Density Altitude Charts 4-13
    Takeoff Data Charts 4-14
    Climb and Cruise Performance Data 4-15
    Landing Performance Data 4-16
    Combined Graphs 4-16

CHAPTER 5—WEATHER

INTRODUCTION 5-1

OBSERVATIONS 5-1
    Surface Aviation Weather Observations 5-1
    Upper Air Observations 5-1
    Radar Observation 5-1

SERVICE OUTLETS 5-2
    FAA Flight Service Station (FSS) 5-2
    Pilot's Automatic Telephone Weather Answering System (PATWAS) 5-2
    Transcribed Information Briefing Service (TIBS) 5-2
    Direct User Access Terminal Service (DUATS) 5-2
    Transcribed Weather Broadcast (TWEB) 5-2

WEATHER BRIEFING 5-2
    Standard Briefing 5-2
    Abbreviated Briefing 5-3
    Outlook Briefing 5-3

NATURE OF THE ATMOSPHERE 5-3
    Oxygen and the Human Body 5-4
    Significance of Atmospheric Pressure 5-4
        Measurement of Atmospheric Pressure 5-4
        Effect of Altitude on Atmospheric Pressure 5-4
        Effect of Altitude on Flight 5-4
        Effect of Differences in Air Density 5-6
        Pressure Recorded in "Millibars" 5-6
        Wind 5-6

THE CAUSE OF ATMOSPHERIC CIRCULATION 5-6
    Wind Patterns 5-7
    Convection Currents 5-8
        Effect of Obstructions on Wind 5-10
    Low-Level Wind Shear 5-11
    Wind and Pressure Representation on Surface Weather Maps 5-12

MOISTURE AND TEMPERATURE 5-14
    Relative Humidity 5-14
    Temperature/Dewpoint Relationship 5-14
    Methods by Which Air Reaches the Saturation Point 5-14
    Effect of Temperature on Air Density 5-14
    Effect of Temperature on Flight 5-14
    Effect of High Humidity on Air Density 5-15
    Effect of High Humidity on Flight 5-15
    Dew and Frost 5-15
    Fog 5-15
    Clouds 5-15
    Ceiling 5-18
    Visibility 5-19
    Precipitation 5-19

AIR MASSES AND FRONTS 5-19
  Warm Front 5-19
    Flight Toward an Approaching Warm Front 5-20
  Cold Front 5-21
    Fast-Moving Cold Fronts 5-21
    Flight Toward an Approaching Cold Front 5-21
    Comparison of Cold Fronts with Warm Fronts 5-22
  Wind Shifts 5-22
  Occluded Front 5-22

AVIATION WEATHER REPORTS, FORECASTS, AND WEATHER CHARTS 5-24
  Aviation Weather Reports 5-25
    Aviation Routine Weather Report (METAR) 5-25
    Pilot Weather Reports (PIREPs) 5-28
    Radar Weather Reports (RAREPs) 5-28
  Aviation Forecasts 5-29
    Terminal Aerodrome Forecasts (TAF) 5-29
    Area Forecast (FA) 5-30
    In-Flight Weather Advisories 5-31
    Significant Meteorological Information (SIGMET) 5-31
    Airmen's Meteorological Information (AIRMET) 5-32
    Convective Significant Meteorological Information 5-32
    Winds and Temperatures Aloft Forecast (FD) 5-32
  Weather Charts 5-32
    Surface Analysis Chart 5-33
    Weather Depiction Chart 5-34
    Radar Summary Chart 5-34
    Significant Weather Prognostic Charts 5-34

CHAPTER 6—AIRPORT OPERATIONS

INTRODUCTION 6-1

TYPES OF AIRPORTS 6-1
  Controlled Airport 6-1
  Uncontrolled Airport 6-1

SOURCES FOR AIRPORT DATA 6-1
  Aeronautical Charts 6-1
  Airport/Facility Directory (A/FD) 6-1
  Notices to Airmen (NOTAMs) 6-3

AIRPORT MARKINGS AND SIGNS 6-3
  Runway Markings 6-3
  Taxiway Markings 6-4
  Other Markings 6-4
  Airport Signs 6-4

Airport lighting 6-4

Airport Beacon 6-5
Approach Light Systems 6-6
Visual Glideslope Indicators 6-6
Visual Approach Slope Indicator (VASI) 6-6
Other Glidepath Systems 6-6
Runway Lighting 6-7
Runway End Identifier Lights (REIL) 6-7
Runway Edge Lights 6-7
In-Runway Lighting 6-7
Control of Airport Lighting 6-8
Taxiway Lights 6-8
Obstruction Lights 6-8

Wind direction indicators 6-8

Radio communications 6-8

Radio License 6-9
Radio Equipment 6-9
Radio Procedures 6-10
Lost Communication Procedures 6-10

AIR TRAFFIC SERVICES 6-11

Primary Radar 6-11
Air Traffic Control Radar Beacon System (**ATCRBS**) 6-12
Transponder 6-12
Radar Traffic Information Service 6-12

WAKE TURBULENCE 6-13

Vortex Generation 6-13
Vortex Strength 5-13
Vortex Behavior 5-13
Vortex Avoidance Procedures 5-14

COLLISION AVOIDANCE 5-14

Clearing Procedures i-15

CHAPTER 7—AIRSPACE

Introduction 7-1

Controlled airspace 7-1

Class A Airspace 7-1
Class B Airspace 7-1
Class C Airspace 7-1
Class D Airspace 7-1
Class E Airspace 7-3

UNCONTROLLED AIRSPACE 7-3
    Class G Airspace 7-3

SPECIAL USE AIRSPACE 7-3
    Prohibited Areas 7-3
    Restricted Areas 7-3
    Warning Areas 7-3
    Military Operation Areas 7-4
    Alert Areas 7-4
    Controlled Firing Areas 7-4
    National Security Areas 7-4

OTHER AIRSPACE AREAS 7-4
    Airport Advisory Areas 7-4
    Military Training Routes 7-4
    Temporary Flight Restrictions 7-4
    Parachute Jump Areas 7-4
    Published VFR Routes 7-4

CHAPTER 8—NAVIGATION

INTRODUCTION 8-1

AERONAUTICAL CHARTS 8-1
    Sectional Charts 8-1
    Visual Flight Rule (VFR) Terminal Area Charts 8-1
    World Aeronautical Charts 8-1

LATITUDE AND LONGITUDE (MERIDIANS AND PARALLELS) 8-3
    Time Zones 8-3
    Measurement of Direction 8-4
    Variation 8-4
    Deviation 8-5

EFFECT OF WIND 8-7

BASIC CALCULATIONS 8-8
    Converting Minutes to Equivalent Hours 8-8
    Converting Knots to Miles Per Hour 8-9
    Fuel Consumption 8-9
    Flight Computers 8-9
    Plotter 8-9

PILOTAGE 8-9

DEAD RECKONING 8-11
    The Wind Triangle or Vector Analysis 8-11

FLIGHT PLANNING 8-13
    Assembling Necessary Material 8-13
    Weather Check 8-13
    Use of the Airport/Facility Directory 8-15
    Airplane Flight Manual or Pilot's Operating Handbook 8-15

CHARTING THE COURSE 8-15
    Steps in Charting the Course 8-15

FILING A VFR FLIGHT PLAN 8-17

RADIO NAVIGATION 8-18
    Very High Frequency (VHF) Omnidirectional Range (VOR) 8-18
        Using the VOR 8-20
        Tracking with Omni 8-20
    Tips on Using the VOR 8-21
    Automatic Direction Finder 8-22
    Other Navigational Systems 8-24

CHAPTER 9—AEROMEDICAL INFORMATION

INTRODUCTION 9-1

OBTAINING A MEDICAL CERTIFICATE 9-1

HEALTH FACTORS AFFECTING PILOT PERFORMANCE 9-2
    Alcohol 9-2
    Fatigue 9-2
    Anxiety 9-2
    Stress 9-2
    Emotion 9-3
    Tobacco 9-3

ENVIRONMENTAL FACTORS WHICH AFFECT PILOT PERFORMANCE 9-3
    Hypoxia 9-3
    Hyperventilation in Flight 9-4
    Middle Ear Discomfort or Pain 9-4
    Spatial Disorientation and Illusions in Flight 9-4
    Motion Sickness 9-5
    Carbon Monoxide Poisoning 9-5
    Decompression Sickness After Scuba Diving 9-5
    Vision in Flight 9-6

CHAPTER 1

PRINCIPLES OF FLIGHT

INTRODUCTION

There are certain laws of nature or physics that apply to any object that is lifted from the Earth and moved through the air. To analyze and predict airplane performance under various operating conditions, it is important that pilots gain as much knowledge as possible concerning the laws and principles that apply to flight.

The principles of flight discussed in this chapter are intended primarily for beginning pilots, and are not intended as a detailed and complete explanation of the complexities of aerodynamics.

FORCES ACTING ON THE AIRPLANE IN FLIGHT

When in flight, there are certain forces acting on the airplane. It is the primary task of a pilot to control these forces so as to direct the airplane's speed and flightpath in a safe and efficient manner. To do this the pilot must understand these forces and their effects. [Figure 1-1]

Among the aerodynamic forces acting on an airplane during flight, four are considered to be basic because they act upon the airplane during all maneuvers. These basic forces are :

- Lift
- Gravity (Weight)
- Thrust
- Drag

While in steady-state flight, the attitude, direction, and speed of the airplane will remain constant until one or more of the basic forces changes in magnitude. In unaccelerated flight (steady flight) the opposing forces are in equilibrium. Lift and thrust are considered as positive forces, while weight and drag are considered as negative forces, and the sum of the opposing forces is zero. In other words, lift equals weight and thrust equals drag.

When pressure is applied to the airplane controls, one or more of the basic forces changes in magnitude and becomes greater than the opposing force, causing the airplane to accelerate or move in the direction of the applied force. For example, if power is applied (increasing thrust) and altitude is maintained, the airplane will accelerate.

As speed increases, drag increases, until a point is reached where drag again equals thrust, and the airplane will continue in steady flight at a higher speed. As another example, if power is applied while in level flight, and a climb attitude is established, the force of lift would increase during the time back elevator pressure is applied; but after a steady-state climb is established, the force of lift would be approximately equal to the force of weight. The airplane does not climb because lift is greater than in level flight, but because thrust is greater than drag, and because a component of thrust is developed which acts upward, perpendicular to the flightpath.

Airplane designers make an effort to increase the performance of the airplane by increasing the efficiency of the desirable forces of lift and thrust while reducing, as much as possible, the undesirable forces of weight and drag. Nonetheless, compromise must be made to satisfy the function and desired performance of the airplane.

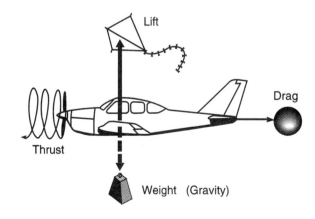

FIGURE 1-1.—Forces acting on the airplane in flight.

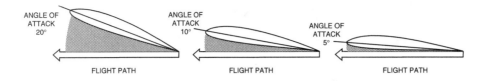

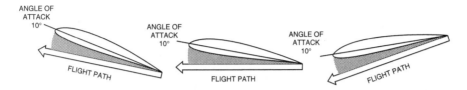

FIGURE 1-2.—(Above) The angle of attack is the angle between the wing chord and the flightpath. (Below) The angle of attack is always based on the flightpath, not the ground.

Terms and Definitions

Before discussing the four forces further, it will be helpful to define some of the terms used extensively in this section.

- **Acceleration**—the force involved in overcoming inertia, and which is defined as a change of velocity per unit of time.
- **Airfoil**—any surface designed to obtain reaction such as lift from the air through which it moves.
- **Angle of Attack**—the angle between the chord line of the wing and the direction of the relative wind. [Figure 1-2]
- **Angle of Incidence**—the angle formed by the chord line of the wing and the longitudinal axis of the airplane. It is determined during the design of the airplane and is the angle at which the wing is attached to the fuselage. Therefore, it is a fixed angle and cannot be changed by the pilot. Angle of incidence should not be confused with angle of attack. [Figure 1-3]

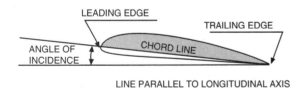

FIGURE 1-3.—Cross sectional view of an airfoil.

- **Camber**—the curvature of the airfoil from the leading edge to the trailing edge. "Upper camber" refers to the curvature of the upper surface; "lower camber" refers to the curvature of the lower surface; and "mean camber" refers to the mean line which is equidistant at all points between the upper and lower surfaces. [Figure 1-4]

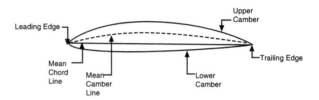

FIGURE 1-4.—Nomenclature of airfoil section.

- **Chord**—an imaginary straight line drawn from the leading edge to the trailing edge of a cross section of an airfoil. [Figure 1-3]
- **Component**—one of the various forces or parts of a combination of forces. Figure 1-5 illustrates the component of lift vertically and the component of drag horizontally.

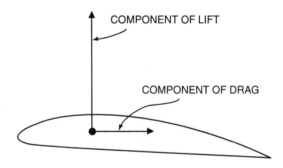

FIGURE 1-5.—Component forces.

- **Relative Wind**—the direction of the airflow produced by an object moving through the air. The relative wind for an airplane in flight flows in a direction parallel with and opposite to the direction of flight. Therefore, the actual flightpath of the airplane determines the direction of the relative wind. [Figure 1-6]
- **Speed**—the distance traveled in a given time.

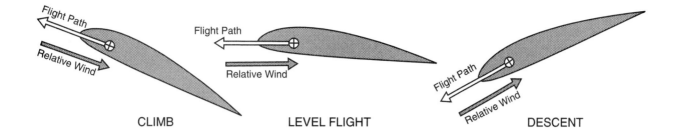

CLIMB   LEVEL FLIGHT   DESCENT

FIGURE 1-6.—Relationship between flightpath and relative wind.

• **Vectors**—the graphic representation of a force drawn in a straight line which indicates direction by an arrow and magnitude by its length. When an object is being acted upon by two or more forces, the combined effect of these forces may be represented by a resultant vector. After the vectors have been resolved, the resultant may be measured to determine the direction and magnitude of the combined forces. [Figure 1-7]

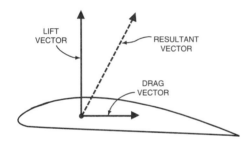

FIGURE 1-7.—Vectors.

• **Velocity**—the speed or rate of movement in a certain direction.
• **Wing Area**—the total surface of the wing (square feet), which includes control surfaces and may include wing area covered by the fuselage (main body of the airplane), and engine nacelles.
• **Wing Planform**—the shape or form of a wing as viewed from above. It may be long and tapered, short and rectangular, or various other shapes. [Figure 1-8]
• **Wingspan**—the maximum distance from wingtip to wingtip.

Lift

Lift is the upward force created by an airfoil when it is moved through the air. Although lift may be exerted to some extent by many external parts of the airplane, there are three principal airfoils on an airplane—the wing, propeller, and horizontal tail surfaces.

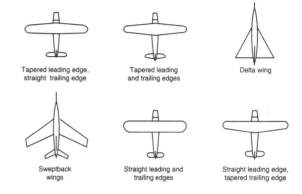

FIGURE 1-8.—Wing planforms.

To understand how an airplane wing produces lift, Bernoulli's Principle and one of Newton's Laws should be reviewed.

Bernoulli's Principle states in part that "the internal pressure of a fluid (liquid or gas) decreases at points where the speed of the fluid increases." In other words, high speed flow is associated with low pressure, and low speed flow with high pressure.

This principle is made apparent by changes in pressure of fluid flowing within a pipe where the inside diameter of the pipe decreases, similar to a venturi tube. [Figure 1-9]

In the wide section of the gradually narrowing pipe, the fluid flows at a lower speed, producing a higher pressure. As the pipe narrows, it still contains the same amount of fluid; but because the passageway is constricted, the fluid flows at a higher speed producing a lower pressure. This principle is also applicable to an airplane wing, since it is designed and constructed with a curve or camber. [Figure 1-9] When air flows along the upper wing surface, it travels a greater distance than the airflow along the lower wing surface. Therefore, as established by Bernoulli's Principle, the pressure above the wing is less than it is below the wing, generating a lift force over the upper curved surface of the wing in the direction of the low pressure.

BERNOULLI'S PRINCIPLE, which explains how lift is created by an airplane's wing, is depicted in these three diagrams. A fluid traveling through a constriction in a pipe (above) speeds up, and at the same time the pressure it exerts on the pipe decreases.

THE CONSTRICTED AIRFLOW shown here, formed by two opposed airplane wings, is analogous to the pinched-pipe situation at left: air moving between the wings accelerates, and this increase in speed results in lower pressure between the curved surfaces.

THE SAME PRINCIPLE applies when the air is disturbed by a single wing. The accelerating airflow over the top surface exerts less pressure than the airflow across the bottom. It is this continuing difference in pressure that creates and sustains lift.

FIGURE 1-9.—Bernoulli's Principle applied to airfoils.

Since for every action there is an equal and opposite reaction (Newton's Third Law of Motion), an additional upward force is generated as the lower surface of the wing deflects the air downward. Thus both the development of low pressure above the wing and reaction to the force and direction of air as it is deflected from the wing's lower surface contribute to the total lift generated. [Figure 1-10]

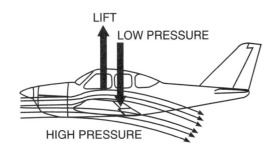

FIGURE 1-10.—Wing deflecting the air downward.

The amount of lift generated by the wing depends upon several factors:

- speed of the wing through the air,
- angle of attack,
- planform of the wing,
- wing area, and
- the density of the air.

Lift acts upward and perpendicular to the relative wind and to the wingspan. Although lift is generated over the entire wing, an imaginary point is established which represents the resultant of all lift forces. This point is called center of lift. [Figure 1-11]

This single point is the center of lift, sometimes referred to as the center of pressure. The location of the center of pressure relative to the center of gravity (weight) is very important from the standpoint of airplane stability. Stability will be covered in more detail later.

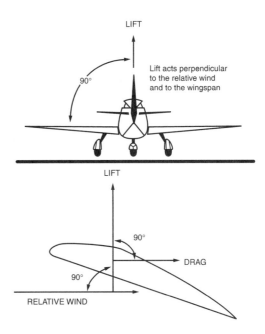

FIGURE 1-11.—Relationship between relative wind, lift, and drag.

Gravity (Weight)

Gravity is the downward force which tends to draw all bodies vertically toward the center of the Earth. The airplane's center of gravity (CG) is the point on the airplane at which all weight is considered to be concentrated. For example, if an airplane were suspended from a rope attached to the center of gravity, the airplane would balance. [Figure 1-12]

FIGURE 1-12.—Airplane suspended from the center of gravity.

The center of gravity is located along the longitudinal centerline of the airplane (imaginary line from the nose to the tail) and somewhere near the center of lift of the wing. The location of the center of gravity depends upon the location and weight of the load placed in the airplane. This is controlled through weight and balance calculations made by the pilot prior to flight. The exact location of the center of gravity is important during flight, because of its effect on airplane stability and performance.

Thrust

The propeller, acting as an airfoil, produces the thrust, or forward force that pulls (pushes) the airplane through the air. It receives its power directly from the engine, and is designed to displace a large mass of air to the rear. It is this rearward displacement that develops the forward thrust that carries the airplane through the air. This thrust must be strong enough to counteract the forces of drag and to give the airplane the desired forward motion. The direction of this thrust force is referred to as the thrust line.

Drag

Drag is the rearward acting force which resists the forward movement of the airplane through the air. Drag acts parallel to and in the same direction as the relative wind. [Figure 1-13]

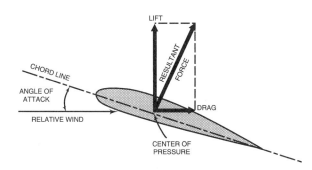

FIGURE 1-13.—Drag acts parallel to and in the same direction as the relative wind.

Every part of the airplane which is exposed to the air while the airplane is in motion produces some resistance and contributes to the total drag. Total drag may be classified into two main types:

- Induced Drag
- Parasite Drag

Induced Drag

Induced drag is the undesirable but unavoidable byproduct of lift, and increases in direct proportion to increases in angle of attack. The greater the angle of attack up to the critical angle, the greater the amount of lift developed, and the greater the induced drag. The airflow around the wing is deflected downward, producing a rearward component to the lift vector which is induced drag. The amount of air deflected downward decreases greatly at higher angles of attack; therefore, the higher the angle of attack or the slower the airplane is flown, the greater the induced drag.

Parasite Drag

Parasite drag is the resistance of the air produced by any part of the airplane that does not produce lift.

Several factors affect parasite drag. When each factor is considered independently, it must be assumed that other factors remain constant. These factors are:

- The more streamlined an object is, the less the parasite drag.
- The more dense the air moving past the airplane, the greater the parasite drag.
- The larger the size of the object in the airstream, the greater the parasite drag.
- As speed increases, the amount of parasite drag increases. If the speed is doubled, four times as much drag is produced.

Parasite drag can be further classified into form drag, skin friction, and interference drag. Form drag is caused by the frontal area of the airplane components being exposed to the airstream. A similar reaction is illustrated by figure 1-14, where the side of a flat plate is exposed to the airstream. This drag is caused by the form of the plate, and is the reason streamlining is necessary to increased airplane efficiency and speed. Figure 1-14 also illustrates that when the face of the plate is parallel to the airstream, the largest part of the drag is skin friction.

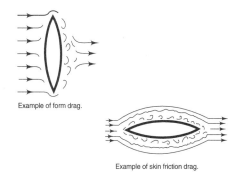

Example of form drag.

Example of skin friction drag.

FIGURE 1-14.—Form drag and skin friction drag.

Skin friction drag is caused by air passing over the airplane's surfaces and increases considerably if the airplane surfaces are rough and dirty.

Interference drag is caused by interference of the airflow between adjacent parts of the airplane such as the intersection of wings and tail sections with the fuselage. Fairings are used to streamline these intersections and decrease interference drag.

It is the airplane's total drag that determines the amount of thrust required at a given airspeed. Figure 1-15 illustrates the variation in parasite, induced, and total drag with speed for a typical airplane in steady, level flight. Thrust must equal drag in steady flight; therefore, the curve for the total drag also represents the thrust required.

Also note in figure 1-15, that the airspeed at which minimum drag occurs is the same airspeed at which the maximum lift-drag ratio (L/D) takes place. At this point the least amount of power is required for both maximum lift and minimum total drag. This is important for determining maximum endurance and range for the airplane.

The force of drag can be controlled to a certain extent by the pilot. Loading the airplane properly, retracting the landing gear and flaps when not used, and keeping the surface of the airplane clean, all help to reduce the total drag.

Relationship Between Angle of Attack and Lift

As stated previously, the angle of attack is the acute angle between the relative wind and the chord line of the wing. At small angles of attack, most of the wing lift is a result of the difference in pressure between the upper and lower surfaces of the wing (Bernoulli's Principle). Additional lift is generated by the equal and opposite reaction of the airstream being deflected downward from the wing (Newton's Law). As the angle of attack is increased, the airstream is forced to travel faster because of the greater distance over the upper surface of the wing, creating a greater pressure differential between the upper and lower surfaces. At the same time, the airstream is deflected downward at a greater angle, causing an increased opposite reaction. Both the increased pressure differential and increased opposite reaction increase lift and also drag. Therefore as angle of attack is increased, lift is increased up to the critical angle of attack. [Figure 1-16]

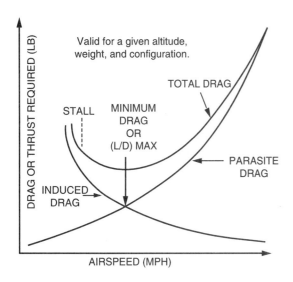

FIGURE 1-15.—Typical airplane drag curves.

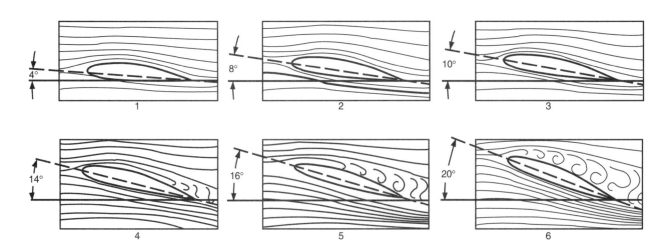

FIGURE 1-16.—Flow of air around a wing at various angles of attack.

When the angle of attack is increased to approximately 15° to 20° (critical angle of attack) on most airfoils, the airstream can no longer follow the upper curvature of the wing because of the excessive change in direction. As the critical angle of attack is approached, the airstream begins separating from the rear of the upper wing surface. As the angle of attack is further increased, the separation moves forward to the area of the highest camber. This causes a swirling or burbling of the air as it attempts to follow the upper surface of the wing.

When the critical angle of attack is reached, the turbulent airflow, which appeared near the trailing edge of the wing at lower angles of attack, quickly spreads forward over the entire upper wing surface. This results in a sudden increase in pressure on the upper wing surface and a considerable loss of lift. Due to the loss of lift and increase in form drag, the remaining lift is insufficient to support the airplane, and the wing stalls. [Figure 1-16]

To recover from a stall, the angle of attack must be decreased so that the airstream can once again flow smoothly over the wing surface. Remember that the angle of attack is the angle between the chord line and the relative wind, not the chord line and the horizon. Therefore, an airplane can be stalled in any attitude of flight with respect to the horizon, if the angle of attack is increased up to and beyond the critical angle of attack.

Relationship of Thrust and Drag in Straight-and-Level Flight

During straight-and-level flight, thrust and drag are equal in magnitude if a constant airspeed is being maintained. When the thrust of the propeller is increased, thrust momentarily exceeds drag and the airspeed will increase, provided straight-and-level flight is maintained. As stated previously, with an increase in airspeed, drag increases rapidly. At some new and higher airspeed, thrust and drag forces again become equalized and speed again becomes constant.

If all the available power is used, thrust will reach its maximum, airspeed will increase until drag equals thrust, and once again the airspeed will become constant. This will be the top speed for that airplane in that configuration and attitude.

When thrust becomes less than drag, the airplane will decelerate to a slower airspeed, provided straight-and-level flight is maintained, and thrust and drag again become equal. Of course if the airspeed becomes too slow, or more precisely, if the angle of attack is too great, the airplane will stall.

Relationship Between Lift and Weight in Straight-and-Level Flight

A component of lift, the upward force on the wing, always acts perpendicular to the direction of the relative wind. In straight-and-level flight (constant altitude) lift counterbalances the airplane weight. When lift and weight are in equilibrium, the airplane neither gains nor loses altitude. If lift becomes less than weight, the airplane will enter a descent; if lift becomes greater than weight, the airplane will enter a climb. Once a steady-state climb or descent is established, the relationship of the four forces will no longer be the same as in straight-and-level flight. However, for all practical purposes, lift still equals weight for small angles of climb or descent.

Factors Affecting Lift and Drag

A number of the factors that influence lift and drag include:

- Wing Area
- Airfoil Shape
- Wing Design
- Airspeed
- Air Density

A change in any of these factors affects the relationship between lift and drag. When lift is increased, drag is increased, or when lift is decreased, drag is decreased.

Effect of Wing Area on Lift and Drag
The lift and drag acting on a wing are proportional to the wing area. This means that if the wing area is doubled, other variables remaining the same, the lift and drag created by the wing will be doubled.

Effect of Airfoil Shape on Lift and Drag
Generally, the more curvature there is to the upper surface of an airfoil, the more lift is produced (up to a point). High-lift wings have a large convex curvature on the upper surface and a concave lower surface. Most airplanes have wing flaps which, when lowered, cause an ordinary wing to approximate this condition by increasing the curvature of the upper surface and creating a concave lower surface, thus increasing lift on the wing. A lowered aileron also accomplishes this by increasing the curvature of a portion of the wing and thereby increasing the angle of attack, which in turn increases lift and also drag. A raised aileron reduces lift on the wing by decreasing the curvature of a portion of the wing and decreasing the angle of

attack. The elevators can change the curvature and angle of attack of the horizontal tail surfaces, changing the amount and direction of lift. The rudder accomplishes the same thing for the vertical tail surfaces.

Many people believe that the only hazard of in-flight icing is the weight of the ice which forms on the wings. It is true that ice formation will increase weight, but equally important is that ice formation will alter the shape of the airfoil and adversely affect all aspects of airplane performance and control.

As the ice forms on the airfoil, especially the leading edge, the flow of air over the wing is disrupted. This disruption of the smooth airflow causes the wing to lose part or all of its lifting efficiency. Also, drag is increased substantially.

Even a slight coating of frost on the wings can prevent an airplane from becoming airborne because the smooth flow of air over the wing surface is disrupted and the lift capability of the wing is destroyed. Even more hazardous is becoming airborne with frost on the wing, because performance and control could be adversely affected. This is why it is extremely important that all frost, snow, and ice be removed from the airplane before takeoff.

Effect of Wing Design on Stall

The type of wing design for a particular airplane depends almost entirely on the purpose for which that airplane is to be used. If speed is the prime consideration, a tapered wing is more desirable than a rectangular wing, but a tapered wing with no twist has undesirable stall characteristics. Assuming equal wing area, the tapered wing produces less drag than the rectangular wing because there is less area at the tip of the tapered wing. The elliptical wing is more efficient (greater lift for the amount of drag), but does not have as good stall characteristics as the rectangular wing.

To achieve good stall characteristics, the root of the wing should stall first, with the stall pattern progressing outward to the tip. This type of stall pattern decreases undesirable rolling tendencies and increases lateral control when approaching a stall. It is undesirable that the wingtip stalls first, particularly if the tip of one wing stalls before the tip of the other wing, which usually happens.

A desirable stall pattern can be accomplished by:

• designing the wing with a twist so that the tip has a lower angle of incidence and therefore a lower angle of attack when the root of the wing approaches the critical angle of attack;

• designing slots near the leading edge of the wingtip to allow air to flow smoothly over that part of the wing at higher angles of attack, therefore allowing the root of the wing to stall first; and

• attaching stall or spoiler strips on the leading edge near the wing root. This strip breaks up the airflow at higher angles of attack and produces the desired effect of the root area of the wing stalling first.

Effect of Airspeed on Lift and Drag

An increase in the velocity of the air passing over the wing (airspeed) increases lift and drag. Lift is increased because:

• the increased impact of the relative wind on the wing's lower surface creates a greater amount of air being deflected downward;

• the increased speed of the relative wind over the upper surface creates a lower pressure on top of the wing (Bernoulli's Principle); and

• a greater pressure differential between the upper and lower wing surface is created. Drag is also increased, since any change that increases lift also increases drag.

Tests show that lift and drag vary as the square of the velocity. The velocity of the air passing over the wing in flight is determined by the airspeed of the airplane. This means that if an airplane doubles its speed, it quadruples the lift and drag (assuming that the angle of attack remains the same).

Effect of Air Density on Lift and Drag

Lift and drag vary directly with the density of the air. As air density increases, lift and drag increase and as air density decreases, lift and drag decrease. Air density is affected by pressure, temperature, and humidity. At an altitude of 18,000 feet, the density of the air is half the air density at sea level. Therefore, if an airplane is to maintain the same lift at high altitudes, the amount of air flowing over the wing must be the same as at lower altitudes. To do this the speed of the air over the wings (airspeed) must be increased. This is why an airplane requires a longer takeoff distance to become airborne at higher altitudes than with similar conditions at lower altitudes. [Figure 1-17]

Because air expands when heated, warm air is less dense than cool air. When other conditions remain the same, an airplane will require a longer takeoff run on a hot day than on a cool day. [Figure 1-17]

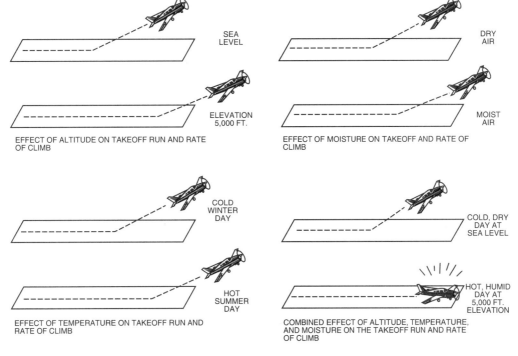

FIGURE 1-17.—Effect of altitude, temperature, and humidity on takeoff run and rate of climb.

Because water vapor weighs less than an equal amount of dry air, moist air (high relative humidity) is less dense than dry air (low relative humidity). Therefore, when other conditions remain the same, the airplane will require a longer takeoff run on a humid day than on a dry day. This is especially true on a hot, humid day because the air can hold much more water vapor than on a cool day. The more moisture in the air, the less dense the air. [Figure 1-17]

Less dense air also produces other performance losses beside the loss of lift. Engine horsepower falls off and propeller efficiency decreases because of power loss and propeller blades, being airfoils, are less effective when air is less dense. Since the propeller is not pulling with the force and efficiency it would were the air dense, it takes longer to obtain the necessary forward speed to produce the required lift for takeoff, thus the airplane requires a longer takeoff run. The rate of climb will also be less for the same reasons.

From the preceding discussion, it is obvious that a pilot should be cognizant of the effects of high altitude, hot temperature, and high moisture content (high relative humidity). A combination of these three conditions could be disastrous, especially when combined with a short runway, a heavily loaded airplane, or other takeoff-limiting conditions.

TURNING TENDENCY (TORQUE EFFECT)

By definition, "torque" is a force, or combination of forces, that produces or tends to produce a twisting or rotating motion of an airplane.

An airplane propeller spinning clockwise, as seen from the rear, produces forces that tend to twist or rotate the airplane in the opposite direction, thus turning the airplane to the left. Airplanes are designed in such a manner that the torque effect is not noticeable to the pilot when the airplane is in straight-and-level flight with a cruise power setting.

The effect of torque increases in direct proportion to engine power, airspeed, and airplane attitude. If the power setting is high, the airspeed slow, and the angle of attack high, the effect of torque is greater. During takeoffs and climbs, when the effect of torque is most pronounced, the pilot must apply sufficient right rudder pressure to counteract the left-turning tendency and maintain a straight takeoff path.

Several forces are involved in the insistent tendency of an airplane of standard configuration to turn to the left. All of these forces are created by the rotating propeller. How they are actually created varies greatly from one explanation to the next.

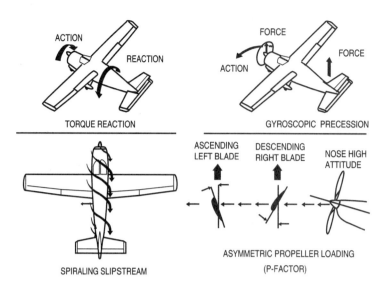

FIGURE 1-18.—Factors which cause left-turning tendency.

Individual explanation of these forces is perhaps the best approach to understanding the reason for the left-turning tendency.

The four forces are:

- Torque Reaction
- Spiraling Slipstream
- Gyroscopic Precession
- Asymmetric Propeller Loading ("P" Factor)

Torque Reaction

This is based on Newton's Law of action and reaction. Applying this law to an airplane with a propeller rotating in a clockwise direction, as seen from the rear, a force is produced which tends to roll the entire airplane about its longitudinal axis in a counterclockwise direction. To better understand this concept, consider the air through which the propeller rotates as a restraining force. This restraining force acts opposite to the direction the propeller rotates, creating a tendency for the airplane to roll to the left. [Figure 1-18]

Spiraling Slipstream

This theory is based on the reaction of the air to a rotating propeller blade. As the airplane propeller rotates through the air in a clockwise direction, as viewed from the rear, the propeller blade forces the air rearward in a spiraling clockwise direction of flow around the fuselage. A portion of this spiraling slipstream strikes the left side of the vertical stabilizer forcing the airplane's tail to the right and the nose to the left, causing the airplane to rotate around the vertical axis. The portion of the spiraling slipstream traveling under the fuselage is not obstructed, therefore, creating a different resistance between the obstructed and the unobstructed flow which causes the left-turning tendency. [Figure 1-18]

Gyroscopic Precession

This theory is based on one of the gyroscopic properties which apply to any object spinning in space, even a rotating airplane propeller. As the nose of the airplane is raised or lowered, or moved left or right, a deflective force is applied to the spinning propeller which results in a reactive force known as precession. Precession is the resultant action or deflection of a spinning wheel (propeller in this case) when a force is applied to its rim. This resultant force occurs 90° ahead in the direction of rotation, and in the direction of the applied force. [Figure 1-18]

Asymmetric Propeller Loading ("P" Factor)

The effects of "P" factor or asymmetric propeller loading usually occur when the airplane is flown at a high angle of attack.

The downward moving blade, which is on the right side of the propeller arc, as seen from the rear, has a higher angle of attack, greater action and reaction, and therefore higher thrust than the upward moving blade on the left. This results in a tendency for the airplane to yaw around the vertical axis to the left. Again this is most pronounced when the engine is operating at a high power setting and the airplane is flown at a high angle of attack. [Figure 1-18]

Corrections for Turning Tendency or Torque During Flight

Since the airplane is flown in cruising flight most of the time, airplane manufacturers design the airplane with certain built-in corrections that counteract the left-turning tendency or torque effect during straight-and-level cruising flight only. This correction eliminates the necessity of applying constant rudder pressure. Because the effect of torque varies to such an extent during climbs and changes in angle of attack, it is impractical for airplane designers to correct for the effect of torque except during straight-and-level flight. Consequently, the pilot is provided other means such as rudder and trim controls to counteract the turning effect during conditions other than straight-and-level flight.

Many manufacturers "cant" the airplane engine slightly so that the thrust line of the propeller points slightly to the right. This counteracts much of the left-turning tendency of the airplane during various conditions of flight.

Other manufacturers, when designing the airplane, increase the angle of incidence of the left wing slightly, which increases the angle of attack and therefore increases the lift on this wing. The increased lift counteracts left-turning tendency in cruising flight. The increase in lift will, however, increase drag on the left wing and, to compensate for this, the vertical stabilizer is offset slightly to the left.

Torque corrections for flight conditions other than cruising flight must be accomplished by the pilot. This is done by applying sufficient rudder to overcome the left-turning tendency. For example, in a straight climb, right rudder pressure is necessary to keep the airplane climbing straight.

When thinking of "torque" such things as reactive force, spiraling slipstream, gyroscopic precession, and asymmetric propeller loading ("P" factor) must be included, as well as any other power-induced forces that tend to turn the airplane.

AIRPLANE STABILITY

Stability is the inherent ability of a body, after its equilibrium is disturbed, to develop forces or moments that tend to return the body to its original position. In other words, a stable airplane will tend to return to the original condition of flight if disturbed by a force such as turbulent air. This means that a stable airplane

is easy to fly; however, this does not mean that a pilot can depend entirely on stability to return the airplane to the original condition. Even in the most stable airplanes, there are conditions that will require the use of airplane controls to return the airplane to the desired attitude. However, a pilot will find that a well designed airplane requires less effort to control the airplane because of the inherent stability.

Stability is classified into three types:

- Positive Stability
- Neutral Stability
- Negative Stability

Positive Stability

Positive stability can be illustrated by a ball inside of a bowl. If the ball is displaced from its normal resting place at the bottom of the bowl, it will eventually return to its original position at the bottom of the bowl. [Figure 1-19]

Neutral Stability

Neutral stability can be illustrated by a ball on a flat plane. If the ball is displaced, it will come to rest at some new, neutral position and show no tendency to return to its original position. [Figure 1-19]

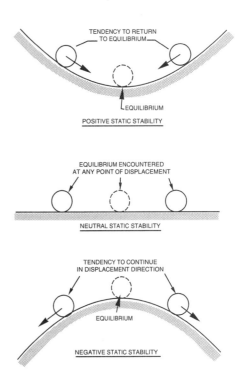

FIGURE 1-19.—Types of stability.

Negative Stability

Negative stability is in fact instability and can be illustrated by a ball on the top of an inverted bowl. Even the slightest displacement of the ball will activate greater forces which will cause the ball to continue to move in the direction of the applied force. It should be obvious that airplanes should display positive stability, or perhaps neutral stability, but never negative stability. [Figure 1-19]

Stability may be further classified as static and/or dynamic. Static stability means that if the airplane's equilibrium is disturbed, forces will be activated which will initially tend to return the airplane to its original position. However, these restoring forces may be so great that they will force the airplane beyond the original position and continue in that direction. On the other hand, dynamic stability is a property which dampens the oscillations set up by a statically stable airplane, enabling the oscillations to become smaller and smaller in magnitude until the airplane eventually settles down to its original condition of flight. Therefore, an airplane should possess positive stability which is both static and dynamic in nature. [Figure 1-20]

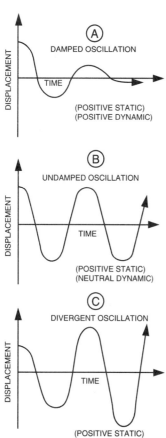

FIGURE 1-20.—*Relationship of oscillation and stability.*

Before further discussion on stability, the axes of rotation will be reviewed because that is where stability has its effect.

The airplane has three axes of rotation around which movement takes place. These are:

• lateral axis, an imaginary line from wingtip to wingtip,
• longitudinal axis, an imaginary line from the nose to the tail, and
• vertical axis, an imaginary line extending vertically through the intersection of the lateral and longitudinal axes.

The airplane can rotate around all three of these axes simultaneously or it can rotate around just one axis. [Figure 1-21] Think of these axes as imaginary axles around which the airplane turns, much as a wheel would turn around axles positioned in these same three planes. The three axes intersect at the center of gravity and each one is perpendicular to the other two.

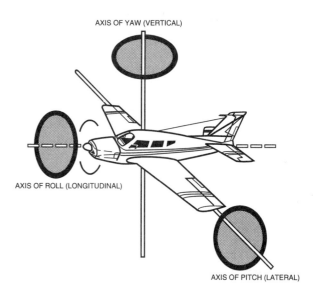

FIGURE 1-21.—*Axes of rotation.*

Rotation about the lateral axis is called pitch and is controlled by the elevators. This rotation is referred to as longitudinal control or longitudinal stability.

Rotation about the longitudinal axis is called roll and is controlled by the ailerons. This rotation is referred to as lateral control or lateral stability.

Rotation about the vertical axis is called yaw and is controlled by the rudder. This rotation is referred to as directional control or directional stability.

Stability of the airplane then, is the combination of forces that act around these three axes to keep the pitch attitude of the airplane in a normal level flight attitude with respect to the horizon, the wings level, and the nose of the airplane directionally straight along the desired path of flight.

Longitudinal Stability about the Lateral Axis

Longitudinal stability is important to the pilot because it determines to a great extent the pitch characteristics of the airplane, particularly as this relates to the stall characteristics. It would be unsafe and uncomfortable for the pilot if an airplane continually displayed a tendency to either stall or dive when the pilot's attention was diverted for some reason. If properly designed, the airplane will not display these unstable tendencies when the airplane is loaded according to the manufacturer's recommendations.

The location of the center of gravity with respect to the center of lift determines to a great extent the longitudinal stability of the airplane.

Figure 1-22 illustrates neutral longitudinal stability. Note that the center of lift is directly over the center of gravity or weight. An airplane with neutral stability will produce no inherent pitch moments around the center of gravity.

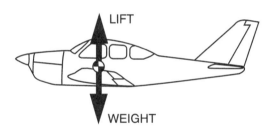

FIGURE 1-22.—Neutral stability.

Figure 1-23 illustrates the center of lift in front of the center of gravity. This airplane would display negative stability and an undesirable pitchup moment during flight. If disturbed, the up and down pitching moment will tend to increase in magnitude. This condition can occur, especially if the airplane is loaded so that the center of gravity is rearward of the airplane's aft loading limits.

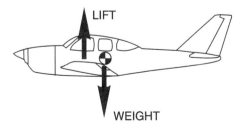

FIGURE 1-23.—Negative stability.

Figure 1-24 shows an airplane with the center of lift behind the center of gravity. Again, this produces negative stability. Some force must balance the down force of the weight. This is accomplished by designing the airplane in such a manner that the air flowing downward behind the trailing edge of the wing strikes the upper surface of the horizontal stabilizer (except on T-tails which have the elevator located on the top instead of below the vertical fin). This creates a downward tail force to counteract the tendency to pitch down and provides positive stability.

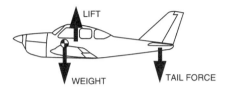

FIGURE 1-24.—Positive stability.

To further explain, if the nose is pitched down and the control released, the airspeed will increase. This, in turn, will increase the downwash on the tail's horizontal stabilizer forcing the nose up (except on T-tails). Conversely, if the nose is pitched up and the control released, the airspeed will diminish, thus decreasing the downwash on the horizontal stabilizer. This permits the nose to pitch downward. There is one speed only for each degree of angle of attack and eventually, after several pitch oscillations, the airplane tends to stabilize at the airspeed (angle of attack) for which it is trimmed.

The above concept is of prime importance to the pilot. A common misconception about longitudinal stability is that an airplane is stable in respect to the horizon. This would be an undesirable characteristic of an airplane. Keep in mind that longitudinal stability is with respect only to airspeed (angle of attack).

The foregoing explanation of longitudinal stability needs some qualification because during certain flight maneuvers, the airplane is not entirely "speed seeking," but "angle of attack seeking." This can be demonstrated by placing the airplane in a power-off glide and trimming the airplane for a specific speed. Then if the throttle is opened suddenly, the airplane will nose up and finally assume an attitude that results in a speed considerably less than that of the power-off glide. This is because of additional forces developed by the propeller blast over the horizontal stabilizer (except T-tails), and the fact that the airplane is stable only with relation to airflow, or the relative wind. In other words, the stable airplane is not concerned with its own attitude relative to the Earth or horizon, but with the relative wind. It will always tend to maintain an alignment with the relative wind.

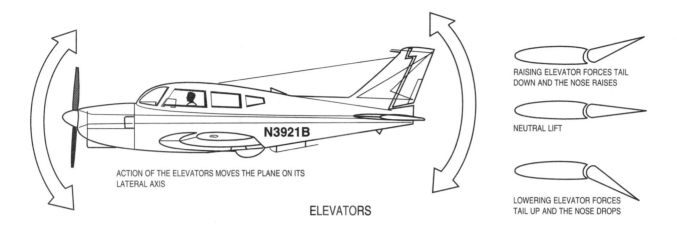

ACTION OF THE ELEVATORS MOVES THE PLANE ON ITS LATERAL AXIS

RAISING ELEVATOR FORCES TAIL DOWN AND THE NOSE RAISES

NEUTRAL LIFT

LOWERING ELEVATOR FORCES TAIL UP AND THE NOSE DROPS

ELEVATORS

FIGURE 1-25.—Effect of elevators.

Longitudinal Control (Pitch) about the Lateral Axis

In the previous discussion, the one speed or angle of attack concept was used to explain how longitudinal stability was attained. It is important for the pilot to know that the airplane is stable at various speeds or angles of attack, not just one. The controls, which allow the pilot to depart from the one speed or angle of attack concept or the controls used to give the pilot longitudinal control around the lateral axis, are the elevators and the elevator trim tab. [Figures 1-25 and 1-26]

Elevators in the neutral position

Up position of the elevators is required to hold the nose in the level flight attitude

Trim tab must be adjusted downward to hold elevators in this position to relieve the pressure on the control wheel

FIGURE 1-26.—Effect of trim tabs.

The function of the elevator control is to provide a means by which the wing's angle of attack may be changed.

On most airplanes the elevators are movable control surfaces hinged to the horizontal stabilizer, and attached to the control column in the cockpit by mechanical linkage. This allows the pilot to change the angle of attack of the entire horizontal stabilizer. The horizontal stabilizer normally has a negative angle of attack to provide a downward force rather than a lifting force. If the pilot applies back elevator pressure, the elevator is raised, increasing the horizontal stabilizer's negative angle of attack and consequently increasing the downward tail force. This forces the tail down, increasing the angle of attack of the wings. Conversely, if forward pressure is applied to the elevator control, the elevators are lowered, decreasing the horizontal stabilizer's negative angle of attack and consequently decreasing the downward force on the tail. This decreases the angle of attack of the wings. [Figure 1-25]

The elevator trim tab is a small auxiliary control surface hinged at the trailing edge of the elevators. The elevator trim tab acts on the elevators, which in turn acts upon the entire airplane. This trim tab is a part of the elevator but may be moved upward or downward independently of the elevator itself. It is controlled from the cockpit by a control which is separate from the elevator control. The elevator trim tab allows the pilot to adjust the angle of attack for a constant setting and therefore eliminates the need to exert continuous pressure on the elevator control to maintain a constant angle of attack. An upward deflection of the trim tab will force the elevator downward with the same result as moving the elevator downward with the elevator control, and conversely a downward deflection of the trim tab will force the elevator upward. The direction the trim tab is deflected will always cause the entire elevator to be deflected in the opposite direction. [Figure 1-26]

Lateral Stability about the Longitudinal Axis

Lateral stability is the stability displayed around the longitudinal axis of the airplane. An airplane that tends to return to a wings-level attitude after being displaced from a level attitude by some force such as turbulent air is considered to be laterally stable.

Three factors that affect lateral stability are:

- Dihedral
- Sweepback
- Keel Effect

Dihedral

Dihedral is the angle at which the wings are slanted upward from the root to the tip. [Figure 1-27] The stabilizing effect of dihedral occurs when the airplane sideslips slightly as one wing is forced down in turbulent air. This sideslip results in a difference in the angle of attack between the higher and lower wing with the greatest angle of attack on the lower wing. The increased angle of attack produces increased lift on the lower wing with a tendency to return the airplane to wings-level flight. Note the direction of the relative wind during a slip by the arrows in figure 1-27.

FIGURE 1-27.—Effect of dihedral.

Sweepback

Sweepback is the angle at which the wings are slanted rearward from the root to the tip. The effect of sweepback in producing lateral stability is similar to that of dihedral, but not as pronounced. If one wing lowers in a slip, the angle of attack on the low wing increases, producing greater lift. This results in a tendency for the lower wing to rise, and return the airplane to level flight. Sweepback augments dihedral to achieve lateral stability. Another reason for sweepback is to place the center of lift farther rearward, which affects longitudinal stability more than it does lateral stability. [Figure 1-28]

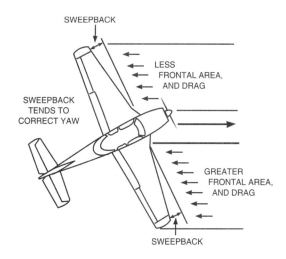

FIGURE 1-28.—Effect of sweepback.

Keel Effect

Keel effect depends upon the action of the relative wind on the side area of the airplane fuselage. In a slight slip, the fuselage provides a broad area upon which the relative wind will strike, forcing the fuselage to parallel the relative wind. This aids in producing lateral stability. [Figure 1-29]

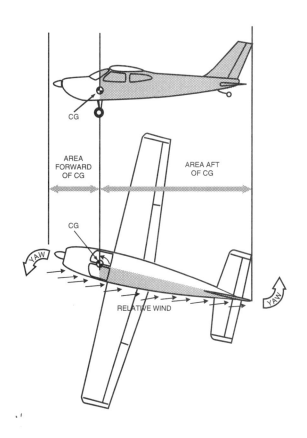

FIGURE 1-29.—Keel effect.

Lateral Control about the Longitudinal Axis

Lateral control is obtained through the use of ailerons, and on some airplanes the aileron trim tabs. The ailerons are movable surfaces hinged to the outer trailing edge of the wings, and attached to the cockpit control column by mechanical linkage. Moving the control wheel or stick to the right raises the aileron on the right wing and lowers the aileron on the left wing. Moving the control wheel or stick to the left reverses this and raises the aileron on the left wing and lowers the aileron on the right wing. When an aileron is lowered, the angle of attack on that wing will increase, which increases the lift. This permits rolling the airplane laterally around the longitudinal axis. [Figure 1-30]

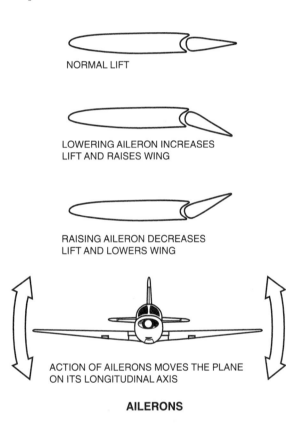

NORMAL LIFT

LOWERING AILERON INCREASES
LIFT AND RAISES WING

RAISING AILERON DECREASES
LIFT AND LOWERS WING

ACTION OF AILERONS MOVES THE PLANE
ON ITS LONGITUDINAL AXIS

AILERONS

FIGURE 1-30.—Effect of ailerons.

Many airplanes are equipped with an aileron trim tab which is a small movable part of the aileron hinged to the trailing edge of the main aileron. These trim tabs can be moved independently of the ailerons. Aileron trim tabs function similar to the elevator trim tabs. Moving the trim tabs produces an effect on the aileron which in turn affects the entire airplane. If the trim tab is deflected upward, the aileron is deflected downward, increasing the angle of attack on that wing, resulting in greater lift on that wing. The reverse is true if the trim tab is deflected downward.

Lateral Stability or Instability in Turns

Because of lateral stability, most airplanes will tend to recover from shallow banks automatically. However, as the bank is increased, the wing on the outside of the turn travels faster than the wing on the inside of the turn. The increased speed increases the lift on the outside wing, causing a destabilizing rolling moment or an overbanking tendency. The angle of bank will continue to increase into a steeper and steeper bank unless the pilot applies a slight amount of control pressure to counteract this tendency. The overbanking tendency becomes increasingly significant when the angle of bank reaches more than 30°.

During a medium banked turn, an airplane tends to hold its bank constant and requires less control input on the part of the pilot. This is because the stabilizing moments of lateral stability and the destabilizing moment of overbanking very nearly cancel each other out. A pilot can discover these various areas of bank through experimentation.

Directional Stability about the Vertical Axis (YAW)

Directional stability is displayed around the vertical axis and depends to a great extent on the quality of lateral stability. If the longitudinal axis of an airplane tends to follow and parallel the flightpath of the airplane through the air, whether in straight flight or curved flight, that airplane is considered to be directionally stable.

Directional stability is accomplished by placing a vertical stabilizer or fin to the rear of the center of gravity on the upper portion of the tail section. The surface of this fin acts similar to a weather vane and causes the airplane to weather vane into the relative wind. If the airplane is yawed out of its flightpath, either by pilot action or turbulence, during straight flight or turn, the relative wind would exert a force on one side of the vertical stabilizer and return the airplane to its original direction of flight.

Wing sweepback aids in directional stability. If the airplane is rotated about the vertical axis, the airplane will be forced sideways into the relative wind. Because of sweepback this causes the leading wing to present more frontal area to the relative wind than the trailing wing. This increased frontal area creates more drag, which tends to force the airplane to return to its original direction of flight.

The combined effects of the vertical stabilizer (fin) and sweepback can be compared with feathers of an arrow. It would be difficult to imagine an arrow traveling through the air sideways at any appreciable rate of speed.

Directional Control about the Vertical Axis (YAW)

Directional control about the vertical axis of the airplane is obtained through the use of the rudder. The rudder is a movable surface hinged to the trailing edge of the vertical stabilizer (fin) and attached by mechanical linkage to the rudder pedals located in the cockpit. By pressing the right rudder pedal, the rudder is deflected to the right, which causes the relative wind to deflect the tail to the left and the nose to the right. If left rudder pressure is applied, the reverse action occurs and the nose is deflected to the left. It should be understood that the purpose of the rudder during flight is to control yaw and not to turn the airplane. [Figure 1-31]

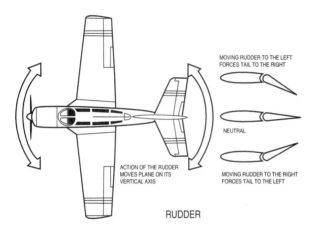

MOVING RUDDER TO THE LEFT
FORCES TAIL TO THE RIGHT

NEUTRAL

ACTION OF THE RUDDER
MOVES PLANE ON ITS
VERTICAL AXIS

MOVING RUDDER TO THE RIGHT
FORCES TAIL TO THE LEFT

RUDDER

FIGURE 1-31.—Effect of rudder.

Some airplanes are equipped with a rudder trim tab, which reacts in a similar manner on the rudder as does the aileron trim tab on the aileron and the elevator trim tab on the elevator.

The amount of control which the pilot has over the airplane is dependent upon the speed of the airflow striking the control surfaces. Effective airplane stability also depends upon speed of the airplane through the air. The greater the airspeed the greater the effect of stability as a restoring force.

LOADS AND LOAD FACTORS

An airplane is designed and certificated for a certain maximum weight during flight. This weight is referred to as the maximum certificated gross weight.

It is important that the airplane be loaded within the specified weight limits before flight, because certain flight maneuvers will impose an extra load on the airplane structure which may, particularly if the airplane is overloaded, impose stresses which will exceed the design capabilities of the airplane. Overstressing the airplane can also occur if the pilot engages in maneuvers creating high loads, regardless of how the airplane is loaded.

These maneuvers not only increase the load that the airplane structure must support, but also increase the airplane's stalling speed.

The following will explain how extra load is imposed upon the airplane during flight.

During flight, the wings of an airplane will support the maximum allowable gross weight of the airplane. So long as the airplane is moving at a steady rate of speed and in a straight line, the load imposed upon the wings will remain constant.

A change in speed during straight flight will not produce any appreciable change in load, but when a change is made in the airplane's flightpath, an additional load is imposed upon the airplane structure. This is particularly true if a change in direction is made at high speeds with rapid forceful control movements.

According to certain laws of physics, a mass (airplane in this case) will continue to move in a straight line unless some force intervenes, causing the mass (airplane) to assume a curved path. During the time the airplane is in a curved flightpath, it still attempts, because of inertia, to force itself to follow straight flight. This tendency to follow straight flight, rather than curved flight, generates a force known as centrifugal force which acts toward the outside of the curve.

Any time the airplane is flying in a curved flightpath with a positive load, the load the wings must support will be equal to the weight of the airplane plus the load imposed by centrifugal force. A positive load occurs when back pressure is applied to the elevator, causing centrifugal force to act in the same direction as the force of weight. A negative load occurs when forward pressure is applied to the elevator control, causing centrifugal force to act in a direction opposite to that of the force of weight.

Curved flight producing a positive load is a result of increasing the angle of attack and consequently the lift. Increased lift always increases the positive load imposed upon the wings. However, the load is increased only at the time the angle of attack is being increased. Once the angle of attack is established, the load remains constant. The loads imposed on the wings in flight are stated in terms of load factor.

Category	Permissible Maneuvers	Limit load Factor*
Normal	1—Any maneuver incident to normal flying. 2—Stalls (except whip stalls). 3—Lazy eights, chandelles, and steep turns in which the angle of bank does not exceed 60°.	3.8
Utility	1—All operations in the normal category. 2—Spins (if approved for that airplane). 3—Lazy eights, chandelles, and steep turns in which the angle of bank is more than 60°.	4.4
Acrobatic	No restrictions except those shown to be necessary as a result of required flight tests.	6.0

*To the limit loads given, a safety factor of 50 percent is added.

FIGURE 1-32.—Airplane categories.

Load factor is the ratio of the total load supported by the airplane's wing to the actual weight of the airplane and its contents; i.e., the actual load supported by the wings divided by the total weight of the airplane. For example, if an airplane has a gross weight of 2,000 pounds and during flight is subjected to aerodynamic forces which increase the total load the wing must support to 4,000 pounds, the load factor would be 2.0 (4,000/2,000 = 2). In this example, the airplane wing is producing "lift" that is equal to twice the gross weight of the airplane.

Another way of expressing load factor is the ratio of a given load to the pull of gravity; i.e., to refer to a load factor of three, as "3 G's," where "G" refers to the pull of gravity. In this case the weight of the airplane is equal to "1 G," and if a load of three times the actual weight of the airplane were imposed upon the wing due to curved flight, the load factor would be equal to "3 G's."

Load Factors and Airplane Design

To be certificated by the Federal Aviation Administration (FAA), the structural strength (load factor) of airplanes must conform with prescribed standards set forth by Title 14 of the Code of Federal Regulations (14 CFR).

All airplanes are designed to meet certain strength requirements depending upon the intended use of the airplanes. Classification of airplanes as to strength and operational use is known as the category system.

The category of each airplane can be readily identified by a placard or document (Airworthiness Certificate) in the cockpit which states the operational category or categories in which that airplane is certificated.

The category, maneuvers that are permitted, and the maximum safe load factors (limit load factors)

specified for these airplanes are listed in figure 1-32.

It should be noted that there is an increase in limit load factor with an increasing severity of maneuvers permitted. Small airplanes may be certificated in more than one category if the requirements for each category are met.

This system provides a means for the pilot to determine what operations can be performed in a given airplane without exceeding the load limit. Pilots are cautioned to operate the airplane within the load limit for which the airplane is designed so as to enhance safety and still benefit from the intended utilization of the airplane.

Effect of Turns on Load Factor

A turn is made by banking the airplane so that lift from the wings pulls the airplane from its straight flightpath. It is not within the scope of this handbook to discuss the mathematics of the turn. However, in any airplane at any airspeed, if a constant altitude is maintained during the turn, the load factor for a given degree of bank is the same. For any given angle of bank, the rate of turn varies with the airspeed. In other words, if the angle of bank is held constant and the airspeed is increased, the rate of turn will decrease; or if the airspeed is decreased, the rate of turn will increase. Because of this, there is no change in centrifugal force for any given bank. Therefore, the load factor remains the same.

Figures 1-33 and 1-34 reveal an important fact about load factor in turns. The load factor increases at a rapid rate after the angle of bank reaches 50°. The wing must produce lift equal to this load factor if altitude is to be maintained.

It should also be noted how rapidly load factor increases as the angle of bank approaches 90°. The 90° banked, constant altitude turn is not

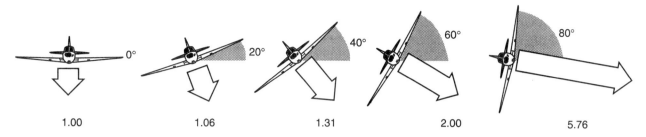

| 1.00 | 1.06 | 1.31 | 2.00 | 5.76 |

FIGURE 1-33.—*The load supported by the wings increases as the angle of bank increases. The increase is shown by the relative lengths of the white arrows. Figures below the arrows indicate the increase in load factor. For example, the load factor during a 60° bank is 2.00, and the load supported by the wings is twice the weight of the airplane in level flight.*

mathematically possible. An airplane can be banked to 90°, but a continued coordinated turn is impossible at this bank angle without losing altitude.

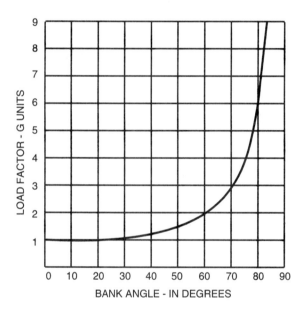

Figure 1-34.—Load factor chart.

At an angle of bank of slightly more than 80°, the load factor exceeds 6, which is the limit load factor of an acrobatic airplane.

The approximate maximum bank for conventional light airplanes is 60° which produces a load factor of 2. An additional 10° of bank will increase the load factor by approximately 1 G, bringing it dangerously close to the point at which structural damage or complete failure may occur in these airplanes. [Figure 1-34]

Effect of Load Factor on Stalling Speed

Any airplane, within the limits of its structure and the strength of the pilot, can be stalled at any airspeed. At a given airspeed, the load factor increases as angle of attack increases, and the wing stalls because the angle of attack has been increased to a certain angle. Therefore, there is a direct relationship between the load factor imposed upon the wing and its stalling characteristics.

When a sufficiently high angle of attack is reached, the smooth flow of air over an airfoil breaks up and tears away, producing the abrupt change of characteristics and loss of lift which is defined as a stall.

A rule for determining the speed at which a wing will stall is that the stalling speed increases in proportion to the square root of the load factor. To further explain, the load factor produced in a 75° banked turn is 4. Applying the rule, the square root of 4 is 2. This means that an airplane with a normal unaccelerated stalling speed of 50 knots can be stalled at twice that speed or 100 knots, by inducing a load factor of 4. If the airplane were capable of withstanding a load factor of 9, this airplane could be stalled at a speed of 150 knots. [Figure 1-34]

Since the load factor squares as the stalling speed doubles, tremendous loads may be imposed on structures by stalling an airplane at relatively high airspeeds. An airplane which has a normal unaccelerated stalling speed of 50 knots will be subjected to a load factor of 4 G's when forced into an accelerated stall at 100 knots. As seen from this example, it is easy to impose a load beyond the design strength of the conventional airplane.

Reference to the chart in figure 1-35 will show that banking an airplane just over 75° in a steep turn increases the stalling speed by 100 percent. If the normal unaccelerated stalling speed is 45 knots, the pilot must keep the airspeed above 90 knots in a 75° bank to prevent sudden entry into a violent power stall. This same effect will take place in a quick pullup from a dive or maneuver producing load factors above 1 G. Accidents have resulted from sudden, unexpected loss of control, particularly in a steep turn near the ground.

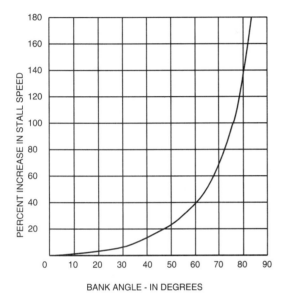

FIGURE 1-35.—Stall speed chart.

The maximum speed at which an airplane can be safely stalled is the design maneuvering speed. The design maneuvering speed is a valuable reference point for the pilot. When operating below this speed, a damaging positive flight load should not be produced because the airplane should stall before the load becomes excessive. Any combination of flight control usage, including full deflection of the controls, or gust loads created by turbulence should not create an excessive air load if the airplane is operated below maneuvering speed. (Pilots should be cautioned that certain adverse wind shear or gusts may cause excessive loads even at speeds below maneuvering speed.)

Design maneuvering speed can be found in the Pilot's Operating Handbook or on a placard within the cockpit. It can also be determined by multiplying the normal unaccelerated stall speed by the square root of the limit load factor. A rule of thumb that can be used to determine the maneuvering speed is approximately 1.7 times the normal stalling speed.

Thus, an airplane which normally stalls at 35 knots should never be stalled when the airspeed is above 60 knots (35 knots x 1.7 = 59.5 knots).

A knowledge of this must be applied from two points of view by the competent pilot: the danger of inadvertently stalling the airplane by increasing the load factor such as in a steep turn or spiral; and that intentionally stalling an airplane above its design maneuvering speed imposes a tremendous load factor on the structure.

Effect of Speed on Load Factor

The amount of excess load that can be imposed on the wing depends on how fast the airplane is flying. At slow speeds, the maximum available lifting force of the wing is only slightly greater than the amount necessary to support the weight of the airplane. Consequently, the load factor should not become excessive even if the controls are moved abruptly or the airplane encounters severe gusts, as previously stated. The reason for this is that the airplane will stall before the load can become excessive. However, at high speeds, the lifting capacity of the wing is so great that a sudden movement of the elevator controls or a strong gust may increase the load factor beyond safe limits. Because of this relationship between speed and safety, certain "maximum" speeds have been established. Each airplane is restricted in the speed at which it can safely execute maneuvers, withstand abrupt application of the controls, or fly in rough air. This speed is referred to as the design maneuvering speed, which was discussed previously.

Summarizing, at speeds below design maneuvering speed, the airplane should stall before the load factor can become excessive. At speeds above maneuvering speed, the limit load factor for which an airplane is stressed can be exceeded by abrupt or excessive application of the controls or by strong turbulence.

Effect of Flight Maneuvers on Load Factor

Load factors apply to all flight maneuvers. In straight-and-level unaccelerated flight, a load factor of 1G is always present, but certain maneuvers are known to involve relatively high load factors.

• **Turns**—As previously discussed, increased load factors are a characteristic of all banked turns. Load factors become significant both to flight performance and to the load on wing structure as the bank increases beyond approximately 45°.

- **Stalls**—The normal stall entered from straight-and-level flight, or an unaccelerated straight climb, should not produce added load factors beyond the 1G of straight-and-level flight. As the stall occurs, however, this load factor may be reduced toward zero, the factor at which nothing seems to have weight, and the pilot has the feeling of "floating free in space." In the event recovery is made by abruptly moving the elevator control forward, a negative load is created which raises the pilot from the seat. This is a negative wing load and usually is so small that there is little effect on the airplane structure. The pilot should be cautioned, however, to avoid sudden and forceful control movements because of the possibility of exceeding the structural load limits.

During the pullup following stall recovery, however, significant load factors are often encountered. These may be increased by excessively steep diving, high airspeed, and abrupt pullups to level flight. One usually leads to the other, thus increasing the resultant load factor. The abrupt pullup at a high diving speed may easily produce critical loads on structures, and may produce recurrent or secondary stalls by building up the load factor to the point that the speed of the airplane reaches the stalling airspeed during the pullup.

- **Advanced Maneuvers**—Spins, chandelles, lazy eights, and snap maneuvers will not be covered in this handbook. However, before attempting these maneuvers, pilots should be familiar with the airplane being flown, and know whether or not these maneuvers can be safely performed.

Effect of Turbulence on Load Factor

Turbulence in the form of vertical air currents can, under certain conditions, cause severe load stress on an airplane wing.

When an airplane is flying at a high speed with a low angle of attack, and suddenly encounters a vertical current of air moving upward, the relative wind changes to an upward direction as it meets the airfoil. This increases the angle of attack of the wing.

If the air current is well defined and travels at a significant rate of speed upward (15 to 30 feet per second), a sharp vertical gust is produced which will have the same effect on the wing as applying sudden sharp back pressure on the elevator control.

All certificated airplanes are designed to withstand loads imposed by turbulence of considerable intensity. Nevertheless, gust load factors increase with increasing airspeed. Therefore it is wise, in extremely rough air, as in thunderstorm or frontal conditions, to reduce the speed to the design maneuvering speed. As a general rule, when severe turbulence is encountered, the airplane should be flown at the maneuvering speed shown in the FAA-approved Airplane Flight Manual, Pilot's Operating Handbook, or placard in the airplane. This is the speed least likely to result in structural damage to the airplane, even if full control travel is used, and yet allows a sufficient margin of safety above stalling speed in turbulent air.

Placarded "never exceed speeds" are determined for smooth air only. High dive speeds or abrupt maneuvering in gusty air at airspeeds above the maneuvering speed may place damaging stress on the whole structure of an airplane. Stress on the structure means stress on any vital part of the airplane. The most common failures due to load factors involve rib structure within the leading and trailing edges of wings.

The cumulative effect of such loads over a long period of time may tend to loosen and weaken vital parts so that actual failure may occur later when the airplane is being operated in a normal manner.

Determining Load Factors in Flight

The leverage in the control systems of different airplanes varies; some types are balanced control surfaces while others are not. (A balanced control surface is an aileron, rudder, or elevator designed in such a manner as to put each side of its hinged axis in balance with the other side.) Therefore the pressure exerted by the pilot on the controls cannot be used as a means to determine the load factor produced in different airplanes. Load factors are best judged by feel through experience. They can be measured by an instrument called an accelerometer, but since this instrument is not commonly used in general aviation-type airplanes, developing the ability to judge load factors from the feel of their effect on the body is important. One indication the pilot will have of increased load factor is the feeling of increased body weight. In a 60° bank, the body weight would double. A knowledge of the principles outlined above is essential to estimate load factors.

In view of the foregoing discussion on load factors, a few suggestions can be made to avoid overstressing the structure of the airplane:

- Operate the airplane in conformance with the Pilot's Operating Handbook.
- Avoid abrupt control usage at high speeds.

- Reduce speed if turbulence of any great intensity is encountered in flight, or abrupt maneuvers are to be performed.
- Reduce weight of airplane before flight if intensive turbulence or abrupt maneuvering is anticipated.
- Avoid turns using an angle of bank in excess of 60°.

Forces Acting on the Airplane when at Airspeeds Slower than Cruise

At a constant cruise speed, maintaining straight-and-level flight, the force of thrust and drag act opposite to each other and parallel to the flightpath. These opposing forces are equal in magnitude. Also, the force of lift is equal in magnitude to the force of weight.

While maintaining straight-and-level flight at constant airspeeds slower than cruise, the opposing forces must still be equal in magnitude, but some of these forces are separated into components. In this flight condition, the actual thrust no longer acts parallel and opposite to the flightpath and drag. Actual thrust is inclined upward as illustrated in figure 1-36.

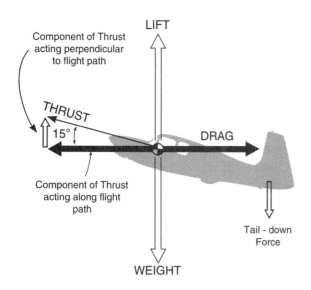

FIGURE 1-36.—The forces on the airplane in straight-and-level flight at airspeeds slower than cruise.

Note that now thrust has two components; one acting perpendicular to the flightpath in the direction of lift, while the other acts along the flightpath. Because the actual thrust is inclined, its magnitude must be greater than drag if its component of thrust along the flightpath is to equal drag. Also note that a component of thrust acts 90° to the flightpath, and

thus acts in the same direction as wing lift. Figure 1-37 also illustrates that the forces acting upward (wing lift and the component of thrust) equal the forces acting downward (weight and tail-down force).

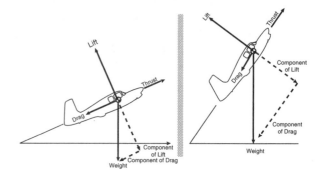

FIGURE 1-37.—Forces acting on an airplane in a climb.

Wing loading (wing lift) is actually less at slow speeds than at cruise speeds because the vertical component of thrust helps support the airplane.

To summarize, in straight-and-level flight at slow speeds, the actual thrust is greater than drag, and wing lift is less than at cruise speed.

Forces in a Climb

The forces acting on an airplane during a climb are illustrated in figure 1-37. When the airplane is in equilibrium, the weight can be resolved into two components: one opposing the lift, and the other acting in the same direction as the drag along the line of the relative wind. The requirements for equilibrium are: the thrust must equal the sum of the drag and the opposing component of the weight; and the lift must equal its opposing component of the weight. The steeper the angle of climb, the shorter becomes the length of the component of lift, and simultaneously the component of drag becomes longer. Therefore, the lift requirement decreases steadily as the angle of climb steepens until, in a true vertical climb, if this were possible, the wings would supply no lift and the thrust would be the only force opposing both the drag and the weight, which would be acting downward in opposition.

At a constant power setting, a given rate of climb can be obtained either by climbing steeply at a low airspeed or by climbing on a shallow path at high airspeed. At one extreme, if the airspeed is too low, the induced drag rises to a figure at which all thrust available is required to overcome the drag and none is available for climbing. At the other extreme, if the speed is the maximum obtainable in level flight, again all the power is being used to overcome the drag and there is no rate of climb. Between these two extremes lies a speed, or a small band of speeds, which will achieve the best rate of climb. The best rate of climb is achieved not at the steepest angle, but at some combination of moderate angle and optimum airspeed at which the greatest amount of excess power is available to climb the airplane after the drag has been balanced.

Figure 1-38 shows that the speed for minimum drag or the lowest point on the power-required curve, although low, is not the lowest possible that can be flown without stalling. The increase in power required at the lowest speeds (to the left of the minimum power-required point) is caused by the rapidly rising effects of induced drag at the lower speeds.

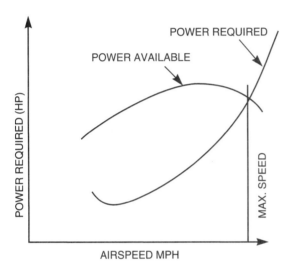

FIGURE 1-38.—*Power available vs. power required.*

The propeller driven airplane, under the same set of circumstances and for a given rated horsepower, suffers a gradual loss of propeller efficiency and, therefore, a gradual loss of thrust at both ends of its speed range.

The vertical distance between the power-available and power-required curves represents the power available for climbing at the particular speed. The best climbing airspeed is that at which excess power is at a maximum so that after expending some power in overcoming drag, the maximum amount of power remains available for climbing the airplane. At the intersection of the curves, all the available power is being used to overcome drag, leaving none available for climbing. Of course at the lower range, excess power for climb soon becomes available if the angle of attack is reduced to allow an increase in speed. [Figure 1-38]

The thrust horsepower of piston engines decreases with altitude. Even if it is possible to prolong sea-level power to some greater altitude by supercharging, or some other method of power boosting, the power will inevitably decline when the boosting method employed reaches an altitude at which it can no longer maintain a set power. At higher altitudes, the power-available curves are lowered. Since power required increases with true airspeed (velocity), the thrust horsepower required to fly at any desired indicated airspeed increases with altitude.

In summarizing, it is a fallacy to think that an airplane climbs because of "excess lift." It does not; the airplane climbs because of power available over power required.

Forces in a Glide

The forces acting on an airplane in a glide are illustrated in figure 1-39. For a steady glide with the engine providing no thrust, the lift, drag, and weight forces must be in equilibrium. The illustration shows that weight is balanced by the resultant of lift and drag. The lift vector, acting as it does at right angles to the path of flight, will now be tilted forward, while the drag vector will be tilted upward and will continue to act opposite to the path of flight. From the illustration, it can be seen that the geometry of the vectors is such that the angle between the lift vector and the resultant is the same as that between the glidepath and the horizontal. This angle (X) between the glidepath and the horizontal is called the glide angle. Further examination of this diagram will show that as drag is reduced and speed increased, the smaller will be the glide angle; therefore, the steepness of the glidepath depends on the ratio of lift to drag. When gliding at the angle of attack for best L/D, least drag is experienced, and the flattest glide will result. The L/D is a measure of the gliding efficiency or aerodynamic cleanness of the airplane. If the L/D is 11/1, it means that lift is 11 times greater than drag.

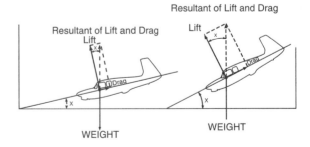

FIGURE 1-39.—*Forces acting on an airplane in a glide.*

If the gliding airplane is flying at an airspeed just above the stall, it is operating at maximum angle of attack and therefore, maximum lift. This, however, does not produce the best glide angle for maximum glide distance because the induced drag at this point is high. By reducing the angle of attack, the airspeed increases and, although lift is less at the lower angle of attack, the airplane travels farther per increment of altitude lost because of greatly reduced drag. The increased range can be accomplished up to a point, by decreasing angle of attack and induced drag.

At some point, the best glide angle will be achieved. If airspeed continues to increase, the parasite drag begins to rise sharply and the airplane will again start losing more altitude per increment of distance traveled. The extreme of this is when the nose is pointed straight down.

It can be shown that best glide distance is obtained when L/D is at maximum. This optimum condition is determined for each type of airplane and the speed at which it occurs is used as the recommended best range glide speed for the airplane. It will vary somewhat for different airplane weights, so the airspeed for a representative operational condition is generally selected.

If several instances of the optimum glidepath were plotted by an observer on the ground under varying conditions of wind, they would be found to be inconsistent. However, the actual gliding angle of the airplane with respect to the moving air mass remains unchanged. Starting from a given altitude, a glide into the wind at optimum glide airspeed covers less distance over the ground than a glide downwind. Since in both cases the rate of descent is the same, the measured angle as seen by a ground observer is governed only by the groundspeed, being steeper at the lower groundspeed when gliding into the wind. The effect of wind, therefore, is to decrease range when gliding with a headwind component, and to increase it when gliding downwind. The endurance of the glide is unaffected by wind.

Variations in gross weight do not affect the gliding angle provided the optimum indicated airspeed for each gross weight is used. The fully loaded airplane will sink faster but at a greater forward speed, and although it would reach the ground much quicker, it would have traveled exactly the same distance as the lighter airplane, and its glide angle would have been the same.

An inspection of figure 1-39 will show that an increase in the weight factor is equivalent to adding thrust to the weight component along the glidepath. This means more speed and, therefore, more lift and drag which lengthen the resultant vector until the

geometric balance of the diagram is restored. This is done without affecting the gliding angle. The higher speed corresponding to the increased weight is provided automatically by the larger component of weight acting along the glidepath, and this component grows or diminishes in proportion to the weight. Since the gliding angle is unaffected, range also is unchanged.

Although range is not affected by changes in weight, endurance decreases with addition of weight and increases with reduction of weight. If two airplanes having the same L/D, but different weights, start a glide from the same altitude, the heavier airplane, gliding at a higher airspeed, will cover the distance between the starting point and touch down in a shorter time. Both, however, will cover the same distance. Therefore, the endurance of the heavier airplane is less.

Turns During Flight

Many pilots do not reach a complete understanding of what makes an airplane turn. Such an understanding is certainly worthwhile, since many accidents occur as a direct result of losing control of the airplane while in turning flight.

In review, the airplane is capable of movement around the three axes. It can be pitched around the lateral axis, rolled around the longitudinal axis, and yawed around the vertical axis. Yawing around the vertical axis causes most misunderstanding about how and why an airplane turns. First, it should be kept in mind that the rudder does not turn the airplane in flight.

Although most pilots know that an airplane is banked to make a turn, few know the reason why. The answer is quite simple. The airplane must be banked because the same force (lift) that sustains the airplane in flight is used to make the airplane turn. The airplane is banked and back elevator pressure is applied. This changes the direction of lift and increases the angle of attack on the wings, which increases the lift. The increased lift pulls the airplane around the turn. The amount of back elevator pressure applied, and therefore the amount of lift, varies directly with the angle of bank used. As the angle of bank is steepened, the amount of back elevator pressure must be increased to hold altitude.

In level flight, the force of lift acts opposite to and exactly equal in magnitude to the force of gravity. Gravity tends to pull all bodies to the center of the Earth; therefore, this force always acts in a vertical plane with respect to the Earth. On the other hand, total lift always acts perpendicular to the relative wind, which for the purposes of this discussion is considered to be the same as acting perpendicular to the lateral axis of the wind.

With the wings level, lift acts directly opposite to gravity. However, as the airplane is banked, gravity still acts in a vertical plane, but lift will now act in an inclined plane.

As illustrated in figure 1-40, the force of lift can be resolved into two components, vertical and horizontal. During the turn entry, the vertical component of lift still opposes gravity, and the horizontal component of lift must overcome apparent centrifugal force. Consequently, the total lift must be sufficient to counteract both of these forces.

The total resultant lift acts opposite to the total resultant load. So long as these opposing forces are equal to each other in magnitude, the airplane will maintain a constant rate of turn. If the pilot moves the controls in such a manner as to change the magnitude of any of the forces, the airplane will accelerate or decelerate in the direction of the applied force. This will result in changing the rate at which the airplane turns.

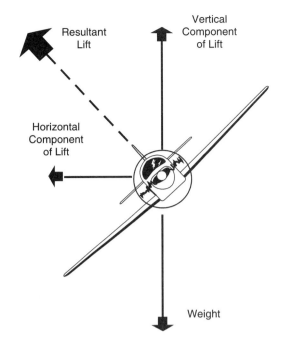

FIGURE *1-40.—Forces acting on an airplane in a turn.*

CHAPTER 2

AIRPLANES AND ENGINES

INTRODUCTION

One of the most important activities in promoting safety in aviation is the airworthiness certification of airplanes. Each airplane certificated by the Federal Aviation Administration (FAA) has been manufactured under rigid specifications of design, materials, workmanship, construction, and performance. This certification process provides adequate assurance that the airplane will not fail from a structural standpoint if the airplane is properly maintained and flown within the limitations clearly specified. However, this may not be true if the airplane is abused, improperly maintained, or flown without regard to its limitations.

The goal of airplane designers and manufacturers is to obtain maximum efficiency, combined with adequate strength. Excessive strength requires additional weight which lowers the efficiency of the airplane by reducing its speed and the amount of useful load it can carry.

This chapter covers the airplane's structure, flight control systems, wing flaps, landing gear, engine operation, engine accessories, and associated engine instruments. Also included is material related to aircraft documents, aircraft maintenance, and inspection procedures.

AIRPLANE STRUCTURE

As stated in Chapter 1, Principles of Flight, the required structural strength is based on the intended use of the airplane. An airplane which is to be used for normal flying does not need the strength of an airplane which is intended to be used for acrobatic flight or other special purposes, some of which involve significant in-flight stresses.

Numerous wing designs have been developed in an effort to determine the best type for a specific purpose. Basically, all wings are similar to those used by the Wright brothers and other pioneers. Modifications have been made, however, to increase lifting capacity, reduce drag, increase structural strength, and generally improve flight characteristics. Wing designs are subjected to thorough analysis before being approved for use on certificated airplanes. Strength tests determine the effect of strains and stresses which might be encountered in flight.

Airplane strength is measured basically by the total load which the wings are capable of carrying without permanent damage to the wing structure. The load imposed upon the wings depends upon the type of flight in which the airplane is engaged. The wing must support not only the weight of the airplane, but the additional loads caused during certain flight maneuvers such as turns and pullouts from dives. Turbulent air also creates additional loads and these loads increase as the severity of the turbulence increases.

To permit the utmost efficiency of construction without sacrificing safety, the FAA has established several categories of airplanes with minimum strength requirements for each. Limitations of each airplane are available to the pilot through markings on instruments, placards on instrument panels, operating limitations attached to Airworthiness Certificates, Aircraft Flight Manual, or Pilot's Operating Handbook.

FLIGHT CONTROL SYSTEMS

The flight control systems in most general aviation airplanes consist of the cockpit controls, cables, pulleys, and linkages connected to the movable control surfaces outside the airplane.

There are three primary and two secondary flight control systems. The primary flight control systems consist of the elevator, aileron, and rudder, which are essential in controlling the aircraft. The secondary control systems consist of the trim tabs and wing flaps. The trim tabs enable the pilot to trim out control pressures, and the flaps enable the pilot to change the lifting characteristics of the wing and also to decrease the speed at which the wing stalls. All of the flight control systems, except the wing flaps, were discussed in Chapter 1, Principles of Flight. The flaps will be discussed at this point.

Wing Flaps

Wing flaps are a movable part of the wing, normally hinged to the inboard trailing edge of each wing. Flaps are extended or retracted by the pilot. Extending the flaps increases the wing camber, wing area (some types), and the angle of attack of the wing. This increases wing lift and also increases induced drag. The increased lift enables the pilot to make steeper approaches to a landing without an increase in airspeed. Their use at recommended settings also provides increased lift under certain takeoff conditions. When the flaps are no longer needed, they can be retracted.

Pilots are cautioned to operate the flaps within the airspeed limitations set forth for the particular airplane being flown. If the speed limitations are exceeded, the increased drag forces created by extending the flaps could result in structural damage to the airplane.

Figure 2-1 shows the four types of flaps in general use. The plain or simple flap is a portion of the trailing edge of the wing on a hinged pivot which allows the flap to be moved downward, thereby changing the chord line, angle of attack, and the camber of the wing. The split flap is a hinged portion of the bottom surface of the wing only, which when extended increases the angle of attack by changing the chord line. The Fowler flap, when extended, not only tilts downward but also slides rearward on tracks. This increases angle of attack, wing camber, and wing area, thereby providing added lift without significantly increasing drag. The slotted flap in addition to changing the wing's camber and chord line also lets a portion of high pressure air beneath the wing travel through a slot. This increases the velocity of air and increases lift.

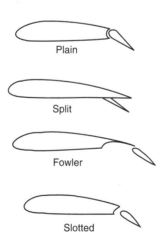

Plain

Split

Fowler

Slotted

FIGURE 2-1.—Wing flaps.

With all four types of flaps, the practical effect of the flap is to permit a steeper angle of descent without an increase in airspeed. Extended flaps also permit a slower speed to be used on an approach and landing, thus reducing the distance of the landing roll.

Landing Gear

The landing gear system supports the airplane during the takeoff run, landing, taxiing, and when parked. These ground operations require that the landing gear be capable of steering, braking, and absorbing shock.

A steerable nose gear or tailwheel permits the airplane to be controlled by the pilot throughout all operations while on the ground. Individual brakes installed on each main wheel permit the pilot to use either brake individually as an aid to steering or, by applying both brakes simultaneously, the pilot can decelerate or stop the airplane. Hydraulic shock struts or leaf springs are installed in the various types of landing gear systems to absorb the impact of landings, or the shock of taxiing over rough ground.

There are two basic types of landing gear used on light airplanes. These are:

- Conventional Landing Gear
- Tricycle Landing Gear

Conventional Landing Gear

The conventional landing gear, which was used on most airplanes manufactured years ago, is still used on some airplanes designed for operations on rough fields. This landing gear system consists of two main wheels and a tailwheel. Shock absorption is usually provided on the main landing gear by inflated tires and shock absorbers while it is provided on the tailwheel by a spring assembly to which the tailwheel is bolted. The tailwheel is usually steerable by the rudder pedals through at least 15° on each side of a center point beyond which it becomes full swiveling.

Tricycle Landing Gear

The tricycle landing gear is used on most airplanes produced today. This gear has advantages over the conventional gear because it provides easier ground handling characteristics. The main landing gear is constructed similar to the main landing gear on the conventional system, but is located further rearward on the airplane. The nose gear is usually steerable by the rudder pedals.

Some airplanes are equipped with a retractable landing gear. Retracting the gear reduces the drag, and increases the airspeed without additional power.

The landing gear normally retracts into the wing or fuselage through an opening which is covered by doors after the gear is retracted. This provides for the unrestricted flow of air across the opening which houses the gear. The retraction or extension of the landing gear is accomplished either electrically or hydraulically by landing gear controls from within the cockpit. Indicators are provided in the cockpit to indicate whether the wheels are extended and locked, or retracted. In retractable landing gear installations, a system is provided for emergency gear extension in the event the normal landing gear mechanism fails to lower the gear.

ELECTRICAL SYSTEM

Electrical energy is required to operate navigation and communication radios, lights, and other airplane equipment.

Many airplanes in the past were not equipped with an electrical system. They were equipped with a magneto system which supplied electrical energy to the engine ignition system only. Modern airplanes still use an independent magneto system, but in addition are equipped with an electrical system. The magneto system does not depend upon the airplane electrical system for operation. In other words, the airplane electrical system can be turned off in flight and the engine will continue to operate efficiently, utilizing the electrical energy provided by the magnetos.

Most airplanes are equipped with a 14- or 28-volt direct-current electrical system. The 28-volt system provides an electrical reserve capacity for more complex systems, including additional electrical energy for starting.

A basic airplane electrical system consists of the following components:

- Alternator or generator
- Battery
- Master or battery switch
- Alternator or generator switch
- Bus bar, fuses, and circuit breakers
- Voltage regulator
- Ammeter
- Starting motor
- Associated electrical wiring
- Accessories

Engine-driven alternators or generators supply electric current to the electrical system and also maintain a sufficient electrical charge in the battery which is used primarily for starting.

There are several basic differences between alternators and generators. Most generators will not produce a sufficient amount of electrical current at low engine revolutions per minute (RPM) to operate the entire electrical system. Therefore, during operations at low engine RPM's, the electrical needs must be drawn from the battery, which in a short time may be depleted.

An alternator, however, produces a sufficient amount of electrical current at slower engine speeds by first producing alternating current which is converted to direct current. Another advantage is that the electrical output of an alternator is more constant throughout the ranges of engine speeds. Alternators are also lighter in weight, less expensive to maintain, and less prone to become overloaded during conditions of heavy electrical loads.

Electrical energy stored in a battery provides a source of electricity for starting the engine and a limited supply of electricity for use in the event the alternator or generator fails.

Some airplanes are equipped with receptacles to which external auxiliary power units (APU) can be connected to provide electrical energy for starting. These are very useful, especially during cold weather starting. Care must be exercised in starting engines using an APU.

A master switch is installed on airplanes to provide a means for the pilot to turn the electrical system "on" and "off." Turning the master switch "on" provides electrical energy to all the electrical equipment circuits with the exception of the ignition system. Although additional electrical equipment may be found in some airplanes, the following list the equipment most commonly found which uses the electrical system for its source of energy:

• Position lights	• Anticollision lights
• Landing lights	• Taxi lights
• Interior cabin lights	• Instrument lights
• Radio equipment	• Turn indicator
• Fuel gauges	• Electric fuel pump
• Stall warning system	• Pitot heat

Some airplanes are equipped with a battery switch which controls the electrical power to the airplane in a manner similar to the master switch. In addition, an alternator switch is installed which permits the pilot to exclude the alternator from the electrical system in the event of alternator failure. With the alternator switch "off," the entire electrical load is placed on the battery. Therefore, all nonessential electrical equipment should be turned off to conserve the energy stored in the battery.

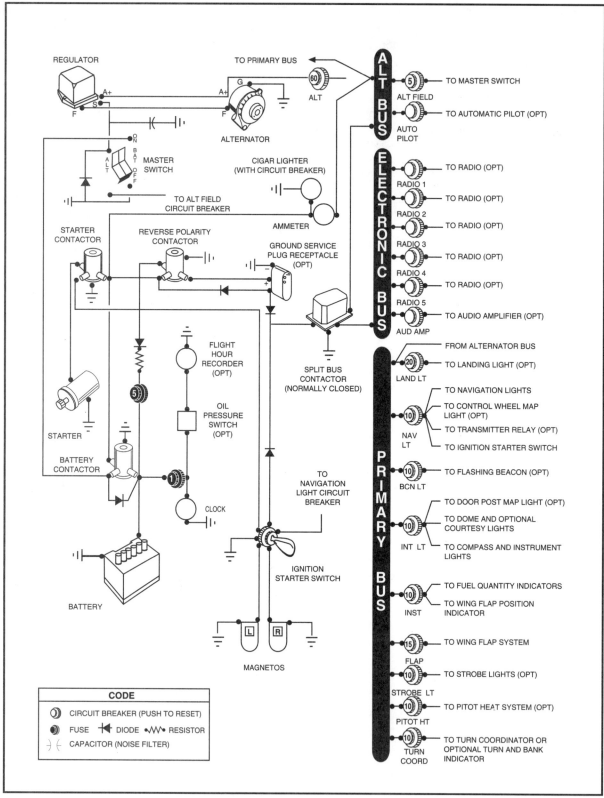

FIGURE 2-2.—Electrical system schematic.

A bus bar is used as a terminal in the airplane electrical system to connect the main electrical system to the equipment using electricity as a source of power. This simplifies the wiring system and provides a common point from which voltage can be distributed throughout the system. [Figure 2-2]

Fuses or circuit breakers are used in the electrical system to protect the circuits and equipment from electrical overload. Spare fuses of the proper amperage limit should be carried in the airplane to replace defective or blown fuses. Circuit breakers have the same function as a fuse but can be manually reset, rather than replaced, if an overload condition occurs in the electrical system. Placards at the fuse or circuit breaker location identify the circuit by name and show the amperage limit. [Figure 2-3]

An ammeter is an instrument used to monitor the performance of the airplane electrical system. Not all airplanes are equipped with an ammeter. Some are equipped with a light which, when lighted, indicates a discharge in the system as a generator/alternator malfunction.

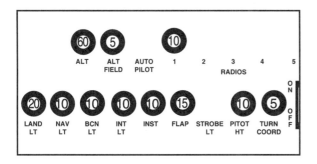

FIGURE 2-3.—Circuit breaker panel.

An ammeter shows if the alternator/generator is producing an adequate supply of electrical power to the system by measuring the amperes of electricity. This instrument also indicates whether the battery is receiving an electrical charge. The face of some ammeters is designed with a zero point in the upper center of the dial and a plus value to the right of center; a negative value is to the left. A vertical needle swings to the right or left, depending upon the performance of the electrical system. If the needle indicates a plus value, it means that the battery is being charged. After power is drawn from the battery for starting, the needle will indicate a noticeable plus charge value for a short period of time, and then stabilize to a lower plus charge value. [Figure 2-4]

FIGURE 2-4.—Loadmeter and ammeter.

If the needle indicates a minus value, it means that the generator or alternator output is inadequate and energy is being drawn from the battery to supply the system. This could be caused by either a defective alternator/generator or by an overload in the system, or both. Full scale ammeter discharge or rapid fluctuation of the needle usually means generator/alternator malfunction. If this occurs, the pilot should cut the generator/alternator out of the system and conserve battery power by reducing the load on the electrical system.

The loadmeter type of ammeter shows the load being placed on the alternator. [Figure 2-4]

A voltage regulator controls the rate of charge to the battery by stabilizing the generator or alternator electrical output. The generator/alternator voltage output is usually slightly higher than the battery voltage. For example, a 12-volt battery would be fed by a generator/alternator system of approximately 14 volts. The difference in voltage keeps the battery charged.

ENGINE OPERATION

Knowledge of a few general principles of engine operation will help the pilot obtain increased dependability and efficiency from the engine and, in many instances, this knowledge will help in avoiding engine failure.

In this short chapter, it is impractical to discuss in detail the various types of engines and the finer points of operation which can be learned only through experience. Information from the manufacturer's instruction manual; familiarity with the operating limitations for the airplane engine; and specific advice from a flight instructor, combined with the information contained within this section, should provide adequate information to operate an airplane engine satisfactorily.

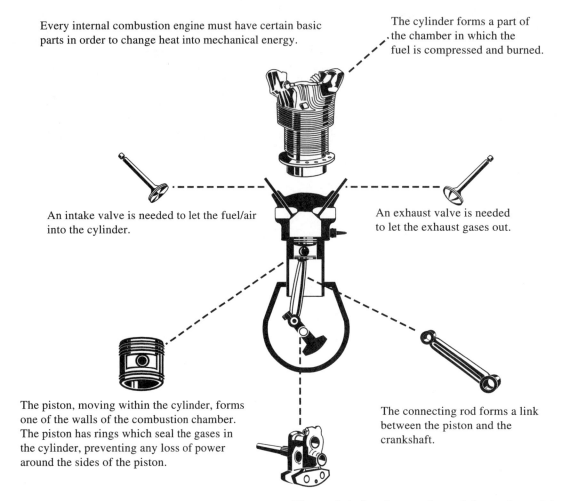

Every internal combustion engine must have certain basic parts in order to change heat into mechanical energy.

The cylinder forms a part of the chamber in which the fuel is compressed and burned.

An intake valve is needed to let the fuel/air into the cylinder.

An exhaust valve is needed to let the exhaust gases out.

The piston, moving within the cylinder, forms one of the walls of the combustion chamber. The piston has rings which seal the gases in the cylinder, preventing any loss of power around the sides of the piston.

The connecting rod forms a link between the piston and the crankshaft.

The crankshaft and connecting rod change the straight line motion of the piston to a rotary turning motion. The crankshaft in an aircraft engine also absorbs the power or work from all the cylinders and transfers it to the propeller.

FIGURE 2-5.—Basic parts of a reciprocating engine.

How an Engine Operates

Most light airplane engines are internal combustion of the reciprocating type which operate on the same principle as automobile engines. They are called reciprocating engines because certain parts move back and forth in contrast to a circular motion such as a turbine. Some smaller airplanes are equipped with turbine engines, but this type will not be discussed in this handbook. As shown in figure 2-5, the reciprocating engine consists of cylinders, pistons, connecting rods, and a crankshaft. One end of a connecting rod is attached to a piston and the other end to the crankshaft.

This connecting rod converts the straight-line motion of the piston to the rotary motion of the crankshaft, which turns the propeller. At the closed end of the cylinder, there are normally two spark plugs which ignite the fuel, and two openings over which valves open and close. One valve (the intake valve) when open admits the mixture of fuel and air, and the other (the exhaust valve) when open permits the burned gases to escape. For the engine to complete one cycle, the piston must complete four strokes. This requires two revolutions of the crankshaft. The four strokes are the intake, compression, power, and exhaust. The following describes one cycle of engine operation.

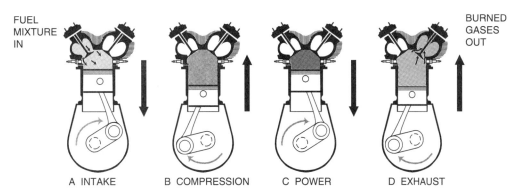

FUEL MIXTURE IN

BURNED GASES OUT

A INTAKE   B COMPRESSION   C POWER   D EXHAUST

FIGURE 2-6.—Four strokes of the piston produce: (A) fuel mixture (light blue) is drawn into cylinder by downward stroke, (B) mixture (darker blue) is compressed by upward stroke, (C) spark ignites mixture (red) forcing piston downward and producing power that turns propeller, (D) burned gases (light red) pushed out of cylinder by upward stroke.

Diagram A of figure 2-6 shows the piston moving away from the cylinder head. The intake valve is opened and the fuel/air mixture is drawn into the cylinder. This is the intake stroke.

Diagram B shows the piston returning to the top of the cylinder. Both valves are closed, and the fuel/air mixture is compressed. This is the compression stroke.

Diagram C shows that when the piston is approximately at the top of the cylinder head, a spark from the plugs ignites the mixture, which burns at a controlled rate. Expansion of the burning gas exerts pressure on the piston, forcing it downward. This is the power stroke.

Diagram D shows that just before the piston completes the power stroke the exhaust valve starts to open, and the burned gases are forced out as the piston returns to the top of the cylinder. This is the exhaust stroke. The cycle is then ready to begin again as shown in Diagram A.

From this description, notice that each cylinder of the engine delivers power only once in every four strokes of the piston or every two revolutions of the crankshaft. The momentum of the crankshaft carries the piston through the other three strokes although the diagram shows the action of only one cylinder. To increase power and gain smoothness of operation, other cylinders are added and the power strokes are timed to occur at successive intervals during the revolution of the crankshaft.

Aircraft engines are classified by the various ways the cylinders are arranged around the central crankcase. Most general aviation airplane engines are classed as the horizontally opposed, which have the cylinder banks arranged in two rows, directly opposite to each other and using the same crankshaft.

Larger and more powerful reciprocating engines are classed as radial engines. In these engines, the cylinders are placed in a circular pattern around the crankcase, which is placed in the center of the circle.

Other engine classifications are the in-line engine with the cylinders placed in one straight row, and the "vee" type with the cylinders placed in two rows forming a "V" similar to the V-8 engine used in automobiles.

Cooling System

The burning fuel within the cylinders produces intense heat, most of which is expelled through the exhaust. Much of the remaining heat, however, must be removed to prevent the engine from overheating. In practically all automobile engines, excess heat is carried away by a coolant circulating around the cylinder walls.

Most light airplane engines are air cooled. The cooling process is accomplished by cool air being forced into the engine compartment through openings in front of the engine cowl. This ram air is routed by baffles over fins attached to the engine cylinders, and other parts of the engine, where the air absorbs the engine heat. Expulsion of the hot air takes place through one or two openings at the rear bottom of the engine cowling.

Some airplanes are equipped with a device known as cowl flaps which are used to control engine temperatures during various flight operations. Cowl flaps are hinged covers which fit over the opening through which the hot air is expelled. By adjusting the cowl flap opening, the pilot can regulate the engine temperature during flight. If the engine temperature is low, the cowl flaps can be closed, thereby restricting the flow of expelled hot air and increasing engine temperature. If the engine temperature is high, the cowl flaps can be opened to permit a greater flow of air through the system, thereby decreasing the engine temperature. Usually during low airspeed and high power operations such as takeoffs and climbs, the cowl flaps are opened. During higher speed and lower power operations such as cruising flight and descents, the cowl flaps are closed.

Under normal operating conditions in airplanes not equipped with cowl flaps, the engine temperature can be controlled by changing the airspeed or the power output of the engine. High engine temperatures can be decreased by increasing the airspeed and/or reducing the power.

The oil temperature gauge indicates the temperature of the oil which is heated by the engine; therefore, this gauge gives an indirect and delayed indication of rising engine temperature. However, the oil temperature gauge should be used for determining engine temperature if this is the only means available.

Many airplanes are equipped with a cylinder-head temperature gauge. This is an additional instrument which will indicate a direct and immediate cylinder temperature change. This instrument is calibrated in degrees Celsius or Fahrenheit, and is usually color coded with a green arc to indicate the normal operating range. A red line on the instrument indicates maximum allowable cylinder head temperature.

To avoid excessive cylinder head temperatures, a pilot can open the cowl flaps, increase airspeed, enrich the mixture, or reduce power. Any of these procedures will aid in reducing the engine temperature.

When an airplane engine is operated on the ground, very little air flows past the cylinders (particularly if the engine is closely cowled) and overheating is likely to occur. Overheating may also occur during a prolonged climb, because the engine at this time is usually developing high power at relatively slow airspeed.

Operating the engine at higher than its designed temperature can cause loss of power, excessive oil consumption, and detonation. It will also lead to serious permanent damage, such as, scoring the cylinder walls, damaging the pistons and rings, and burning and warping the valves. To aid the pilot in avoiding excessive temperatures, engine temperature instruments in the cockpit should be monitored in flight.

Ignition System

The function of the ignition system is to provide a spark to ignite the fuel/air mixture in the cylinder. The magneto ignition system is used on most aircraft engines because it does not depend on an external source of energy such as the electrical system.

Magnetos are self-contained engine driven units supplying ignition current. However, the magneto must be actuated by rotating the engine before current is supplied to the ignition system. The aircraft battery furnishes electrical power to operate the starter system; the starter system actuates the rotating element of the magneto; and the magneto then furnishes the spark to each cylinder to ignite the fuel/air mixture. After the engine starts, the starter system is disengaged, and the battery no longer has any part in the actual operation of the engine. If the battery (or master) switch is turned "OFF," the engine will continue to run. However, this should not be done since battery power is necessary at low engine RPM to operate other electrical equipment (radio, lights, etc.). When the generator or alternator is operating, the battery will be charging.

Most aircraft engines are equipped with a dual ignition system; that is, two magnetos to supply the electrical current to two spark plugs for each combustion chamber. One magneto system supplies the current to one set of plugs; the second magneto system supplies the current to the other set of plugs. This is the reason that the ignition switch has four positions: "OFF," "LEFT," "RIGHT," and "BOTH." With the switch in the "L" or "R" position, only one magneto is supplying current and only one set of spark plugs is firing. With the switch in the "BOTH" position, both magnetos are supplying current and both sets of spark plugs are firing. The main advantages of the dual system are: increased safety, in case one magneto system fails, the engine may be operated on the other system until a landing can be made; and improved burning and combustion of the mixture, and consequently improved performance.

NOTE: To ensure that both ignition systems are operating properly, each system is checked during the engine runup prior to flight. This check should be accomplished in accordance with the manufacturer's recommendations in the Aircraft Flight Manual or Pilot's Operating Handbook.

It is important to turn the ignition switch to "BOTH" for flight and completely "OFF" when shutting down the engine after flight. Even with the electrical master switch "OFF" and the ignition switch on either "BOTH" or "LEFT" or "RIGHT" magnetos, the engine could fire if the propeller is moved from outside the airplane. Also, if the magneto switch ground wire is disconnected or broken, the magneto is "ON" even though the ignition switch is in the "OFF" position.

Fuel System

The function of the fuel system is to provide a means of storing fuel in the airplane and transferring this fuel to the airplane engine. Fuel systems are classified according to the method used to furnish fuel to the engine from the fuel tanks. The two classifications are the "gravity feed" and the "fuel pump system."

The gravity feed system utilizes the force of gravity to transfer the fuel from the tanks to the engine. This system can be used on high-wing airplanes if the fuel tanks are installed in the wings. This places the fuel tanks above the carburetor and the fuel is gravity fed through the system and into the carburetor.

If the design of the airplane is such that gravity cannot be used to transfer fuel, fuel pumps are installed. This is true on low-wing airplanes where the fuel tanks in the wings are located below the carburetor.

Two fuel pump systems are used on most airplanes. The main pump system is engine driven and an auxiliary electric driven pump is provided for use in the event the engine pump fails. The auxiliary pump, commonly know as the "boost pump," provides added reliability to the fuel system, and is also used as an aid in engine starting. The electric auxiliary pump is controlled by a switch in the cockpit.

Because of variation in fuel system operating procedures, the pilot should consult the Aircraft Flight Manual or Pilot's Operating Handbook for specific operating procedures.

Fuel Tanks, Selectors, Strainers, and Drains

Most airplanes are designed to use space in the wings to mount fuel tanks. All tanks have filler openings which are covered by a cap. This system also includes lines connecting to the engine, a fuel gauge, strainers, and vents which permit air to replace the fuel consumed during flight. Fuel overflow vents are provided to discharge fuel in the event the fuel expands because of high temperatures. Fuel tank sump drains are located at the bottom of the tanks from which water and other sediment can be drained from the tanks.

Fuel lines pass through a selector assembly located in the cockpit which provides a means for the pilot to turn the fuel "off," "on," or to select a particular tank from which to draw fuel. The fuel selector assembly may be a simple "on/off" valve, or a more complex arrangement which permits the pilot to select individual tanks or use all tanks at the same time.

Airplanes are equipped with fuel strainers, called sumps, located at the low point in the fuel lines between the fuel selector and the carburetor. The strainer filters the fuel and traps water and sediment in a container which can be drained to remove foreign matter from the fuel.

Fuel Primer

A manual fuel primer is installed in some airplanes to aid in starting the engine, particularly when the weather is cold. Activating the primer draws fuel from the tanks and vaporizes the fuel directly into the cylinders through small fuel lines. When engines are cold and do not generate sufficient heat to vaporize the fuel, the primer is used not only to start the engine, but to keep the engine running until sufficient engine heat is generated.

Fuel Pressure Gauge

If a fuel pump is installed in the fuel system, a fuel pressure gauge is also included. This gauge indicates the pressure in the fuel lines. The normal operating pressure can be found in the Airplane Flight Manual or on the gauge by color coding.

Induction, Carburetion, and Injection Systems

In reciprocating aircraft engines, the function of the induction system is to complete the process of taking in outside air, mixing it with fuel, and delivering this mixture to the cylinders. The system includes the air scoops and ducts, the carburetor or fuel injection system, the intake manifold, and (if installed) the turbo or superchargers.

Two types of induction systems are commonly used in light airplane engines: (1) carburetor system, which mixes the fuel and air in the carburetor before this mixture enters the intake manifold, and (2) fuel injection system in which the fuel and air are mixed just prior to entering each cylinder. The fuel injection system does not utilize a carburetor.

Carburetor System

The carburetor system uses one of two types of carburetor: (1) the float-type carburetor, which is generally installed in airplanes equipped with small horsepower engines, and (2) the pressure type, used in higher horsepower engines. The pressure type will not be discussed in this handbook, but many aspects of each are similar.

In the operation of the carburetor system, the outside air first flows through an air filter, usually located at an air intake in the front part of the engine cowling. This filtered air flows into the carburetor and through a venturi, a narrow throat in the carburetor. When the air flows through the venturi, a low pressure area is created, which forces the fuel to flow through a main fuel jet located at the throat and into the airstream where it is mixed with the flowing air. [Figure 2-7]

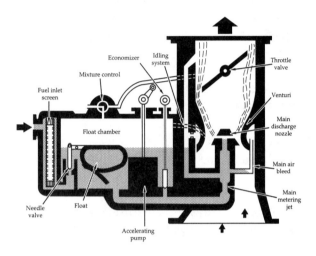

FIGURE 2-7.—A float-type carburetor.

The fuel/air mixture is then drawn through the intake manifold and into the combustion chambers where it is ignited. The "float-type carburetor" acquires its name from a float which rests on fuel within the float chamber. A needle attached to the float opens and closes an opening in the fuel line. This meters the correct amount of fuel into the carburetor, depending upon the position of the float, which is controlled by the level of fuel in the float chamber. When the level of the fuel forces the float to rise, the needle closes the fuel opening and shuts off the fuel flow to the carburetor. It opens when the engine requires additional fuel.

Mixture Control

A "mixture control" in the cockpit is provided to change the fuel flow to the engine to compensate for varying air densities as the airplane changes altitude.

Carburetors are normally calibrated at sea level pressure to meter the correct amount of fuel with the mixture control in a "full rich" position. As altitude increases, air density decreases. This means that a given volume of air does not weigh as much at higher altitudes because it does not contain as many air molecules. As altitude increases, the weight of air decreases, even though the volume of air entering the carburetor remains the same. To compensate for this difference, the mixture control is used to adjust the ratio of fuel-to-air mixture entering the combustion chamber. This also regulates fuel consumption.

If the fuel/air mixture is too rich, i.e., too much fuel in terms of the weight of air, excessive fuel consumption, rough engine operation, and appreciable loss of power will occur. Because of excessive fuel, a cooling effect takes place which causes below normal temperatures in the combustion chambers. This cooling results in spark plug fouling. Conversely, operation with an excessively lean mixture, i.e., too little fuel in terms of the weight of air, will result in rough engine operation, detonation, overheating, and a loss of power.

To summarize, as the airplane climbs and the atmospheric pressure decreases, there is a corresponding decrease in the weight of air passing through the induction system. The volume of air, however, remains constant, and since it is the volume of airflow which determines the pressure drop at the throat of the venturi, the carburetor tends to meter the same amount of fuel to this thin air as to the dense air at sea level. Therefore, the mixture becomes richer as the airplane gains altitude. The mixture control prevents this by decreasing the rate of fuel discharge to compensate for the decrease in air density. However, the mixture must be enriched when descending from altitude.

Follow the manufacturer's recommendation for the particular airplane being flown to determine the proper leaning/enriching procedures.

Carburetor Icing

The vaporization of fuel, combined with the expansion of air as it flows through the carburetor, causes a sudden cooling of the mixture. The temperature of the air passing through the carburetor may drop significantly within a fraction of a second. Water vapor in the air is "squeezed out" by this cooling and, if the temperature in the carburetor reaches 0 °C (32 °F) or below, the moisture will be deposited as frost or ice inside the carburetor passages. Even a slight accumulation of this deposit will reduce power and may lead to complete engine failure, particularly when the throttle is partly or fully closed. [Figure 2-8]

Conditions Conducive to Carburetor Icing

On dry days, or when the temperature is well below freezing, the moisture in the air is not generally enough to cause trouble. But if the temperature is between -7 °C (20 °F) and 21 °C (70 °F), with visible moisture or high humidity, the pilot should be constantly on the alert for carburetor ice. During low or closed throttle settings, an engine is particularly susceptible to carburetor icing.

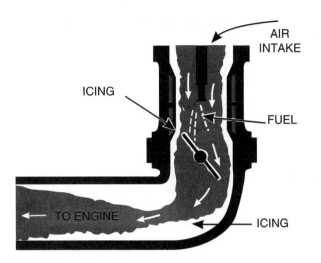

FIGURE 2-8.—Formation of ice (white) in the fuel intake system may reduce or block fuel flow (red) to the engine.

Indications of Carburetor Icing

For airplanes with fixed-pitch propellers, the first indication of carburetor icing is loss of RPM. For airplanes with controllable-pitch (constant-speed) propellers, the first indication is usually a drop in manifold pressure. In both cases, a roughness in engine operation may develop later. There will be no reduction in RPM in airplanes with constant-speed propellers, since propeller pitch is automatically adjusted to compensate for the loss of power, thus maintaining constant RPM.

Use of Carburetor Heat

The carburetor heater is an anti-icing device that preheats the air before it reaches the carburetor. This preheating can be used to melt any ice or snow entering the intake, to melt ice that forms in the carburetor passages (provided the accumulation is not too great), and to keep the fuel mixture above the freezing temperature to prevent formation of carburetor ice.

When conditions are conducive to carburetor icing during flight, periodic checks should be made to detect its presence. If detected, full carburetor heat should be applied immediately, and it should be left in the "on" position until the pilot is certain that all the ice has been removed. If ice is present, applying partial heat or leaving heat on for an insufficient time might aggravate the situation.

When heat is first applied, there will be a drop in RPM in airplanes equipped with fixed-pitch propellers; there will be a drop in manifold pressure in airplanes equipped with controllable-pitch propellers. If no carburetor ice is present, there will be no further change in RPM or manifold pressure until the carburetor heat is turned off; then the RPM or manifold pressure will return to the original reading before heat was applied. If carburetor ice is present, there will normally be a rise in RPM or manifold pressure after the initial drop (often accompanied by intermittent engine roughness); and then, when the carburetor heat is turned "off," the RPM or manifold pressure will rise to a setting greater than that before application of the heat. The engine should also run more smoothly after the ice has been removed.

Whenever the throttle is closed during flight, the engine cools rapidly and vaporization of the fuel is less complete than if the engine is warm. Also, in this condition, the engine is more susceptible to carburetor icing. Therefore, if the pilot suspects carburetor-icing conditions and anticipates closed-throttle operation, the carburetor heat should be turned to "full-on" before closing the throttle, and left on during the closed-throttle operation. The heat will aid in vaporizing the fuel and preventing carburetor ice. Periodically, however, the throttle should be opened smoothly for a few seconds to keep the engine warm, otherwise the carburetor heater may not provide enough heat to prevent icing.

Use of carburetor heat tends to reduce the output of the engine and also to increase the operating temperature. Therefore, the heat should not be used when full power is required (as during takeoff) or during normal engine operation except to check for the presence or removal of carburetor ice. In extreme cases of carburetor icing, after the ice has been removed, it may be necessary to apply just enough carburetor heat to prevent further ice formation. However, this must be done with caution. Check the engine manufacturer's recommendations for the correct use of carburetor heat.

The carburetor heat should be checked during the engine runup. To properly perform this inspection, the manufacturer's recommendations should be followed.

Carburetor Air Temperature Gauge

Some airplanes are equipped with a carburetor air temperature gauge which is useful in detecting potential icing conditions. Usually, the face of the gauge is calibrated in degrees Celsius (C), with a yellow arc indicating the carburetor air temperatures at which icing may occur. This yellow arc ranges between -15 °C and +5 °C. If the air temperature and moisture content of the air are such that the carburetor icing is improbable, the engine can be operated with the indicator in the yellow range with no adverse effects. However, if the atmospheric conditions are conducive to carburetor icing, the indicator must be kept outside the yellow arc by application of carburetor heat.

Certain carburetor air temperature gauges have a red radial which indicates the maximum permissible carburetor inlet air temperature recommended by the engine manufacturer; also, a green arc which indicates the normal operating range.

Outside Air Temperature Gauge

Most airplanes are equipped with an outside air temperature gauge (OAT) calibrated in both degrees Celsius and Fahrenheit. It is used not only for obtaining the outside or ambient air temperature for calculating true airspeed, but also is useful in detecting potential icing conditions.

Fuel Injection System

Fuel injection systems have replaced carburetors on some engines. In this system, the fuel is normally injected either directly into the cylinders or just ahead of the intake valve. The fuel injection system is generally considered to be less susceptible to icing than the carburetor system. Impact icing of the air intake, however, is a possibility in either system. Impact icing occurs when ice forms on the exterior of the airplane and results in clogging openings such as the air intake for the injection system.

There are several types of fuel injection systems in use today. Although there are variations in design, the operational methods of each are generally similar. Most designs include an engine-driven fuel pump, a fuel/air control unit, fuel distributor, and discharge nozzles for each cylinder.

Some of the advantages of fuel injection are:

- Reduction in evaporative icing.
- Better fuel flow.
- Faster throttle response.
- Precise control of mixture.
- Better fuel distribution.
- Easier cold weather starts.

Disadvantages are usually associated with:

- Difficulty in starting a hot engine.
- Vapor locks during ground operations on hot days.
- Problems associated with restarting an engine that quits because of fuel starvation.

The air intake for the fuel injection system is somewhat similar to that used in the carburetor system. The fuel injection system, however, is equipped with an alternate air source located within the engine cowling. This source is used if the external air source is obstructed by ice or by other matter. The alternate air source is usually operated automatically with a backup manual system that can be used if the automatic feature malfunctions.

Proper Fuel is Essential

There are several grades of aviation fuel available; therefore, care must be exercised to assure that the correct aviation grade is being used for the specific type of engine. It can be harmful to the engine and dangerous to the flight if the wrong kind of fuel is used. It is the pilot's responsibility to obtain the proper grade of fuel. The proper grade is stated in the Aircraft Flight Manual or Pilot's Operating Handbook, on placards in the cockpit, and next to the filler caps.

The proper fuel for an engine will burn smoothly from the spark plug outward, exerting a smooth pressure downward on the piston. Using low-grade fuel or too lean a mixture can cause detonation. Detonation or knock is a sudden explosion or shock, to a small area of the piston top, similar to striking it with a hammer. Detonation produces extreme heat which often progresses into preignition, causing structural stresses on parts of the engine. Therefore, to prevent detonation, the pilot should use the proper grade of fuel, maintain a sufficiently rich mixture, and maintain engine temperatures within the recommended limits. [Figure 2-9]

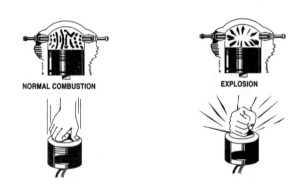

NORMAL COMBUSTION   EXPLOSION

FIGURE 2-9.—Normal combustion and explosive combustion.

Aviation gasolines are identified by octane or performance numbers (grades) which designate the antiknock value or knock resistance of the fuel mixture in the engine cylinder. The higher the grade of gasoline, the more pressure the fuel can withstand without detonating.

Airplane engines are designed to operate using a specific grade of fuel as recommended by the manufacturer. Lower numbered octane fuel is used in lower compression engines because these fuels ignite at a lower temperature. Higher octane fuels are used in higher compression engines because they must ignite at higher temperatures but not prematurely. If the proper grade of fuel is not available, it is possible, but not desirable, to use the next higher grade as a substitute.

Dyes are added to aviation fuels to assist in identification of the proper fuel grade.

GRADE	COLOR
80	RED
100	GREEN
100LL	BLUE
TURBINE	COLORLESS

It should be noted that if fuel grades are mixed together they will become clear or colorless.

Fuel Contamination

Water and dirt in fuel systems are dangerous; the pilot must either eliminate or prevent contamination. Of the accidents attributed to powerplant failure from fuel contamination, most have been traced to:

• Inadequate preflight inspection by the pilot.
• Servicing of aircraft with improperly filtered fuel from small tanks or drums.
• Storing aircraft with partially filled fuel tanks.
• Lack of proper maintenance.

To help alleviate these problems, fuel should be drained from the fuel strainer quick drain and from each fuel tank sump into a transparent container and be checked for dirt and water. Experiments have shown that when the fuel strainer is being drained, water in the tank may not appear until all the fuel has been drained from the lines leading to the tank. This indicates that the water remains in the tank and is not forcing the fuel out of the fuel lines leading to the fuel strainer. Therefore, drain enough fuel from the fuel strainer to be certain that fuel is being drained from the tank. The amount will depend on the length of fuel line from the tank to the drain. If water is found in the first sample, drain further samples until no trace appears.

Experiments have also shown that water will still remain in the fuel tanks after the drainage from the fuel strainer had ceased to show any trace of water. This residual water can be removed only by draining the fuel tank sump drains.

The pilot should be able to identify suspended water droplets in the fuel from a cloudy appearance of the fuel; or the clear separation of water from the colored fuel which occurs after the water has settled to the bottom of the tank. Water is the principal contaminant of fuel, and to increase flight safety, the fuel sumps should be drained during preflight.

In addition to the above measures, the following should be considered. The fuel tanks should be filled after each flight, or at least after the last flight of the day. This will prevent moisture condensation within the tank since no air space will be left. If the pilot chooses to refuel with only the amount that can be carried on the next flight—perhaps a day later—there is an added risk of fuel contamination by moisture condensation within the tank. Each additional day may add to the amount of moisture condensation within the tank or tanks.

Another preventive measure the pilot can take is to avoid refueling from cans and drums. This practice introduces a major likelihood of fuel contamination.

As has been pointed out, the practice of using a funnel and chamois skin when refueling from cans or drums is hazardous under any condition, and should be discouraged. It is recognized, of course, that in remote areas or in emergency situations, there may be no alternative to refueling from sources with inadequate anticontamination systems, and a chamois skin and funnel may be the only possible means of filtering fuel.

In addition, it should be clearly understood that the use of a chamois will not always assure decontaminated fuel. Worn out chamois will not filter water; neither will a new, clean chamois that is already water-wet or damp. Most imitation chamois skins will not filter water. There are many filters available that are more effective than the old chamois and funnel system.

Refueling Procedures

Static electricity, formed by the friction of air passing over the surfaces of an airplane in flight and by the flow of fuel through the hose and nozzle, creates a fire hazard during refueling. To guard against the possibility of a spark igniting fuel fumes, a ground wire should be attached to the aircraft before the cap is removed from the tank. The refueling nozzle should be grounded to the aircraft before refueling is begun and throughout the refueling process. The fuel truck should also be grounded to the aircraft and the ground.

If fueling from drums or cans is necessary, proper bonding and grounding connections are extremely important, since there is an ever present danger of static discharge and fuel vapor explosion. Nylon, dacron, or wool clothing are especially prone to accumulate and discharge static electricity from the person to the funnel or nozzle. Drums should be placed near grounding posts and the following sequence of connections observed:

- Drum to ground.
- Ground to aircraft.
- Drum to aircraft.
- Nozzle to aircraft before the aircraft tank cover is opened.
- When disconnecting, reverse the order.

The passage of fuel through a chamois increases the charge of static electricity and the danger of sparks. The aircraft must be properly grounded and the nozzle, chamois filter, and funnel bonded to the aircraft. If a can is used, it should be connected to either the grounding post or the funnel. Under no circumstances should a plastic bucket or similar nonconductive container be used in this operation.

Oil System

Proper lubrication of the engine is essential to the extension of engine life and prevention of excessive maintenance.

The oil system provides a means of storing and circulating oil throughout the internal components of a reciprocating engine. Lubricating oil serves two purposes: (1) it furnishes a coating of oil over the surfaces of the moving parts, preventing direct metal-to-metal contact and the generation of heat, and (2) it absorbs and dissipates, through the oil cooling system, part of the engine heat produced by the internal combustion process.

Usually the engine oil is stored in a sump at the bottom of the engine crankcase. An opening to the oil sump is provided through which oil can be added and a dipstick is provided to measure the oil level in the sump.

A pump forces oil from the sump to the various parts of the engine that require lubrication. The oil then drains back to the sump for recirculation.

Each engine is equipped with an oil pressure gauge and an oil temperature gauge which are monitored to determine that the oil system is functioning properly.

Oil pressure gauges indicate pounds of pressure per square inch (PSI), and are color coded with a green arc to indicate the normal operating range. Also, at each end of the arc, some gauges have a red line to indicate high oil pressure, and another red line to indicate low oil pressure.

The oil pressure indication varies with the temperature of the oil. If the oil temperature is cold, the pressure will be higher than if the oil is hot.

A loss of oil pressure is usually followed by engine failure. If this occurs while on the ground, the pilot must shut the engine down immediately; if in the air, land at a suitable emergency landing site.

The oil temperature gauge is calibrated in either Celsius or Fahrenheit and color coded in green to indicate the normal temperature operating range.

It is important that the pilot check the oil level before each flight. Starting a flight with an insufficient oil supply can lead to serious consequences. The airplane engine will burn off a certain amount of oil during operation, and beginning a flight when the oil level is low will usually result in an insufficient supply of oil before the flight terminates.

There are many different types of oil manufactured for aviation use. The engine manufacturer's recommendation should be followed to determine the type and weight of oil to use. This information can be found in the Aircraft Flight Manual or Pilot's Operating Handbook, or on placards on or near the oil filler cap.

PROPELLER

A detailed discussion of the propeller is quite complex and beyond the intended scope of this handbook. However, the following material is offered as an introduction to the function of the propeller.

A propeller is a rotating airfoil, and is subject to induced drag, stalls, and other aerodynamic principles that apply to any airfoil. It provides the necessary thrust to pull, or in some cases push, the airplane through the air. This is accomplished by using engine power to rotate the propeller which in turn generates thrust in much the same way as a wing produces lift. The propeller has an angle of attack which is the angle between the chord line of the propeller's airfoil and its relative wind (airflow opposite to the motion of the blade).

A propeller blade is twisted. The blade angle changes from the hub to the tip with the greatest angle of incidence, or highest pitch, at the hub and the smallest at the tip. [Figure 2-10]

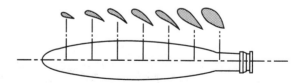

FIGURE 2-10.—Changes in propeller blade angle from hub to tip.

The reason for the twist is to produce uniform lift from the hub to the tip. As the blade rotates, there is a difference in the actual speed of the various portions of the blade. The tip of the blade travels faster than that part near the hub because the tip travels a greater distance than the hub in the same length of time. Changing the angle of incidence (pitch) from the hub to the tip to correspond with the speed produces uniform lift throughout the length of the blade. If the propeller blade was designed with the same angle of incidence throughout its entire length, it would be extremely inefficient because as airspeed increases in flight, the portion near the hub would have a negative angle of attack while the blade tip would be stalled. [Figure 2-11]

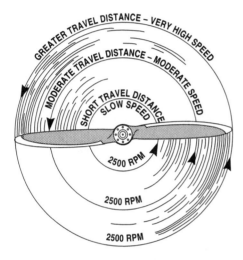

FIGURE 2-11.—Relationship of travel distance and speed of various portions of propeller blade.

Geometric pitch is the distance in inches that the propeller would move forward in one revolution if it were rotated in a solid medium so as not to be affected by slippage as it is in the air. Effective pitch is the actual distance it moves forward through the air in one revolution. Propeller slip is the difference between the geometric pitch and effective pitch. Pitch is proportional to the blade angle which is the angle between the chord line of the blade and the propeller's plane of rotation. [Figure 2-12]

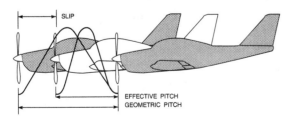

FIGURE 2-12.—Effective and geometric propeller pitch.

Small airplanes are equipped with either one of two types of propellers. One is the fixed-pitch, and the other is the controllable-pitch or constant-speed propeller.

Fixed-Pitch Propeller

The pitch of this propeller is fixed by the manufacturer and cannot be changed by the pilot. There are two types of fixed-pitch propellers; the climb propeller and the cruise propeller. Whether the airplane has a climb or cruise propeller installed depends upon its intended use. The climb propeller has a lower pitch, therefore less drag. This results in the capability of higher RPM and more horsepower being developed by the engine. This increases performance during takeoffs and climbs, but decreases performance during cruising flight.

The cruise propeller has a higher pitch, therefore more drag. This results in lower RPM and less horsepower capability. This decreases performance during takeoffs and climbs, but increases efficiency during cruising flight.

The propeller on a low-horsepower engine is usually mounted on a shaft which may be an extension of the engine crankshaft. In this case, the RPM of the propeller would be the same as the engine RPM.

On higher horsepower engines, the propeller is mounted on a shaft geared to the engine crankshaft. In this type, the RPM of the propeller is different than that of the engine.

If the propeller is a fixed-pitch and the speed of the engine and propeller is the same, a tachometer is the only indicator of engine power.

A tachometer is calibrated in hundreds of RPM, and gives a direct indication of the engine and propeller RPM. The instrument is color coded with a green arc denoting the normal operating range and a red line denoting the maximum continuous operating RPM. Some tachometers have additional marking or interrupted arcs. Therefore, the manufacturer's recommendations should be used as a reference to clarify any misunderstanding of tachometer markings.

The revolutions per minute are regulated by the throttle which controls the fuel/air flow to the engine. At a given altitude, the higher the tachometer reading the higher the power output of the engine.

There is a condition under which the tachometer does not show correct power output of the engine. This occurs when operating altitude increases. For example, 2,300 RPM at 5,000 feet produce less horsepower than 2,300 RPM at sea level. The reason for this is that air density decreases as altitude increases. Power output depends on air density, therefore decreasing the density decreases the power output of the engine. As altitude changes, the position of the throttle must be changed to maintain the same RPM. As altitude is increased, the throttle must be opened further to indicate the same RPM as at a lower altitude.

Controllable-Pitch Propellers

The pitch on these propellers can be changed in flight; therefore, they are referred to as controllable-pitch propellers. These propeller systems vary from a simple two-position propeller to more complex automatic constant-speed propellers.

The number of pitch positions at which the propeller can be set may be limited, such as a two-position propeller with only high or low pitch available. Many other propellers, however, are variable pitch, and can be adjusted to any pitch angle between a minimum and maximum pitch setting.

An airplane equipped with a controllable-pitch propeller has two controls: (1) a throttle control and (2) a propeller control.

The throttle controls the power output of the engine which is registered on the manifold pressure gauge. The manifold pressure gauge is a simple barometer that measures the air pressure in the engine intake manifold in inches of mercury. It is color coded with a green arc indicating the normal operating range.

The propeller control regulates the engine RPM and in turn the propeller RPM. The RPM is registered on the tachometer. The pilot can set the throttle control and propeller control at any desired manifold pressure and RPM setting within the engine operating limitation.

Within a given power setting, when using a constant-speed propeller, the pilot can set the propeller control to a given RPM and the propeller governor will automatically change the pitch (blade angle) to counteract any tendency for the engine to vary from this RPM. For example, if manifold pressure or engine power is increased, the propeller governor automatically increases the pitch of the blade (more propeller drag) to maintain the same RPM.

A controllable-pitch propeller permits the pilot to select the blade angle that will result in the most efficient performance for a particular flight condition. A low blade angle or decreased pitch, reduces the propeller drag and allows more engine power for takeoffs. After airspeed is attained during cruising flight, the propeller blade is changed to a higher angle or increased pitch.

Consequently, the blade takes a larger bite of air at a lower power setting, and therefore increases the efficiency of the flight. This process is similar to shifting gears in an automobile from low gear to high gear.

For any given RPM there is a manifold pressure that should not be exceeded. If manifold pressure is excessive for a given RPM, the pressure within the cylinders could be exceeded, thus placing undue stress on them. If repeated too frequently, this stress could weaken the cylinder components and eventually cause engine failure.

The pilot can avoid conditions that would possibly overstress the cylinders by being constantly aware of the RPM, especially when increasing the manifold pressure. Pilots should conform to the manufacturer's recommendations for power settings of a particular engine so as to maintain the proper relationship between manifold pressure and RPM. Remember, the combination to avoid is a high throttle setting (manifold pressure indication) and a low RPM (tachometer indication).

When both manifold pressure and RPM need to be changed, the pilot can further help avoid engine overstress by making power adjustments in the proper order. When power settings are being decreased, reduce manifold pressure before RPM. When power settings are being increased, reverse the order—increase RPM first, then manifold pressure. If RPM is reduced before manifold pressure, manifold pressure will automatically increase and possibly exceed the manufacturer's tolerances.

Summarizing: In an airplane equipped with a controllable-pitch propeller, the throttle controls the manifold pressure and the propeller control is used to regulate the RPM. Avoid high manifold pressure settings with low RPM. The preceding is a standard procedure for most situations, but with unsupercharged engines it is sometimes modified to take advantage of auxiliary fuel metering devices in the carburetor. These devices function at full throttle settings, providing additional fuel flow. This additional fuel helps cool the engine during takeoffs and full power climbs where engine overheating may be a problem. In such instances, a small reduction in RPM is possible without overstressing the engine, even though the throttle is in the full-power position. If in doubt, the manufacturer's recommendations should be followed.

STARTING THE ENGINE

Before starting the engine, the airplane should be in an area where the propeller will not stir up gravel or dust that could cause damage to the propeller or property. Rules of safety and courtesy should be strictly observed to avoid personal injury or annoyance. The wheels should be chocked and the brakes set to avoid hazards caused by unintentional movement.

Engines Equipped with a Starter

The pilot should be familiar with the manufacturer's recommended starting procedures for the airplane being flown. This information can be found in the Airplane Flight Manual or Pilot's Operating Handbook, or other sources. There are not only different procedures applicable to starting engines equipped with conventional carburetors and those equipped with fuel injection systems, but also between different systems of either carburetion or fuel injection. The pilot should always ascertain that no one is near the propeller, call "clear prop," and wait for a possible response before engaging the propeller. Continuous cranking beyond 30 seconds' duration may damage the starter. In addition, the starter motor should be allowed to cool at least 1 to 2 minutes between cranking periods. If the engine refuses to start under normal circumstances after a reasonable number of attempts, the possibility of problems with ignition or fuel flow should be investigated.

As soon as the engine starts, check for unintentional movement and set power to the recommended warmup RPM. The oil pressure should then be checked to determine that the oil system is functioning properly. If the gauge does not indicate oil pressure within 30 seconds, the engine should be stopped and a check should be made to determine what is causing the lack of oil pressure. If oil is not circulating properly, the engine can be seriously damaged in a short time. During cold weather there will be a much slower response in oil pressure indications than during warmer weather, because colder temperatures cause the oil to congeal (thicken) to a greater extent.

The engine must reach normal operating temperature before it will run smoothly and dependably. Temperature is indicated by the cylinder-head temperature gauge. If the airplane is not equipped with this gauge, the oil temperature gauge must be used. Remember, in this case, that oil warms much slower in cold weather.

Before takeoff the pilot should perform all necessary checks for engine and airplane operation. Follow the manufacturer's recommendations when performing all checks. Always use a checklist; do not rely on memory.

Engines Not Equipped with a Starter

Because of the hazards involved in hand starting airplane engines, every precaution should be exercised. The safety measures previously mentioned should be adhered to, and it is extremely important that a competent pilot be at the controls in the cockpit. Also, the person turning the propeller should be thoroughly familiar with the technique. The following are additional suggestions to aid in increasing the safety factor while hand starting airplanes.

The person who turns the propeller is in charge, and calls out the commands, "gas on, switch off, throttle closed, brakes set." The pilot in the cockpit will check these items and repeat the phrase to assure that there is no misunderstanding. The person propping the airplane should push slightly on the airplane to assure that the brakes are set and are holding firmly. The switch and throttle must not be touched again until the person swinging the prop calls "contact." The pilot will repeat "contact" and then turn on the switch in that sequence—never turn the switch on and then call "contact."

For the person swinging the prop, a few simple precautions will help avoid accidents.

When touching a propeller, always assume that the switch is on, even though the pilot may confirm the statement "switch off." The switches on many engine installations operate on the principle of short circuiting the current. If the switch is faulty, as sometimes happens, it can be in the "off" position and still permit the current to flow to the spark plugs.

Be sure to stand on firm ground. Slippery grass, mud, grease, or loose gravel could cause a slip or fall into or under the propeller.

Never allow any portion of the body to get into the propeller arc of rotation. This applies even though the engine is not being cranked; occasionally, a hot engine will backfire after shutdown when the propeller has almost stopped rotating.

Stand close enough to the propeller to be able to step away as it is pulled down. Standing too far away from the propeller requires leaning forward to reach it. This is an off-balance position and it is possible to fall into the blades as the engine starts. Stepping away after cranking is also a safeguard in the event the brakes do not hold when the engine starts.

When swinging the propeller, always move the blade downward by pushing with the palms of the hands. If the blade is moved upward, or gripped tightly with the fingers and backfiring occurs, it could cause broken fingers or the body to be pulled into the path of the propeller blades.

When removing the chocks from in front of the wheels, it should be remembered that the propeller, when revolving, is almost invisible. There are cases on record where someone intending to remove the chocks walked directly into the propeller.

Unsupervised "hand propping" of an airplane should not be attempted by inexperienced persons. Regardless of the experience level, it should never be attempted by anyone without adhering to adequate safety measures. Uninformed or inexperienced persons or nonpilot passengers should never handle the throttle, brakes, or switches during starting procedures. The airplane should be securely chocked or tied down, and great care should be exercised in setting the throttle. It may be well to turn the fuel selector valve to the "off" position after properly priming the engine and prior to actually attempting the hand start. After it starts, the engine will usually run long enough with the fuel "off" to permit walking around the propeller and turning the fuel selector to the "on" position.

Idling the Engine During Flight

There could be potential problems created by excessive idling of the engine during flight, particularly for long periods of time such as prolonged descents.

Whenever the throttle is closed during flight, the engine cools rapidly and vaporization of fuel is less complete. The airflow through the carburetor system under such conditions may not be of sufficient volume to assure a uniform mixture of fuel and air. Consequently, the engine may cease to operate because the mixture is too lean or too rich. Suddenly opening or closing the throttle could aggravate this condition, and the engine may cough once or twice, sputter, and stop.

Three precautions should be taken to prevent the engine from stopping while idling. First, make sure that the ground idling speed is properly adjusted. Second, do not open or close the throttle abruptly. Third, keep the engine warm during glides by frequently opening the throttle for a few seconds.

EXHAUST GAS TEMPERATURE GAUGE

Many airplanes are equipped with an exhaust gas temperature (EGT) gauge. If properly used, this engine instrument can reduce fuel consumption by 10 percent because of its accuracy in indicating to the pilot the exact amount of fuel that should be metered to the engine.

An EGT gauge measures, in degrees Celsius or Fahrenheit, the temperature of the exhaust gases at the exhaust manifold. This temperature measurement varies with ratio of fuel to air entering the cylinders, and therefore can be used as a basis for regulating the fuel/air mixture. This is possible because this instrument is very sensitive to temperature changes.

Although the manufacturer's recommendation for leaning the mixture should be adhered to, the usual procedure for leaning the mixture on lower horsepower engines when an EGT is available is as follows:

The mixture is leaned slowly while observing the increase in exhaust gas temperature on the gauge. When the EGT reaches a peak, the mixture should be enriched until the EGT gauge indicates a decrease in temperature. The number of degrees drop is recommended by the engine manufacturer, usually approximately 25° to 75°. Engines equipped with carburetors will run rough when leaned to the peak EGT reading, but will run smooth after the mixture is enriched slightly.

AIRCRAFT DOCUMENTS, MAINTENANCE, AND INSPECTIONS

Aircraft Owner Responsibilities

The registered owner of an aircraft is responsible for certain items such as:

• Having a current Airworthiness Certificate and Certificate of Aircraft Registration in the aircraft.
• Maintaining the aircraft in an airworthy condition including compliance with all applicable Airworthiness Directives.
• Assuring that maintenance is properly recorded.
• Keeping abreast of current regulations concerning the operation and maintenance of the aircraft.
• Notifying the FAA Civil Aviation Registry immediately of any change of permanent mailing address, or of the sale or export of the aircraft, or of the loss of U.S. citizenship.

FIGURE 2-13.—AC Form 8050-3, Certificate of Aircraft Registration.

An aircraft must be inspected in accordance with an annual inspection program or with one of the inspection programs outlined in 14 CFR section 91.409, in order to maintain a current Airworthiness Certificate.

Certificate of Aircraft Registration

Before an aircraft can be legally flown, it must be registered with the FAA Civil Aviation Registry and have within it a Certificate of Aircraft Registration issued to the owner as evidence of the registration. [Figure 2-13]

The Certificate of Aircraft Registration will expire when:

• The aircraft is registered under the laws of a foreign country.
• The registration of the aircraft is canceled at the written request of the holder of the certificate.
• The aircraft is totally destroyed or scrapped.
• The ownership of the aircraft is transferred.
• The holder of the certificate loses United States citizenship.
• Thirty days have elapsed since the death of the holder of the certificate.

When the aircraft is destroyed, scrapped, or sold, the previous owner must notify the FAA by filling in the back of the Certificate of Aircraft Registration, and mailing it to the FAA Civil Aviation Registry.

A dealer's aircraft registration certificate is another form of registration certificate, but it is valid only for required flight tests by the manufacturer or in flights that are necessary for the sale of the aircraft by the manufacturer or a dealer. It must be removed by the dealer when the aircraft is sold.

The FAA does not issue any certificate of ownership or endorse any information with respect to ownership on a Certificate of Aircraft Registration.

NOTE: For any additional information concerning the Aircraft Registration Application or the Aircraft Bill of Sale, contact the nearest Flight Standards District Office (FSDO).

Airworthiness Certificate

An Airworthiness Certificate is issued by the FAA only after the aircraft has been inspected and it is found that it meets the requirements of Title 14 of the Code Federal Regulations (14 CFR) and is in a condition for safe operation. Under any circumstances, the aircraft must meet the requirements of the original type certificate. The certificate must be displayed in the aircraft so that it is legible to passengers or crew whenever the aircraft is operated. The Airworthiness Certificate may be transferred with the aircraft except when it is sold to a foreign purchaser.

UNITED STATES OF AMERICA DEPARTMENT OF TRANSPORTATION—FEDERAL AVIATION ADMINISTRATION **STANDARD AIRWORTHINESS CERTIFICATE**			
1. NATIONALITY AND REGISTRATION MARKS	2. MANUFACTURER AND MODEL	3. AIRCRAFT SERIAL NUMBER	4. CATEGORY
N12345	CESSNA C-150L	6969	NORMAL

5. AUTHORITY AND BASIS FOR ISSUANCE

This airworthiness certificate is issued pursuant to the Federal Aviation Act of 1958 and certifies that, as of the date of issuance, the aircraft to which issued has been inspected and found to conform to the type certificate therefor, to be in condition for safe operation, and has been shown to meet the requirements of the applicable comprehensive and detailed airworthiness code as provided by Annex 8 to the Convention on International Civil Aviation, except as noted herein.

Exceptions:

NONE

6. TERMS AND CONDITIONS

Unless sooner surrendered, suspended, revoked, or a termination date is otherwise established by the Administrator, this airworthiness certificate is effective as long as the maintenance, preventative maintenance, and alterations are performed in accordance with Parts 21, 43, and 91 of the Federal Aviation Regulations, as appropriate, and the aircraft is registered in the United States.

DATE OF ISSUANCE	FAA REPRESENTATIVE	DESIGNATION NUMBER
1/29/96	R.E. BARO	AEA-FSDO-03

Any alteration, reproduction, or misuse of this certificate may be punishable by a fine not exceeding $1,000 or imprisonment not exceeding 3 years, or both. THIS CERTIFICATE MUST BE DISPLAYED IN THE AIRCRAFT IN ACCORDANCE WITH APPLICABLE FEDERAL AVIATION REGULATIONS.

FAA FORM 8100-2   (8-82)   GPO 892-804

FIGURE 2-14.—FAA Form 8100-2, Standard Airworthiness Certificate.

The Standard Airworthiness Certificate, is issued for aircraft type certificated in the normal, utility, acrobatic, and transport categories or for manned free balloons. An explanation of each item in the certificate follows: [Figure 2-14]

Item 1. Nationality—The "N" indicates the aircraft is of United States registry. Registration Marks—the number, in this case 12345, is the registration number assigned to the aircraft.

Item 2—Indicates the make and model of the aircraft.

Item 3—Indicates the serial number assigned to the aircraft, as noted on the aircraft data plate.

Item 4—Indicates that the aircraft, in this case, must be operated in accordance with the limitations specified for the "NORMAL" category.

Item 5—Indicates the aircraft has been found to conform to its type certificate and is considered in condition for safe operation at the time of inspection and issuance of the certificate. Any exemptions from the applicable airworthiness standards are briefly noted here and the exemption number given. The word "NONE" is entered if no exemption exists.

Item 6—Indicates the Airworthiness Certificate is in effect indefinitely if the aircraft is maintained in accordance with 14 CFR parts 21, 43, and 91 and the aircraft is registered in the United States. Also included are the date the certificate was issued and the signature and office identification of the FAA representative.

The Special Airworthiness Certificate is issued for all aircraft certificated in other than the Standard classifications (Experimental, Restricted, Limited, and Provisional).

In purchasing an aircraft classed as other than Standard, it is suggested that the local FSDO be contacted for an explanation of the pertinent airworthiness requirements and the limitations of such a certificate.

In summary, the FAA initially determines that the aircraft is in a condition for safe operation and conforms to type design, then issues an Airworthiness Certificate. A Standard Airworthiness Certificate remains in effect as long as the aircraft receives the required maintenance and is properly registered in the United States. Flight safety relies in part on the condition of the aircraft, which may be determined on inspection by mechanics, approved repair stations, or manufacturers who meet specific requirements of 14 CFR part 43.

Aircraft Maintenance

Maintenance means the inspection, overhaul, and repair of aircraft, including the replacement of parts. A PROPERLY MAINTAINED AIRCRAFT IS A SAFE AIRCRAFT.

The purpose of maintenance is to ensure that the aircraft is kept to an acceptable standard of airworthiness throughout its operational life.

Although maintenance requirements will vary for different types of aircraft, experience shows that most aircraft will need some type of preventive maintenance every 25 hours of flying time or less, and minor maintenance at least every 100 hours. This is influenced by the kind of operation, climatic conditions, storage facilities, age, and construction of the aircraft. Most manufacturers supply service information which should be used in maintaining the aircraft.

Inspections

14 CFR part 91 places primary responsibility on the owner or operator for maintaining an aircraft in an airworthy condition. Certain inspections must be performed on the aircraft and the owner must maintain the airworthiness of the aircraft during the time between required inspections by having any unsafe defects corrected.

Title 14 of the Code of Federal Regulations (14 CFR) requires the inspection of all civil aircraft at specific intervals for the purpose of determining the overall condition. The interval depends generally upon the type of operations in which the aircraft is engaged. Some aircraft need to be inspected at least once each 12 calendar months, while inspection is required for others after each 100 hours of operation. In other instances, an aircraft may be inspected in accordance with an inspection system set up to provide for total inspection of the aircraft on the basis of time, time in service, number of system operations, or any combination of these.

Annual Inspection

A reciprocating-powered single-engine aircraft flown for pleasure is required to be inspected at least annually by a certificated airframe and powerplant mechanic holding an Inspection Authorization, or by a certificated repair station that is appropriately rated, or by the manufacturer of the aircraft. The aircraft may not be operated unless the annual inspection has been performed within the preceding 12 calendar months. A period of 12 calendar months extends from any day of any month to the last day of the same month the following year. However, an aircraft with the annual inspection overdue may be operated under a special flight permit for the purpose of flying the aircraft to a location where the annual inspection can be performed.

100-Hour Inspection

A reciprocating-powered single-engine aircraft used to carry passengers or for flight instruction for hire must be inspected within each 100 hours of time in service by a certificated airframe and powerplant mechanic, a certificated repair station that is appropriately rated, or the aircraft manufacturer. An annual inspection is acceptable as a 100-hour inspection, but the reverse is not true.

Other Inspection Programs

The annual and 100-hour inspection requirements do not apply to large airplanes, turbojet or turbo-propeller-powered multiengine airplanes, or to airplanes for which the owner or operator complies with the progressive inspection requirements. Details of these requirements may be determined by reference to 14 CFR parts 43 and 91 and by inquiry at a local FSDO.

Preflight Inspection

The preflight inspection of the airplane is one of the pilot's most important duties. A number of serious airplane accidents have been traced directly to poor preflight inspection practices. The preflight inspection should be a thorough and systematic means by which the pilot determines that the airplane is ready for safe flight.

Most Aircraft Flight Manuals or Pilot's Operating Handbooks contain a section devoted to a systematic method of performing a preflight inspection that should be used by the pilot for guidance.

Preventive Maintenance

Simple or minor preservation operations and the replacement of small standard parts, not involving complex assembly operations, are considered preventive maintenance. A certificated pilot may perform preventive maintenance on any aircraft, owned or operated by the pilot, that is not used in air carrier service. Typical preventive maintenance operations are contained in 14 CFR part 43 which also contains other rules to be followed in the maintenance of aircraft.

Repairs and Alterations

Except as noted under "Preventive Maintenance," all repairs and alterations are classed as either major or minor. Major repairs or alterations must be approved for return to service by an appropriately rated certificated repair station, an airframe and powerplant mechanic holding an Inspection Authorization, or a representative of the Administrator. Minor repairs and alterations may be approved for return to service by a certificated airframe and powerplant mechanic or an appropriately certificated repair station.

Deferred Repair

Within certain guidelines, the pilot in command may defer repairs to nonessential inoperative instruments, and/or equipment while continuing to operate an aircraft (refer to 14 CFR section 91.213).

If the determination is made, for the aircraft without a minimum equipment list (MEL), that instruments or equipment can have repairs deferred, the operative instrument or item of equipment must be deactivated or removed.

When inoperative instruments or items of equipment are removed, a certificated and appropriately rated maintenance person shall perform that task. The cockpit control of the affected device shall be placarded and the discrepancy recorded in the aircraft's maintenance records in accordance with 14 CFR section 43.9.

If instruments or items of equipment are deactivated and the deactivation involves maintenance, it must be accomplished and recorded in accordance with 14 CFR part 43. Deactivated instruments or equipment must be placarded "inoperative."

Special Flight Permits

A special flight permit is an authorization to operate an aircraft that may not currently meet applicable airworthiness requirements, but is safe for a specific flight. Before the permit is issued, an FAA inspector may personally inspect the aircraft or require it to be inspected by a certificated airframe and powerplant mechanic or repair station to determine its safety for the intended flight. The inspection must be recorded in the aircraft records.

The special flight permit is issued to allow the aircraft to be flown to a base where repairs, alterations, or maintenance can be performed; for delivering or exporting the aircraft; or for evacuating an aircraft from an area of impending danger. A special flight permit may be issued to allow the operation of an overweight aircraft for flight beyond its normal range over water or land areas where adequate landing facilities or fuel is not available.

If a special flight permit is needed, assistance and the necessary forms may be obtained from the local FSDO or Designated Airworthiness Representative (DAR).

Airworthiness Directives

A primary safety function of the FAA is to require correction of unsafe conditions found in an aircraft, aircraft engine, propeller, or appliance when such conditions exist and are likely to exist or develop in other products of the same design. The unsafe condition may exist because of a design defect, maintenance, or other causes. 14 CFR part 39, Airworthiness Directives (AD's), defines the authority and responsibility of the Administrator for requiring the necessary corrective action. The AD's are the media used to notify aircraft owners and other interested persons of unsafe conditions and to prescribe the conditions under which the product may continue to be operated.

Airworthiness directives may be divided into two categories: (1) those of an emergency nature requiring immediate compliance upon receipt, and (2) those of a less urgent nature requiring compliance within a relatively longer period of time.

Airworthiness directives are regulatory and must be complied with, unless specific exemption is granted. It is the aircraft owner or operator's responsibility to assure compliance with all pertinent AD's. This includes those AD's that require recurrent or continuing action. For example, an AD may require a repetitive inspection each 50 hours of operation, meaning the particular inspection shall be accomplished and recorded every 50 hours of time in service.

14 CFR requires that a record be maintained that shows the current status of applicable AD's, including the method of compliance, and the signature and certificate number of the repair station or mechanic who performed the work. For ready reference, many aircraft owners have a chronological listing of the pertinent AD's in their logbooks.

The Summary of Airworthiness Directives contains all the valid AD's previously published. The Summary is divided into two areas. The small aircraft and rotorcraft books contain all AD's applicable to small aircraft, i.e., 12,500 pounds or less maximum certificated takeoff weight and AD's applicable to all helicopters. The large aircraft books contain all AD's applicable to large aircraft—those over 12,500 pounds. The Summary of Airworthiness Directives is sold and distributed by the Superintendent of Documents for the FAA in Oklahoma City and is available in paper copy, microfiche, or electronic format. For further information on how to order AD's and the current price, contact:

U.S. Department of Transportation
Federal Aviation Administration
Airworthiness Programs Branch, AFS-610
P.O. Box 26460
Oklahoma City, OK 73125

Telephone Number: (405) 954-4103
Fax: (405) 954-4104

CHAPTER 3

FLIGHT INSTRUMENTS

INTRODUCTION

The use of instruments as an aid to flight enables the pilot to operate the airplane more precisely, and therefore, obtain maximum performance and enhanced safety. This is particularly true when flying greater distances. Manufacturers have provided the necessary flight instruments; however, it is the pilot's responsibility to gain the essential knowledge about how the instruments operate so that they can be used effectively.

This chapter covers the operational aspects of the pitot-static system and associated instruments: the vacuum system and associated instruments; and the magnetic compass.

THE PITOT-STATIC SYSTEM AND ASSOCIATED INSTRUMENTS

There are two major parts of the pitot-static system: (1) impact pressure chamber and lines; and (2) static pressure chamber and lines, which provides the source of ambient air pressure for the operation of the altimeter, vertical speed indicator (vertical velocity indicator), and the airspeed indicator.

Impact Pressure Chamber and Lines

In this system, the impact air pressure (air striking the airplane because of its forward motion) is taken from a pitot tube, which is mounted either on the leading edge of the wing or on the nose, and aligned to the relative wind. On certain aircraft, the pitot tube is located on the vertical stabilizer. These locations provide minimum disturbance or turbulence caused by the motion of the airplane through the air. The static pressure (pressure of the still air) is usually taken from the static line attached to a vent or vents mounted flush with the side of the fuselage. Airplanes using a flush-type static source, with two vents, have one vent on each side of the fuselage. This compensates for any possible variation in static pressure due to erratic changes in airplane attitude.

The openings of both the pitot tube and the static vent should be checked during the preflight inspection to assure that they are free from obstructions. Clogged or partially clogged openings should be cleaned by a certificated mechanic. Blowing into these openings is not recommended because this could damage any of the three instruments. [Figure 3-1]

As the airplane moves through the air, the impact pressure on the open pitot tube affects the pressure in the pitot chamber. Any change of pressure in the pitot chamber is transmitted through a line connected to the airspeed indicator which utilizes impact pressure for its operation.

Static Pressure Chamber and Lines

The static chamber is vented through small holes to the free undisturbed air, and as the atmospheric pressure increases or decreases, the pressure in the static chamber changes accordingly. Again, this pressure change is transmitted through lines to the instruments which utilize static pressure as illustrated in figure 3-1.

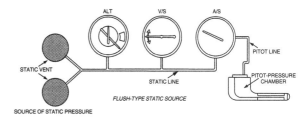

FIGURE 3-1.—Pitot-static system with instruments.

An alternate source for static pressure is provided in some airplanes in the event the static ports become clogged. This source usually is vented to the pressure inside the cockpit. Because of the venturi effect of the flow of air over the cockpit, this alternate static pressure is usually lower than the pressure provided by the normal static air source. When the alternate static source is used, the following differences in the instrument indications usually occur: the altimeter will indicate higher than the actual altitude, the airspeed will indicate greater than the actual airspeed, and the vertical speed will indicate a climb while in level flight.

Altimeter

The altimeter measures the height of the airplane above a given level. Since it is the only instrument that gives altitude information, the altimeter is one of the most important instruments in the airplane. To use the altimeter effectively, the pilot must thoroughly understand its principle of operation and the effect of atmospheric pressure and temperature on the altimeter. [Figure 3-2]

FIGURE 3-2.—Sensitive altimeter. The instrument is adjusted by the knob (lower left) so the current altimeter setting (29.48) appears in the window to the right.

Principle of Operation

The pressure altimeter is simply an aneroid barometer that measures the pressure of the atmosphere at the level where the altimeter is located, and presents an altitude indication in feet. The altimeter uses static pressure as its source of operation. Air is more dense at the surface of the Earth than aloft, therefore as altitude increases, atmospheric pressure decreases. This difference in pressure at various levels causes the altimeter to indicate changes in altitude.

The presentation of altitude varies considerably between different types of altimeters. Some have one pointer while others have more. Only the multipointer type will be discussed in this handbook.

The dial of a typical altimeter is graduated with numerals arranged clockwise from 0 to 9 inclusive as shown in figure 3-2. Movement of the aneroid element

is transmitted through a gear train to the three hands which sweep the calibrated dial to indicate altitude. The shortest hand indicates altitude in tens of thousands of feet; the intermediate hand in thousands of feet; and the longest hand in hundreds of feet, subdivided into 20-foot increments.

This indicated altitude is correct, however, only if the sea level barometric pressure is standard (29.92 in. Hg.), the sea level free air temperature is standard (+15 °C or 59 °F), and furthermore, the pressure and temperature decrease at a standard rate with an increase in altitude. Since atmospheric pressure continually changes, a means is provided to adjust the altimeter to compensate for nonstandard conditions. This is accomplished through a system by which the altimeter setting (local station barometric pressure reduced to sea level) is set to a barometric scale located on the face of the altimeter. Only after the altimeter is set properly will it indicate the correct altitude.

Effect of Nonstandard Pressure and Temperature

If no means were provided for adjusting altimeters to nonstandard pressure, flight could be hazardous. For example, if a flight is made from a high pressure area to a low pressure area without adjusting the altimeter, the actual altitude of the airplane will be LOWER than the indicated altitude, and when flying from a low pressure area to a high pressure area, the actual altitude of the airplane will be HIGHER than the indicated altitude. Fortunately, this error can be corrected by setting the altimeter properly.

Variations in air temperature also affect the altimeter. On a warm day, the expanded air is lighter in weight per unit volume than on a cold day, and consequently the pressure levels are raised. For example, the pressure level where the altimeter indicates 10,000 feet will be HIGHER on a warm day than under standard conditions. On a cold day, the reverse is true, and the 10,000-foot level would be LOWER. The adjustment made by the pilot to compensate for nonstandard pressures does not compensate for nonstandard temperatures. Therefore, if terrain or obstacle clearance is a factor in the selection of a cruising altitude, particularly at higher altitudes, remember to anticipate that COLDER-THAN-STANDARD TEMPERATURE will place the aircraft LOWER than the altimeter indicates. Therefore, a higher altitude should be used to provide adequate terrain clearance.

A memory aid in applying the above is "from a high to a low or hot to cold, look out below."

Setting the Altimeter

To adjust the altimeter for variation in atmospheric pressure, the pressure scale in the altimeter setting window, calibrated in inches of mercury (in. Hg.), is adjusted to correspond with the given altimeter setting. Altimeter settings can be defined as station pressure reduced to sea level, expressed in inches of mercury.

The station reporting the altimeter setting takes an hourly measurement of the station's atmospheric pressure and corrects this value to sea level pressure. These altimeter settings reflect height above sea level only in the vicinity of the reporting station. Therefore, it is necessary to adjust the altimeter setting as the flight progresses from one station to the next.

14 CFR part 91 provides the following concerning altimeter settings: The cruising altitude of an aircraft below 18,000 feet mean sea level (MSL) shall be maintained by reference to an altimeter that is set to the current reported altimeter setting of a station located along the route of flight and within 100 nautical miles (NM) of the aircraft. If there is no such station, the current reported altimeter setting of an appropriate available station shall be used. In an aircraft having no radio, the altimeter shall be set to the elevation of the departure airport or an appropriate altimeter setting available before departure.

Many pilots confidently expect that the current altimeter setting will compensate for irregularities in atmospheric pressure at all altitudes. This is not always true because the altimeter setting broadcast by ground stations is the station pressure corrected to mean sea level. The altimeter setting does not account for the irregularities at higher levels, particularly the effect of nonstandard temperature.

It should be pointed out, however, that if each pilot in a given area were to use the same altimeter setting, each altimeter will be equally affected by temperature and pressure variation errors, making it possible to maintain the desired separation between aircraft.

When flying over high mountainous terrain, certain atmospheric conditions can cause the altimeter to indicate an altitude of 1,000 feet, or more, HIGHER than the actual altitude. For this reason, a generous margin of altitude should be allowed—not only for possible altimeter error, but also for possible downdrafts which are particularly prevalent if high winds are encountered.

To illustrate the use of the altimeter setting system, follow a flight from Love Field, Dallas, Texas, to Abilene Municipal Airport, Abilene, Texas, via Mineral Wells. Before takeoff from Love Field, the pilot receives a current altimeter setting of 29.85 from the control tower or automatic terminal information service (ATIS). This value is set in the altimeter setting window of the altimeter. The altimeter indication should then be compared with the known airport elevation of 485 feet. Since most altimeters are not perfectly calibrated, an error may exist. If an altimeter indication varies from the field elevation more than 75 feet, the accuracy of the instrument is questionable and it should be referred to an instrument technician for recalibration.

When over Mineral Wells, assume the pilot receives a current altimeter setting of 29.94 and applies this setting to the altimeter. Before entering the traffic pattern at Abilene Municipal Airport, a new altimeter setting of 29.69 is received from the Abilene Control Tower, and applied to the altimeter. If the pilot desires to fly the traffic pattern at approximately 800 feet above terrain, and the field elevation of Abilene is 1,778 feet, an indicated altitude of 2,600 feet should be maintained (1,778 feet + 800 feet = 2,578 feet rounded to 2,600 feet).

The importance of properly setting and reading the altimeter cannot be overemphasized. Let's assume that the pilot neglected to adjust the altimeter at Abilene to the current setting, and uses the Mineral Wells setting of 29.94. If this occurred, the airplane, when in the Abilene traffic pattern, would be approximately 250 feet below the proper traffic pattern altitude of 2,600 feet, and the altimeter would indicate approximately 250 feet more than the field elevation (2,028 feet) upon landing.

Actual altimeter setting	29.94
Proper altimeter setting	29.69
Difference	.25

(1 inch of pressure is equal to approximately 1,000 feet of altitude—.25 x 1,000 feet = 250 feet)

The above calculation may be confusing, particularly in determining whether to add or subtract the amount of altimeter error. The following additional explanation is offered and can be helpful in finding the solution to this type of problem.

There are two means by which the altimeter pointers can be moved. One utilizes changes in air pressure while the other utilizes the mechanical makeup of the altimeter setting system.

When the aircraft altitude is changed, the changing pressure within the altimeter case expands or contracts the aneroid barometer which through linkage rotates the pointers. A decrease in pressure causes the altimeter to indicate an increase in altitude, and an increase in pressure causes the altimeter to indicate a decrease in altitude. It is obvious then that if the aircraft is flown from a pressure level of 28.75 in. Hg. to a pressure level of 29.75 in. Hg., the altimeter would show a decrease of approximately 1,000 feet in altitude.

The other method of moving the pointers does not rely on changing air pressure, but the mechanical construction of the altimeter. When the knob on the altimeter is rotated, the altimeter setting pressure scale moves simultaneously with the altimeter pointers. This may be confusing because the numerical values of pressure indicated in the window increase while the altimeter indicates an increase in altitude; or decrease while the altimeter indicates a decrease in altitude. This is contrary to the reaction on the pointers when air pressure changes, and is based solely on the mechanical makeup of the altimeter. To further explain this point, assume that the proper altimeter setting is 29.50 and the actual setting is 30.00 or a .50 difference. This would cause a 500-foot error in altitude. In this case if the altimeter setting is adjusted from 30.00 to 29.50, the numerical value decreases and the altimeter indicates a decrease of 500 feet in altitude. Before this correction was made, the aircraft was flying at an altitude of 500 feet lower than was shown on the altimeter.

Types of Altitude

Knowing the aircraft's altitude is vitally important to the pilot for several reasons. The pilot must be sure that the airplane is flying high enough to clear the highest terrain or obstruction along the intended route; this is especially important when visibility is restricted. To keep above mountain peaks, the pilot must note the altitude of the aircraft and elevation of the surrounding terrain at all times. To reduce the possibility of a midair collision, the pilot must maintain altitudes in accordance with air traffic rules. Often certain altitudes are selected to take advantage of favorable winds and weather conditions. Also, a knowledge of the altitude is necessary to calculate true airspeeds.

Altitude is vertical distance above some point or level used as a reference. There may be as many kinds of altitude as there are reference levels from which altitude is measured and each may be used for specific reasons. Pilots are usually concerned, however, with five types of altitudes:

- **Absolute Altitude**—The vertical distance of an aircraft above the terrain.
- **Indicated Altitude**—That altitude read directly from the altimeter (uncorrected) after it is set to the current altimeter setting.
- **Pressure Altitude**—The altitude indicated when the altimeter setting window (barometric scale) is adjusted to 29.92. This is the standard datum plane, a theoretical plane where air pressure (corrected to

15 °C) is equal to 29.92 in. Hg. Pressure altitude is used for computer solutions to determine density altitude, true altitude, true airspeed, etc.
- **True Altitude**—The true vertical distance of the aircraft above sea level—the actual altitude. (Often expressed in this manner; 10,900 feet MSL.) Airport, terrain, and obstacle elevations found on aeronautical charts are true altitudes.
- **Density Altitude**—This altitude is pressure altitude corrected for nonstandard temperature variations. When conditions are standard, pressure altitude and density altitude are the same. Consequently, if the temperature is above standard, the density altitude will be higher than pressure altitude. If the temperature is below standard, the density altitude will be lower than pressure altitude. This is an important altitude because it is directly related to the aircraft's takeoff and climb performance.

Vertical Speed Indicator

The vertical speed indicator (VSI) or vertical velocity indicator indicates whether the aircraft is climbing, descending, or in level flight. The rate of climb or descent is indicated in feet per minute. If properly calibrated, this indicator will register zero in level flight. [Figure 3-3]

FIGURE 3-3.—*Vertical speed indicator.*

Principle of Operation

Although the vertical speed indicator operates solely from static pressure, it is a differential pressure instrument. The case of the instrument is airtight except for a small connection through a restricted passage to the static line of the pitot-static system.

A diaphragm with connecting linkage and gearing to the indicator pointer is located inside the sealed case. Both the diaphragm and the case receive air from the static line at existing atmospheric pressure. When the aircraft is on the ground or in level flight, the pressures inside the diaphragm and the instrument case remain the same and the pointer is at the zero indication. When the aircraft climbs or descends, the pressure inside the diaphragm changes immediately; but due to the metering action of the restricted passage, the case pressure will remain higher or lower for a short time causing the diaphragm to contract or expand. This causes a differential pressure which is indicated on the instrument needle as a climb or descent.

Airspeed Indicator

The airspeed indicator is a sensitive, differential pressure gauge which measures and shows promptly the difference between (1) pitot, or impact pressure, and (2) static pressure, the undisturbed atmospheric pressure at level flight. These two pressures will be equal when the aircraft is parked on the ground in calm air. When the aircraft moves through the air, the pressure on the pitot line becomes greater than the pressure in the static lines. This difference in pressure is registered by the airspeed pointer on the face of the instrument, which is calibrated in miles per hour (MPH), knots, or both. [Figure 3-4]

FIGURE 3-4.—Airspeed indicator.

Kinds of Airspeed

There are three kinds of airspeed that the pilot should understand:

- Indicated Airspeed
- Calibrated Airspeed
- True Airspeed

Indicated Airspeed
Indicated airspeed (IAS) is the direct instrument reading obtained from the airspeed indicator, uncorrected for variations in atmospheric density, installation error, or instrument error.

Calibrated Airspeed
Calibrated airspeed (CAS) is indicated airspeed corrected for installation error and instrument error. Although manufacturers attempt to keep airspeed errors to a minimum, it is not possible to eliminate all errors throughout the airspeed operating range. At certain airspeeds and with certain flap settings, the installation and instrument error may be several miles per hour. This error is generally greatest at low airspeeds. In the cruising and higher airspeed ranges, indicated airspeed and calibrated airspeed are approximately the same.

It may be important to refer to the airspeed calibration chart to correct for possible airspeed errors because airspeed limitations such as those found on the color-coded face of the airspeed indicator, on placards in the cockpit, or in the Airplane Flight Manual or Owner's Handbook are usually calibrated airspeeds. Some manufacturers use indicated rather than calibrated airspeed to denote the airspeed limitations mentioned.

The airspeed indicator should be calibrated periodically because leaks may develop or moisture may collect in the tubing. Dirt, dust, ice, or snow collecting at the mouth of the tube may obstruct air passage and prevent correct indications, and also vibrations may destroy the sensitivity of the diaphragm.

True Airspeed
The true airspeed indicator (TAS) is calibrated to indicate true airspeed under standard sea level conditions—that is, 29.92 in. Hg. and 15 °C. Because air density decreases with an increase in altitude, the airplane has to be flown faster at higher altitudes to cause the same pressure difference between pitot impact pressure and static pressure. Therefore, for a given true airspeed, indicated airspeed decreases as altitude increases or for a given indicated airspeed, true airspeed increases with an increase in altitude.

A pilot can find true airspeed by two methods. The first method, which is more accurate, involves using a computer. In this method, the calibrated airspeed is corrected for temperature and pressure variation by using the airspeed correction scale on the computer.

A second method, which is a "rule of thumb," can be used to compute the approximate true airspeed. This is done by adding to the indicated airspeed 2 percent of the indicated airspeed for each 1,000 feet of altitude.

Airspeed Indicator Markings

Airplanes weighing 12,500 pounds or less, manufactured after 1945 and certificated by the FAA, are required to have airspeed indicators that conform in a standard color-coded marking system. This system of color-coded markings enables the pilot to determine at a glance certain airspeed limitations which are important to the safe operation of the aircraft. For example, if during the execution of a maneuver, the pilot notes that the airspeed needle is in the yellow arc and is rapidly approaching the red line, immediate corrective action to reduce the airspeed should be taken. It is essential at high airspeed that the pilot use smooth control pressures to avoid severe stresses upon the aircraft structure. [Figure 3-4]

The following is a description of the standard color-code markings on airspeed indicators used on single-engine light airplanes:

• FLAP OPERATING RANGE (the white arc).
• POWER-OFF STALLING SPEED WITH THE WING FLAPS AND LANDING GEAR IN THE LANDING POSITION (the lower limit of the white arc).
• MAXIMUM FLAPS EXTENDED SPEED (the upper limit of the white arc). This is the highest airspeed at which the pilot should extend full flaps. If flaps are operated at higher airspeeds, severe strain or structural failure could result.
• NORMAL OPERATING RANGE (the green arc).
• POWER-OFF STALLING SPEED WITH THE WING FLAPS AND LANDING GEAR RETRACTED (the lower limit of the green arc).
• MAXIMUM STRUCTURAL CRUISING SPEED (the upper limit of the green arc). This is the maximum speed for normal operation.
• CAUTION RANGE (the yellow arc). The pilot should avoid this area unless in smooth air.
• NEVER-EXCEED SPEED (the red line). This is the maximum speed at which the airplane can be operated in smooth air. This speed should never be exceeded intentionally.

Other Airspeed Limitations

There are other important airspeed limitations not marked on the face of the airspeed indicator. These speeds are generally found on placards in view of the pilot and in the Airplane Flight Manual or Pilot's Operating Handbook.

One example is the MANEUVERING SPEED. This is the "rough air" speed and the maximum speed for abrupt maneuvers. If during flight, rough air or severe turbulence is encountered, the airspeed should be reduced to maneuvering speed or less to minimize the stress on the airplane structure.

Other important airspeeds include LANDING GEAR OPERATING SPEED, the maximum speed for extending or retracting the landing gear if using aircraft equipped with retractable landing gear; the BEST ANGLE-OF-CLIMB SPEED, important when a short-field takeoff to clear an obstacle is required; and the BEST RATE-OF-CLIMB SPEED, the airspeed that will give the pilot the most altitude in a given period of time. The pilot who flies the increasingly popular light twin-engine aircraft must know the aircraft's MINIMUM CONTROL SPEED, the minimum flight speed at which the aircraft is satisfactorily controllable when an engine is suddenly made inoperative with the remaining engine at takeoff power. The last two airspeeds are now marked either on the face of the airspeed indicator or on the instrument panel of recently manufactured airplanes.

Descriptions of these airspeed limitations are, through choice, limited to layman's language.

The following are abbreviations for performance speeds:

V_A—design maneuvering speed.
V_C—design cruising speed.
V_F—design flap speed.
V_{FE}—maximum flap extended speed.
V_{LE}—maximum landing gear extended speed.
V_{LO}—maximum landing gear operating speed.
V_{LOF}—lift-off speed.
V_{NE}—never-exceed speed.
V_R—rotation speed.
V_S—the stalling speed or the minimum steady flight speed at which the airplane is controllable.
V_{SO}—the stalling speed or the minimum steady flight speed in the landing configuration.
V_{S1}—the stalling speed or the minimum steady flight speed obtained in a specified configuration.
V_X—speed for best angle of climb.
V_Y—speed for best rate of climb.

GYROSCOPIC FLIGHT INSTRUMENTS

Several flight instruments utilize the properties of a gyroscope for their operation. The most common instruments containing gyroscopes are the turn coordinator, heading indicator, and the attitude indicator. To understand how these instruments operate requires a knowledge of the instrument power systems, gyroscopic principles, and the operating principles of each instrument.

Sources of Power for Gyroscopic Operation

In some airplanes, all the gyros are vacuum, pressure, or electrically operated; in others, vacuum, or pressure systems provide the power for the heading and attitude indicators, while the electrical system provides the power for the turn coordinator.

Vacuum or Pressure System

The vacuum or pressure system spins the gyro by drawing a stream of air against the rotor vanes to spin the rotor at high speeds essentially the same as a water wheel or turbine operates. The amount of vacuum or pressure required for instrument operation varies with manufacture and is usually between 4.5 to 5.5 in. Hg.

Engine-Driven Vacuum Pump

One source of vacuum for the gyros installed in light aircraft is the vane-type engine-driven pump which is mounted on the accessory case of the engine. Pump capacity varies in different aircraft, depending on the number of gyros to be operated.

A typical vacuum system consists of an engine-driven vacuum pump, regulator, air filter, gauge, tubing, and manifolds necessary to complete the connections. The gauge is mounted in the airplane instrument panel and indicates the amount of pressure in the system. [Figure 3-5]

The air filter prevents foreign matter from entering the vacuum or pressure system. Airflow is reduced as the master filter becomes dirty; this results in a lower reading on the vacuum or pressure gauge.

Gyroscopic Principles

Any spinning object exhibits gyroscopic properties; however, a wheel designed and mounted to utilize these properties is called a gyroscope. Two important design characteristics of an instrument gyro are great weight or high density for size and rotation at high speeds with low friction bearings. The mountings of the gyro wheels are called "gimbals" which may be circular rings, rectangular frames, or a part of the instrument case itself.

There are two general types of mountings; the type used depends upon which property of the gyro is utilized. A freely or universally mounted gyroscope is free to rotate in any direction about its center of gravity. Such a wheel is said to have three planes of freedom. The wheel or rotor is free to rotate in any plane in relation to the base and is so balanced that with the gyro wheel at rest, it will remain in the position in which it is placed. Restricted or semirigidly mounted gyroscopes are those mounted so that one of the planes of freedom is held fixed in relation to the base.

There are two fundamental properties of gyroscopic action; rigidity in space, and precession.

Rigidity in space can best be explained by applying Newton's First Law of Motion which states, "a body at rest will remain at rest; or if in motion in a straight line, it will continue in a straight line unless acted upon by an outside force." An example of this law is the rotor of a universally mounted gyro. When the wheel is spinning, it exhibits the ability to remain in its original plane of rotation regardless of how the base is moved. However, since it is impossible to design bearings without some friction present, there will be some deflective force upon the wheel.

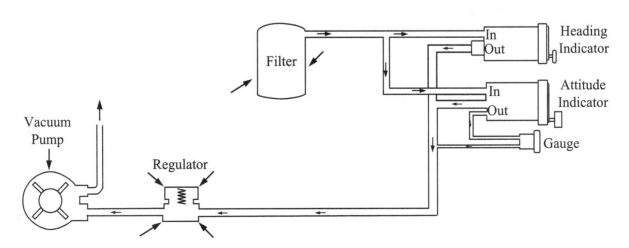

FIGURE 3-5.—Typical pump-driven vacuum system.

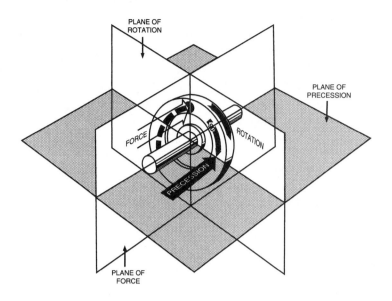

FIGURE 3-6.—Precession of a gyroscope resulting from an applied deflective force.

The flight instruments using the gyroscopic property of rigidity for their operation are the attitude indicator and the heading indicator; therefore, their rotors must be freely or universally mounted.

The second property of a gyroscope—precession—is the resultant action or deflection of a spinning wheel when a deflective force is applied to its rim. When a deflective force is applied to the rim of a rotating wheel, the resultant force is 90° ahead in the direction of rotation and in the direction of the applied force. The rate at which the wheel precesses is inversely proportional to the speed of the rotor and proportional to the deflective force. The force with which the wheel precesses is the same as the deflective force applied (minus the friction in the bearings). If too great a deflective force is applied for the amount of rigidity in the wheel, the wheel precesses and topples over at the same time. [Figure 3-6]

Turn Coordinator

The turn coordinator shows the yaw and roll of the aircraft around the vertical and longitudinal axes.

When rolling in or rolling out of a turn, the miniature airplane banks in the direction of the turn.

The miniature airplane does not indicate the angle of bank, but indicates the rate of turn. When aligned with the turn index, it represents a standard rate of turn of 3° per second. [Figure 3-7]

FIGURE 3-7.—Turn coordinator.

The inclinometer of the turn coordinator indicates the coordination of aileron and rudder. The ball indicates whether the airplane is in coordinated flight or is in a slip or skid. [Figure 3-8]

The Heading Indicator

The heading indicator (or directional gyro) is fundamentally a mechanical instrument designed to facilitate the use of the magnetic compass. Errors in the magnetic compass are numerous, making straight flight and precision turns to headings difficult to accomplish, particularly in turbulent air. A heading indicator, however, is not affected by the forces that make the magnetic compass difficult to interpret. [Figure 3-9]

Coordinated Turn   Skid   Slip

FIGURE 3-8.—Turn coordinator indications.

FIGURE 3-9.—Heading indicator.

The operation of the heading indicator depends upon the principle of rigidity in space. The rotor turns in a vertical plane, and fixed to the rotor is a compass card. Since the rotor remains rigid in space, the points on the card hold the same position in space relative to the vertical plane. As the instrument case and the airplane revolve around the vertical axis, the card provides clear and accurate heading information.

Because of precession, caused chiefly by friction, the heading indicator will creep or drift from a heading to which it is set. Among other factors, the amount of drift depends largely upon the condition of the instrument. If the bearings are worn, dirty, or improperly lubricated, the drift may be excessive.

Bear in mind that the heading indicator is not direction-seeking, as is the magnetic compass. It is important to check the indications frequently and reset the heading indicator to align it with the magnetic compass when required. Adjusting the heading indicator to the magnetic compass heading should be done only when the airplane is in wings-level unaccelerated flight; otherwise erroneous magnetic compass readings may be obtained.

The bank and pitch limits of the heading indicator vary with the particular design and make of instrument. On some heading indicators found in light airplanes, the limits are approximately 55° of pitch and 55° of bank. When either of these attitude limits is exceeded, the instrument "tumbles" or "spills" and no longer gives the correct indication until reset. After spilling, it may be reset with the caging knob. Many of the modern instruments used are designed in such a manner that they will not tumble.

The Attitude Indicator

The attitude indicator, with its miniature aircraft and horizon bar, displays a picture of the attitude of the airplane. The relationship of the miniature aircraft to the horizon bar is the same as the relationship of the real aircraft to the actual horizon. The instrument gives an instantaneous indication of even the smallest changes in attitude. [Figure 3-10]

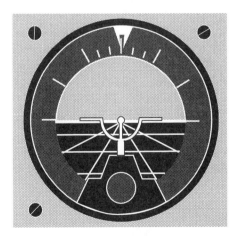

FIGURE 3-10.—Attitude indicator.

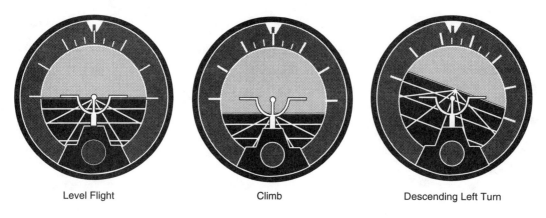

Level Flight   Climb   Descending Left Turn

FIGURE 3-11.—Various indications on the attitude indicator.

The gyro in the attitude indicator is mounted on a horizontal plane and depends upon rigidity in space for its operation. The horizon bar represents the true horizon. This bar is fixed to the gyro and remains in a horizontal plane as the airplane is pitched or banked about its lateral or longitudinal axis, indicating the attitude of the airplane relative to the true horizon.

An adjustment knob is provided with which the pilot may move the miniature airplane up or down to align the miniature airplane with the horizon bar to suit the pilot's line of vision. Normally, the miniature airplane is adjusted so that the wings overlap the horizon bar when the airplane is in straight-and-level cruising flight.

The pitch and bank limits depend upon the make and model of the instrument. Limits in the banking plane are usually from 100° to 110°, and the pitch limits are usually from 60° to 70°. If either limit is exceeded, the instrument will tumble or spill and will give incorrect indications until restabilized. A number of modern attitude indicators will not tumble.

Every pilot should be able to interpret the banking scale. Most banking scale indicators on the top of the instrument move in the same direction from that in which the airplane is actually banked. Some other models move in the opposite direction from that in which the airplane is actually banked. This may confuse the pilot if the indicator is used to determine the direction of bank. This scale should be used only to control the degree of desired bank. The relationship of the miniature airplane to the horizon bar should be used for an indication of the direction of bank. [Figure 3-11]

The attitude indicator is reliable and the most realistic flight instrument on the instrument panel. Its indications are very close approximations of the actual attitude of the airplane.

MAGNETIC COMPASS

Since the magnetic compass works on the principle of magnetism, it is well for the pilot to have at least a basic understanding of magnetism. A simple bar magnet has two centers of magnetism which are called poles. Lines of magnetic force flow out from each pole in all directions, eventually bending around and returning to the other pole. The area through which these lines of force flow is called the field of the magnet. For the purpose of this discussion, the poles are designated "north" and "south." If two bar magnets are placed near each other, the north pole of one will attract the south pole of the other. There is evidence that there is a magnetic field surrounding the Earth, and this theory is applied in the design of the magnetic compass. It acts very much as though there were a huge bar magnet running along the axis of the Earth which ends several hundred miles below the surface. [Figure 3-12]

The lines of force have a vertical component (or pull) which is zero at the Equator but builds to 100 percent of the total force at the poles. If magnetic needles, such as the airplane magnetic compass bars, are held along these lines of force, the vertical component causes one end of the needle to dip or deflect downward. The amount of dip increases as the needles are moved closer and closer to the poles. It is this deflection or dip which causes some of the larger compass errors.

The magnetic compass, which is the only direction-seeking instrument in the airplane, is simple in construction. It contains two steel magnetized needles fastened to a float around which is mounted a compass card. The needles are parallel, with their north-seeking ends pointed in the same direction. The compass card has letters for cardinal headings, and each 30° interval is represented by a number, the last

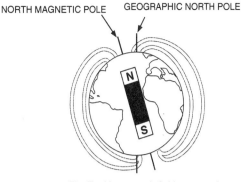

NORTH MAGNETIC POLE   GEOGRAPHIC NORTH POLE

Magnetic field around a bar magnet.

The Earth's magnetic field compared to a bar magnet.

FIGURE 3-12.—Earth's magnetic field.

zero of which is omitted. For example, 30° would appear as a 3 and 300° would appear as 30. Between these numbers, the card is graduated for each 5°. [Figure 3-13]

The float assembly is housed in a bowl filled with acid-free white kerosene. The purposes of the liquid are to dampen out excessive oscillations of the compass card and relieve by buoyancy part of the weight of the float from the bearings. Jewel bearings are used to mount the float assembly on top of a pedestal. A line (called the lubber line) is mounted behind the glass of the instrument that can be used for a reference line when aligning the headings on the compass card.

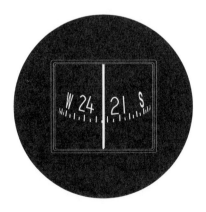

FIGURE 3-13.—Magnetic compass.

Compass Errors

Variation

Although the magnetic field of the Earth lies roughly north and south, the Earth's magnetic poles do not coincide with its geographic poles, which are used in the construction of aeronautical charts. Consequently, at most places on the Earth's surface, the direction-sensitive steel needles which seek the Earth's magnetic field will not point to True North but to Magnetic North. Furthermore, local magnetic fields from mineral deposits and other conditions may distort the Earth's magnetic field and cause an additional error in the position of the compass' north-seeking magnetized needles with reference to True North. The angular difference between True North and the direction indicated by the magnetic compass—excluding deviation error—is variation. Variation is different for different points on the Earth's surface and is shown on the aeronautical charts as broken lines connecting points of equal variation. These lines are isogonic lines. The line where the magnetic variation is zero is an agonic line. Variation will be discussed further in Chapter 8, Navigation.

Deviation

Actually, a compass is very rarely influenced solely by the Earth's magnetic lines of force. Magnetic disturbances from magnetic fields produced by metals and electrical accessories in an aircraft disturb the compass needles and produce an additional error. The difference between the direction indicated by a magnetic compass not installed in an airplane, and one installed in an airplane, is deviation.

If an aircraft changes heading, the compass' direction-sensitive magnetized needles will continue to point in about the same direction while the aircraft turns with relation to it. As the aircraft turns, metallic and electrical equipment in the aircraft change their position relative to the steel needles; hence, their influence on the compass needle changes and deviation changes. Thus, deviation depends, in part, on the heading of the aircraft. Although compensating magnets on the compass are adjusted to reduce this deviation on most headings, it is impossible to eliminate this error entirely on all headings. Therefore, a deviation card, installed in the cockpit in view of the pilot, enables the pilot to maintain the desired magnetic headings. Deviation will be discussed further in Chapter 8, Navigation.

Using the Magnetic Compass

Since the magnetic compass is the only direction-seeking instrument in most airplanes, the pilot must be able to turn the airplane to a magnetic compass heading and maintain this heading. It will help to remember the following characteristics of the magnetic compass which are caused by magnetic dip. These characteristics are only applicable in the Northern Hemisphere. In the Southern Hemisphere the opposite is true.

• If on a northerly heading and a turn is made toward east or west, the initial indication of the compass lags or indicates a turn in the opposite direction. This lag diminishes as the turn progresses toward east or west where there is no turn error.

• If on a southerly heading and a turn is made toward the east or west, the initial indication of the compass needle will indicate a greater amount of turn than is actually made. This lead also diminishes as the turn progresses toward east or west where there is no turn error.

• If a turn is made to a northerly heading from any direction, the compass indication when approaching north lags behind the turn. Therefore, the rollout of the turn is made before the desired heading is reached.

• If a turn is made to a southerly heading from any direction, the compass indication when approaching southerly headings leads behind the turn. Therefore, the rollout is made after the desired heading is passed. The amount of lead or lag is maximum on the north-south headings and depends upon the angle of bank used and geographic position of the airplane with regard to latitude.

• When on an east or west heading, no error is apparent while entering a turn to north or south; however, an increase in airspeed or acceleration will cause the compass to indicate a turn toward north; a decrease in airspeed or acceleration will cause the compass to indicate a turn toward south.

• If on a north or south heading, no error will be apparent because of acceleration or deceleration.

The magnetic compass should be read only when the aircraft is flying straight and level at a constant speed. This will help reduce errors to a minimum.

If the pilot thoroughly understands the errors and characteristics of the magnetic compass, this instrument can become the most reliable means of determining headings.

CHAPTER 4

WEIGHT AND BALANCE
AND
AIRPLANE PERFORMANCE

INTRODUCTION

Airplane performance is the capability of the airplane, if operated within its limitations, to accomplish maneuvers which serve a specific purpose. For example, most present-day airplanes are designed clean and sleek, which results in greater range, speed, payload, and increased efficiency. This type of airplane is preferred for cross-country flights. Airplanes used for short flights and carrying heavy loads, such as those used in certain agricultural operations, are designed differently, but still exhibit good performance for their purpose. Some of the factors which represent good performance are short takeoff and landing distance, increased climb capability, and greater speeds using less fuel.

Because of its effect on performance, airplane weight and balance information is included in this chapter. Also included is an introduction to determining takeoff, cruise, and landing performance. For information relating to weight and balance, takeoff, cruise, and landing performance for a specific make and model of airplane, reference should be made to that Airplane's Flight Manual or Pilot's Operating Handbook.

WEIGHT CONTROL

Weight is the force with which gravity attracts a body toward the center of the Earth. It is a product of the mass of a body and the acceleration acting on the body. Weight is a major problem in airplane construction and operation, and demands respect from all pilots.

The force of gravity continually attempts to pull the airplane down toward Earth. The force of lift is the only force that counteracts weight and sustains the airplane in flight. However, the amount of lift produced by an airfoil is limited by the airfoil design, angle of attack, airspeed, and air density. Therefore, to assure that the lift generated is sufficient to counteract weight, loading the airplane beyond the manufacturer's recommended weight must be avoided. If the weight is greater than the lift generated, altitude cannot be maintained.

Effects of Weight

Any item aboard the airplane which increases the total weight significantly is undesirable as far as performance is concerned. Manufacturers attempt to make the airplane as light as possible without sacrificing strength or safety.

The pilot of an airplane should always be aware of the consequences of overloading. An overloaded airplane may not be able to leave the ground, or if it does become airborne, it may exhibit unexpected and unusually poor flight characteristics. If an airplane is not properly loaded, the initial indication of poor performance usually takes place during takeoff.

Excessive weight reduces the flight performance of an airplane in almost every respect. The most important performance deficiencies of the overloaded airplane are:

- Higher takeoff speed.
- Longer takeoff run.
- Reduced rate and angle of climb.
- Lower maximum altitude.
- Shorter range.
- Reduced cruising speed.
- Reduced maneuverability.
- Higher stalling speed.
- Higher landing speed.
- Longer landing roll.
- Excessive weight on the nosewheel.

The pilot must be knowledgeable in the effect of weight on the performance of the particular airplane being flown. Preflight planning should include a check of performance charts to determine if the airplane's weight may contribute to hazardous flight operations. Excessive weight in itself reduces the safety margins available to the pilot, and becomes even more hazardous when other performance-reducing factors are combined with overweight. The pilot must also consider the consequences of an overweight airplane if an emergency condition arises. If an engine fails on takeoff or ice forms at low altitude, it is usually too late to reduce the airplane's weight to keep it in the air.

Weight Changes

The weight of the airplane can be changed by altering the fuel load. Gasoline has considerable weight—6 pounds per gallon—30 gallons may weigh more than one passenger. But it must be remembered that if weight is lowered by reducing fuel, the range of the airplane is decreased. During flight, fuel burn is normally the only weight change that takes place. As fuel is used, the airplane becomes lighter and performance is improved.

Changes of fixed equipment have a major effect upon the weight of the airplane. An airplane can be overloaded by the installation of extra radios or instruments. Repairs or modifications usually affect the weight of the airplane.

BALANCE, STABILITY, AND CENTER OF GRAVITY

Balance refers to the location of the center of gravity (CG) of an airplane, and is important to airplane stability and safety in flight. The center of gravity is a point at which an airplane would balance if it were suspended at that point.

The prime concern of airplane balancing is the fore and aft location of the CG along the longitudinal axis. Location of the CG with reference to the lateral axis is also important. For each item of weight existing to the left of the fuselage centerline, there is an equal weight existing at a corresponding location on the right. This may be upset, however, by unbalanced lateral loading. The position of the lateral CG is not computed, but the pilot must be aware that adverse effects will certainly arise as a result of a laterally unbalanced condition. Lateral unbalance will occur if the fuel load is mismanaged by supplying the engine(s) unevenly from tanks on one side of the airplane. The pilot can compensate for the resulting

wing-heavy condition by adjusting the aileron trim tab or by holding a constant aileron control pressure. However, this places the airplane controls in an out-of-streamline condition, increases drag, and results in decreased operating efficiency. Since lateral balance is relatively easy to control and longitudinal balance is more critical, further reference to balance in this handbook will mean longitudinal location of the center of gravity. [Figure 4-1]

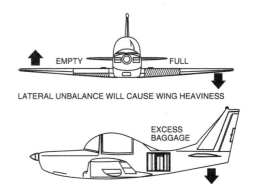

FIGURE 4-1.—Lateral or longitudinal unbalance.

The center of gravity is not necessarily a fixed point; its location depends on the distribution of weight in the airplane. As variable load items are shifted or expended, there is a resultant shift in CG location. The pilot should realize that if the CG of an airplane is displaced too far forward on the longitudinal axis, a nose-heavy condition will result. Conversely, if the CG is displaced too far aft on the longitudinal axis, a tail-heavy condition will result. It is possible that an unfavorable location of the CG could produce such an unstable condition that the pilot could not control the airplane. [Figure 4-1]

In any event, flying an airplane which is out of balance can produce increased pilot fatigue with obvious effects on the safety and efficiency of flight. The pilot's natural correction for longitudinal unbalance is a change of trim to remove the excessive control pressure. Excessive trim, however, has the effect of not only reducing aerodynamic efficiency but also reducing primary control travel distance in the direction the trim is applied.

Effects of Adverse Balance

Adverse balance conditions affect airplane flight characteristics in much the same manner as those mentioned for an excess weight condition. In addition, there are two essential airplane characteristics which may be seriously affected by improper balance; these are stability and control. Loading in a nose-heavy condition causes problems in controlling and raising the nose, especially during takeoff and landing. Loading in a tail-heavy condition has a most serious effect upon longitudinal stability, and can reduce the airplane's capability to recover from stalls and spins. Another undesirable characteristic produced from tail-heavy loading is that it produces very light control forces. This makes it easy for the pilot to inadvertently overstress the airplane.

Limits for the location of the airplane's center of gravity are established by the manufacturer. These are the fore and aft limits beyond which the CG should not be located for flight. These limits are published for each airplane in the Type Certification Data Sheet or Aircraft Specification. If, after loading, the CG is not within the allowable limits, it will be necessary to relocate some items within the airplane before flight is attempted.

The forward center of gravity limit is often established at a location which is determined by the landing characteristics of the airplane. It may be possible to maintain stable and safe cruising flight if the CG is located ahead of the prescribed forward limit; but during landing which is one of the most critical phases of flight, exceeding the forward CG limit may cause problems. Manufacturers purposely place the forward CG limit as far rearward as possible to aid pilots in avoiding damage to the airplane when landing.

A restricted forward center of gravity limit is also specified to assure that sufficient elevator deflection is available at minimum airspeed. When structural limitations or large stick forces do not limit the forward CG position, it is located at the position where full-up elevator is required to obtain a high angle of attack for landing.

The aft center of gravity limit is the most rearward position at which the CG can be located for the most critical maneuver or operation. As the CG moves aft, a less stable condition occurs which decreases the ability of the airplane to right itself after maneuvering or after disturbances by gusts.

For some airplanes the CG limits, both fore and aft, may be specified to vary as gross weight changes. They may also be changed for certain operations such as acrobatic flight, retraction of the landing gear, or the installation of special loads and devices which change the flight characteristics.

The actual location of the CG can be altered by many variable factors and is usually controlled by the pilot. Placement of baggage and cargo items determine the CG location. The assignment of seats to passengers can also be used as a means of obtaining a favorable balance. If the airplane is tail-heavy, it is only logical to place heavy passengers in forward seats.

Management of Weight and Balance Control

Weight and balance control should be a matter of concern to all pilots. The pilot has control over loading and fuel management (the two variable factors which can change both total weight and CG location) of a particular airplane.

The airplane owner or operator should make certain that up-to-date information is available in the airplane for the pilot's use, and should ensure that appropriate entries are made in the airplane records when repairs or modifications have been accomplished. Weight changes must be accounted for and the proper notations made in weight and balance records. The equipment list must be updated if appropriate. Without such information, the pilot has no foundation upon which to base the necessary calculations and decisions.

Terms and Definitions

The pilot should be familiar with terms used in working the problems related to weight and balance. The following list of terms and their definitions is well standardized, and knowledge of these terms will aid the pilot to better understand weight and balance calculations of any airplane.

• **Arm (moment arm)**—is the horizontal distance in inches from the reference datum line to the center of gravity of an item. The algebraic sign is plus (+) if measured aft of the datum, and minus (–) if measured forward of the datum.
• **Center of gravity (CG)**—is the point about which an airplane would balance if it were possible to suspend it at that point. It is the mass center of the airplane, or the theoretical point at which the entire weight of the airplane is assumed to be concentrated. It may be expressed in inches from the reference datum, or in percent of mean aerodynamic chord (MAC).
• **Center of gravity limits**—are the specified forward and aft points within which the CG must be located during flight. These limits are indicated on pertinent airplane specifications.
• **Center of gravity range**—is the distance between the forward and aft CG limits indicated on pertinent airplane specifications.
• **Datum (reference datum)**—is an imaginary vertical plane or line from which all measurements of arm are taken. The datum is established by the manufacturer. Once the datum has been selected, all moment arms and the location of CG range are measured from this point.

- **Delta**—is a Greek letter expressed by the symbol Δ to indicate a change of values. As an example, Δ CG indicates a change (or movement) of the CG.
- **Fuel load**—is the expendable part of the load of the airplane. It includes only usable fuel, not fuel required to fill the lines or that which remains trapped in the tank sumps.
- **Moment**—is the product of the weight of an item multiplied by its arm. Moments are expressed in pound-inches (lb-in). Total moment is the weight of the airplane multiplied by the distance between the datum and the CG.
- **Moment index (or index)**—is a moment divided by a constant such as 100, 1,000, or 10,000. The purpose of using a moment index is to simplify weight and balance computations of airplanes where heavy items and long arms result in large, unmanageable numbers.
- **Mean aerodynamic chord (MAC)**—is the average distance from the leading edge to the trailing edge of the wing.
- **Standard weights**—have been established for numerous items involved in weight and balance computations. These weights should not be used if actual weights are available. Some of the standard weights are:

General aviation—crew
  and passenger .... 170 lb each
Gasoline .... 6 lb/US gal
Oil .... 7.5 lb/US gal
Water .... 8.35 lb/US gal

- **Station**—is a location in the airplane which is identified by a number designating its distance in inches from the datum. The datum is, therefore, identified as station zero. An item located at station +50 would have an arm of 50 inches.
- **Useful load**—is the weight of the pilot, copilot, passengers, baggage, usable fuel, and drainable oil. It is the empty weight subtracted from the maximum allowable gross weight. This term applies to general aviation aircraft only.
- **Weight, basic empty**—consists of the airframe, engines, and all items of operating equipment that have fixed locations and are permanently installed in the airplane. It includes optional and special equipment, fixed ballast, hydraulic fluid, unusable (residual) fuel, and full engine oil (some older aircraft only include undrainable residual oil; refer to the aircraft weight and balance documents).

Control of Loading—General Aviation Airplanes

Before any flight, the pilot should determine the weight and balance condition of the airplane. Simple and orderly procedures, based on sound principles, have been devised by airplane manufacturers for the determination of loading conditions. The pilot must use these procedures and exercise good judgment. In many modern airplanes, it is not possible to fill all seats, baggage compartments, and fuel tanks, and still remain within the approved weight and balance limits. If the maximum passenger load is carried, the pilot must often reduce the fuel load or reduce the amount of baggage.

Basic Principles of Weight and Balance Computations

It might be advantageous at this point to review and discuss some of the basic principles of how weight and balance can be determined. The following method of computation can be applied to any object or vehicle where weight and balance information is essential; but to fulfill the purpose of this handbook, it is directed primarily toward the airplane.

By determining the weight of the empty airplane and adding the weight of everything loaded on the airplane, a total weight can be determined. This is quite simple; but to distribute this weight in such a manner that the entire mass of the loaded airplane is balanced around a point (CG) which must be located within specified limits presents a greater problem, particularly if the basic principles of weight and balance are not understood.

The point where the airplane will balance can be determined by locating the center of gravity, which is, as stated in the definitions of terms, the imaginary point where all the weight is concentrated. To provide the necessary balance between longitudinal stability and elevator control, the center of gravity is usually located slightly forward of the center of lift. This loading condition causes a nosedown tendency in flight, which is desirable during flight at a high angle of attack and slow speeds.

A safe zone within which the balance point (CG) must fall is called the CG range. The extremities of the range are called the forward CG limits and aft CG limits. These limits are usually specified in inches, along the longitudinal axis of the airplane, measured from a datum reference. The datum is an arbitrary point, established by airplane designers, which may vary in location between different airplanes. [Figure 4-2]

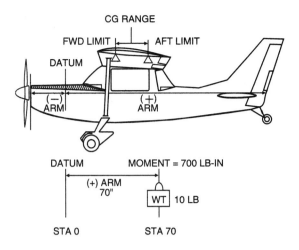

FIGURE 4-2.—Weight and balance illustrated.

The distance from the datum to any component part of the airplane, or any object loaded on the airplane, is called the arm. When the object or component is located aft of the datum, it is measured in positive inches; if located forward of the datum, it is measured as negative inches, or minus inches. The location of the object or part is often referred to as the station. If the weight of any object or component is multiplied by the distance from the datum (arm), the product is the moment. The moment is the measurement of the gravitational force which causes a tendency of the weight to rotate about a point or axis and is expressed in pound-inches. [Figure 4-2]

To illustrate, assume a weight of 50 pounds is placed on the board at a station or point 100 inches from the datum. The downward force of the weight can be determined by multiplying 50 pounds by 100 inches, which produces a moment of 5,000 lb-in. [Figure 4-3]

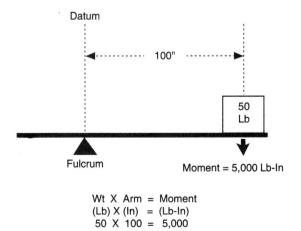

Note: The datum is assumed to be located at the fulcrum.

FIGURE 4-3.—Determining moments.

To establish a balance, a total of 5,000 lb-in must be applied to the other end of the board. Any combination of weight and distance which, when multiplied, produces 5,000 lb-in moment will balance the board. For example, as illustrated in figure 4-4, if a 100-pound weight is placed at a point (station) 25 inches from the datum, and another 50-pound weight is placed at a point (station) 50 inches from the datum, the sum of the product of the two weights and their distances will total a moment of 5,000 lb-in which will balance the board.

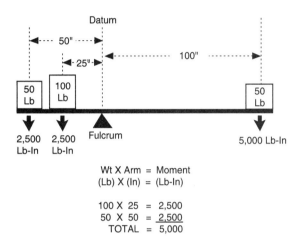

FIGURE 4-4.—Establishing a balance.

Weight and Balance Restrictions

The airplane's weight and balance restrictions should be closely followed. The loading conditions and empty weight of a particular airplane may differ from that found in the Airplane Flight Manual or Pilot's Operating Handbook because modifications or equipment changes may have been made. Sample loading problems in the Airplane Flight Manual or Pilot's Operating Handbook are intended for guidance only; therefore, each airplane must be treated separately. Although an airplane is certified for a specified maximum gross takeoff weight, it will not safely take off with this load under all conditions. Conditions which affect takeoff and climb performance such as high elevations, high temperatures, and high humidity (high density altitudes) may require a reduction in weight before flight is attempted. Other factors to consider prior to takeoff are runway length, runway surface, runway slope, surface wind, and the presence of obstacles. These factors may require a reduction in weight prior to flight.

Some airplanes are designed so that it is impossible to load them in a manner that will place the CG out of limits. These are usually small airplanes with the seats, fuel, and baggage areas located near the CG limit. These airplanes, however, can be overloaded in weight.

Other airplanes can be loaded in such a manner that they will be out of CG limits even though the useful load has not been exceeded.

Because of the effects of an out-of-balance or overweight condition, a pilot should always be sure that an airplane is properly loaded.

DETERMINING LOADED WEIGHT AND CENTER OF GRAVITY

There are various methods for determining the loaded weight and center of gravity of an aircraft. There is the computation method, as well as methods which utilize graphs and tables provided by the aircraft manufacturer.

Computational Method

The computational method involves the application of basic math functions. The following is an example of the computational method:

Given:

Maximum Gross Weight	3400 lb
Center-of-Gravity Range	78-86 in
Front Seat Occupants	340 lb
Rear Seat Occupants	350 lb
Fuel	75 gal
Baggage Area 1	80 lb

To determine the loaded weight and CG, follow these steps.

Step 1—List the weight of the aircraft, occupants, fuel, and baggage. Remember, fuel weighs 6 pounds per gallon.
Step 2—Enter the moment for each item listed. Remember "weight x arm = moment." To simplify calculations, the moments are divided by 100.
Step 3—Total the weight and moments.
Step 4—To determine the CG, divide the moments by the weight.

NOTE: The weight and balance records for a particular aircraft will provide the empty weight and moment as well as the information on the arm distance.

	Weight	Arm	Moment/100
Airplane Empty Weight	2100	78.3	1652.1
Front Seat Occupants	340	85.0	289.0
Rear Seat Occupants	350	121.0	423.5
Fuel	450	75.0	337.5
Baggage Area 1	80.0	150.0	120.0
Total	3330		2822.1/100

2822.1/100 divided by 3330 = 84.7

The total loaded weight of 3,330 pounds does not exceed the maximum gross weight of 3,400 pounds and the CG of 84.7 is within the 78-86 inch range; therefore, the aircraft is loaded within limits.

Graph Method

Another method used to determine the loaded weight and CG is the use of graphs provided by the manufacturers. The following is an example of the graph method. [Figures 4-5 and 4-6]

Given:

Front Seat Occupants	340 lb
Rear Seat Occupants	300 lb
Fuel	40 gal
Baggage Area 1	20 lb

SAMPLE LOADING PROBLEM	SAMPLE AIRPLANE	
	Weight (Lb)	(Lb-In/ 1000)
1. Basic Empty Weight (Use the data pertaining to your airplane as it is presently equipped.) Includes unusable fuel and full oil	1467	57.3
2. Usable Fuel (At 6 Lb/Gal)	240	11.5
Standard Tanks (40 Gal Maximum)		
Long Range Tanks (50 Gal Maximum) . .		
Integral Tanks (62 Gal Maximum).		
Integral Reduced Fuel (42 Gal)		
3. Pilot and Front Passenger (Station 34 to 46) .	340	12.6
4. Rear Passengers	300	21.8
5. Baggage Area 1 or Passenger on Child's Seat (Station 82 to 108, 120 Lb Max)	20	1.9
6. Baggage Area 2 (Station 108 to 142, 50 Lb Max.)		
7. WEIGHT AND MOMENT	2367	104.8

FIGURE 4-5.—Weight and balance data.

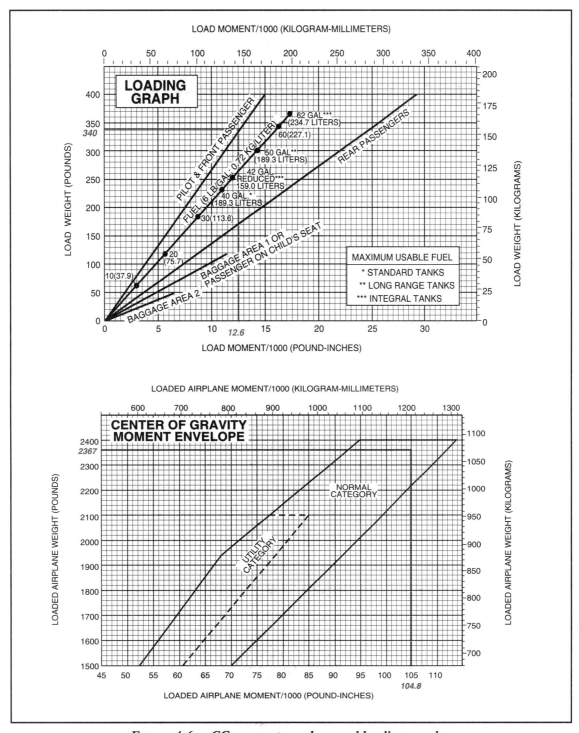

FIGURE 4-6.—CG moment envelope and loading graph.

The same steps should be followed as in the computational method except the graphs provided will calculate the moments and allow the pilot to determine if the aircraft is loaded within limits. To determine the moment using the loading graph, find the weight and draw a line straight across until it intercepts the item for which you are calculating the moment. Then draw a line straight down to determine the moment. (The red line on the loading graph represents the moment for the pilot and front passenger. All other moments were determined in the same way.) Once this has been done for each item, total the weight and moments and draw a line for both weight and moment on the center-of-gravity envelope graph. If the lines intersect within the envelope, the aircraft is loaded within limits. In this sample loading problem, the aircraft is loaded within limits.

USEFUL LOAD WEIGHTS AND MOMENTS

OCCUPANTS

FRONT SEAT ARM 85		REAR SEATS ARM 121	
Weight	Moment/100	Weight	Moment/100
120	102	120	145
130	110	130	157
140	119	140	169
150	128	150	182
160	136	160	194
170	144	170	206
180	153	180	218
190	162	190	230
200	170	200	242

USABLE FUEL

MAIN WING TANKS ARM 75

Gallons	Weight	Moment/100
5	30	22
10	60	45
15	90	68
20	120	90
25	150	112
30	180	135
35	210	158
40	240	180
44	264	198

BAGGAGE OR 5TH SEAT OCCUPANT ARM 140

Weight	Moment/100
10	14
20	28
30	42
40	56
50	70
60	84
70	98
80	112
90	126
100	140
110	154
120	168
130	182
140	196
150	210
160	224
170	238
180	252
190	266
200	280
210	294
220	308
230	322
240	336
250	350
260	364
270	378

AUXILIARY TANKS ARM 94

MAIN WING TANKS ARM 75

Gallons	Weight	Moment/100
5	30	22
10	60	56
15	90	85
19	114	107

*OIL

Quarts	Weight	Moment/100
10	19	5

*Included in basic Empty Weight

Empty Weight ~ 2015
MOM/ 100 ~ 1554

MOMENT LIMITS vs WEIGHT

Moment limits are based on the following weight and center of gravity limit data (landing gear down).

WEIGHT CONDITION	FORWARD CG LIMIT	AFT CG LIMIT
2950 lb (takeoff or landing)	82.1	84.7
2525 lb	77.5	85.7
2475 lb or less	77.0	85.7

Weight	Minimum Moment/100	Maximum Moment/100
2100	1617	1800
2110	1625	1808
2120	1632	1817
2130	1640	1825
2140	1648	1834
2150	1656	1843
2160	1663	1851
2170	1671	1860
2180	1679	1868
2190	1686	1877
2200	1694	1885
2210	1702	1894
2220	1709	1903
2230	1717	1911
2240	1725	1920
2250	1733	1928
2260	1740	1937
2270	1748	1945
2280	1756	1954
2290	1763	1963
2300	1771	1971
2310	1779	1980
2320	1786	1988
2330	1794	1997
2340	1802	2005
2350	1810	2014
2360	1817	2023
2370	1825	2031
2380	1833	2040
2390	1840	2048
2400	1848	2057
2410	1856	2065
2420	1863	2074
2430	1871	2083
2440	1879	2091
2450	1887	2100
2460	1894	2108
2470	1092	2117
2480	1911	2125
2490	1921	2134
2500	1932	2143
2510	1942	2151
2520	1953	2160
2530	1963	2168
2540	1974	2176
2550	1985	2184
2560	1995	2192
2570	2005	2200
2580	2016	2208
2590	2026	2216
2600	2037	2224
2610	2048	2232
2620	2058	2239
2630	2069	2247
2640	2080	2255
2650	2090	2263
2660	2101	2271
2670	2112	2279
2680	2123	2287
2690	2133	2295
2700	2144	2303
2710	2155	2311
2720	2166	2319
2730	2177	2326
2740	2188	2334
2750	2199	2342
2760	2210	2350
2770	2221	2358
2780	2232	2366
2790	2243	2374
2800	2254	2381
2810	2265	2389
2820	2276	2397
2830	2287	2405
2840	2298	2413
2850	2309	2421
2860	2320	2426
2870	2332	2436
2880	2343	2444
2890	2354	2452
2900	2365	3460
2910	2377	2468
2920	2388	2475
2930	2399	2483
2940	2411	2491
2950	2422	2499

SAMPLE LOADING PROBLEM

	WEIGHT	MOMENT/100
BASIC EMPTY WEIGHT	2015	1554
FUEL MAIN TANKS (44 Gal)	264	198
* FRONT SEAT PASSENGERS	300	254
REAR SEAT PASSENGERS	190	230
BAGGAGE	30	42
TOTAL	2799	2278/100

* You can interpolate or, as in this case, add appropriate numbers.

FIGURE 4-7.—Loading schedule placard.

Table Method

The table method applies the same principles as the computational and graph methods. The information and limitations are contained in tables provided by the manufacturer. Figure 4-7 is an example of a table and a weight and balance calculation based on that table. In this problem, the total weight of 2,799 pounds and moment of 2,278\100 is within the limits of the table.

Shifting, Adding, and Removing Weight

A pilot must be able to accurately and rapidly solve any problems which involve the shift, addition, or removal of weight. For example, the pilot may load the aircraft within the allowable takeoff weight limit, then find a CG limit has been exceeded. The most satisfactory solution to this problem is to shift baggage, passengers, or both. The pilot should be able to determine the minimum load shift needed to make the aircraft safe for flight. Pilots should be able to determine if shifting a load to a new location will correct an out-of-limit condition. There are some standardized calculations which can help make these determinations.

Weight Shifting

When weight is shifted from one location to another, the total weight of the aircraft is unchanged. The total moments, however, do change in relation and proportion to the direction and distance the weight is moved. When weight is moved forward, the total moments decrease; when weight is moved aft, total moments increase. The moment change is proportional to the amount of weight moved. Since many aircraft have forward and aft baggage compartments, weight may be shifted from one to the other to change the CG. If starting with a known aircraft weight, CG, and total moments, calculate the new CG (after the weight shift) by dividing the new total moments by the total aircraft weight.

To determine the new total moments, find out how many moments are gained or lost when the weight is shifted. Assume that 100 pounds has been shifted from station 30 to station 150. This movement increases the total moments of the aircraft by 12,000 lb-in.

Moment when
     at station 150 = 100 lb x 150 in = 15,000 lb-in
Moment when
     at station 30 = 100 lb x 30 in = 3,000 lb-in
Moment change   = 12,000 lb-in

By adding the moment change to the original moment (or subtracting if the weight has been moved forward instead of aft), the new total moments are obtained. Then determine the new CG by dividing the new moments by the total weight:

Total moments = 616,000 + 12,000 = 628,000

$$CG = \frac{628,000}{8,000} = 78.5 \text{ in}$$

The shift has caused the CG to shift to station 78.5

A simpler solution may be obtained by using a computer or calculator and a proportional formula. This can be done because the CG will shift a distance which is proportional to the distance the weight is shifted.

EXAMPLE

$$\frac{\text{Weight Shifted}}{\text{Total Weight}} = \frac{\Delta CG \text{ (change of CG)}}{\text{Distance weight is shifted}}$$

$$\frac{100}{8,000} = \frac{\Delta CG}{120}$$

$$\Delta CG = 1.5 \text{ in}$$

The change of CG is added to (or subtracted from when appropriate) the original CG to determine the new CG:

77 + 1.5 = 78.5 inches aft of datum

The shifting weight proportion formula can also be used to determine how much weight must be shifted to achieve a particular shift of the CG. The following problem illustrates a solution of this type.

EXAMPLE

Given:

Aircraft Total Weight .... 7,800 lb
CG .... Station 81.5
Aft CG Limit.. 80.5

Determine how much cargo must be shifted from the aft cargo compartment at station 150 to the forward cargo compartment at station 30 to move the CG to exactly the aft limit.

Solution:

$$\frac{\text{Weight to be Shifted}}{\text{Total Weight}} = \frac{\Delta CG}{\text{Distance Weight Shifted}}$$

$$\frac{\text{Weight to be Shifted}}{7,800} = \frac{1.0 \text{ in}}{120 \text{ in}}$$

$$\text{Weight to be Shifted} = 65 \text{ lb}$$

Weight Addition or Removal

In many instances, the weight and balance of the aircraft will be changed by the addition or removal of weight. When this happens, a new CG must be calculated and checked against the limitations to see if the location is acceptable. This type of weight and balance problem is commonly encountered when the aircraft burns fuel in flight, thereby reducing the weight located at the fuel tanks. Most small aircraft are designed with the fuel tanks positioned close to the CG; therefore, the consumption of fuel does not affect the CG to any great extent.

The addition or removal of cargo presents a CG change problem which must be calculated before flight. The problem may always be solved by calculations involving total moments. A typical problem may involve the calculation of a new CG for an aircraft which, when loaded and ready for flight, receives some additional cargo or passengers just before departure time.

EXAMPLE

Given:

Aircraft Total Weight .... 6,680 lb
CG Station 80.0

Determine the location of the CG if 140 pounds of baggage is added to station 150.

Solution:

$$\frac{\text{Added Weight}}{\text{New Total Weight}} = \frac{\Delta CG}{\text{Distance between weight and old CG}}$$

$$\frac{140}{6,860 + 140} = \frac{\Delta CG}{150 - 80}$$

$$\frac{140}{7,000} = \frac{\Delta CG}{70}$$

$$CG = 1.4 \text{ in aft}$$

Add ΔCG to old CG
New CG = 80.0 in + 1.4 in = 81.4 in

EXAMPLE

Given:

Aircraft Total Weight .... 6,100 lb
CG Station 80.0

Determine the location of the CG if 100 pounds is removed to station 150.

Solution:

$$\frac{\text{Weight Removed}}{\text{New Total Weight}} = \frac{\Delta CG}{\text{Distance between weight and old CG}}$$

$$\frac{100}{6,100 - 100} = \frac{\Delta CG}{150 - 78}$$

$$\frac{100}{6,000} = \frac{\Delta CG}{72}$$

$$CG = 1.2 \text{ in forward}$$

Subtract ΔCG from old CG
New CG = 78 in - 1.2 in = 76.8 in

In the previous examples, the ΔCG is either added or subtracted from the old CG. Deciding which to accomplish is best handled by mentally calculating which way the CG will shift for the particular weight change. If the CG is shifting aft, the ΔCG is added to the old CG; if the CG is shifting forward, the ΔCG is subtracted from the old CG.

AIRPLANE PERFORMANCE

Many accidents occur because pilots fail to understand the effect of varying conditions on airplane performance. In addition to the effects of weight and balance previously discussed, the following factors have a profound effect in changing airplane performance:

- Density Altitude
- Humidity
- Winds
- Runway Surface Conditions
- Runway Gradient

Density Altitude

Air density is perhaps the single most important factor affecting airplane performance. It has a direct bearing on the power output of the engine, efficiency of the propeller, and the lift generated by the wings.

As previously discussed in this handbook, when the air temperature increases, the density of the air decreases. Also, as altitude increases, the density of the air decreases. The density of the air can be described by referring to a corresponding altitude; therefore, the term used to describe air density is density altitude. To avoid confusion, remember that a decrease in air density means a high density altitude; and an increase in air density means a lower density altitude. Density altitude is determined by first finding pressure altitude, and then correcting this altitude for nonstandard temperature variations. It is important to remember that as air density decreases (higher density altitude), airplane performance decreases; and as air density increases (lower density altitude), airplane performance increases.

Effect of Density Altitude on Engine Power and Propeller Efficiency

An increase in air temperature or humidity, or decrease in air pressure resulting in a higher density altitude, significantly decreases power output and propeller efficiency.

The engine produces power in proportion to the weight or density of the air. Therefore, as air density decreases, the power output of the engine decreases. This is true of all engines that are not equipped with a supercharger or turbocharger. Also, the propeller produces thrust in proportion to the mass of air being accelerated through the rotating blades. If the air is less dense, propeller efficiency is decreased.

The problem of high-density altitude operation is compounded by the fact that when the air is less dense, more engine power and increased propeller efficiency are needed to overcome the decreased lift efficiency of the airplane wing. This additional power and propeller efficiency are not available under high-density altitude conditions; consequently, airplane performance decreases considerably.

Humidity

Because of evaporation, the atmosphere always contains some moisture in the form of water vapor. This water vapor replaces molecules of dry air and because water vapor weighs less than dry air, any given volume of moist air weighs less—is less dense—than an equal volume of dry air.

Usually during the operation of small airplanes, the effect of humidity is not considered when determining density altitude; but keep in mind that high humidity will decrease airplane performance which, among other things, results in longer takeoff distances and decreased angle of climb.

Effect of Wind on Airplane Performance

Wind has a direct effect on airplane performance. During takeoff, a headwind will increase the airplane performance by shortening the takeoff distance and increasing the angle of climb. However, a tailwind will decrease performance by increasing the takeoff distance and reducing the angle of climb. The decrease in airplane performance must be carefully considered by the pilot before a downwind takeoff is attempted.

During landing, a headwind will increase airplane performance by steepening the approach angle and reducing the landing distance. A tailwind will decrease performance by decreasing the approach angle and increasing the landing distance. Again, the pilot must take the wind into consideration prior to landing.

During cruise flight, winds aloft have somewhat an opposite effect on airplane performance. A headwind will decrease performance by reducing groundspeed, which in turn increases the fuel requirement for the flight. A tailwind will increase performance by increasing the groundspeed, which in turn reduces the fuel requirement for the flight.

Runway Surface Condition and Gradient

The takeoff distance is affected by the surface condition of the runway. If the runway is muddy, wet, soft, rough, or covered with tall grass, these conditions will act as a retarding force and increase the takeoff distance. Some of these surface conditions may decrease landing roll, but there are certain conditions such as ice or snow covering the surface that will affect braking action and increase the landing roll considerably.

The upslope or downslope of the runway (runway gradient) is quite important when runway length and takeoff distance are critical. Upslope provides a retarding force which impedes acceleration, resulting in a longer ground run on takeoff.

Landing uphill usually results in a shorter landing roll. Downhill operations will usually have the reverse effect of shortening the takeoff distance and increasing the landing roll.

Ground Effect

When an airplane is flown at approximately one wing span or less above the surface, the vertical component of airflow is restricted and modified, and changes occur in the normal pattern of the airflow around the wing and from the wingtips. This change alters the direction of the relative wind in a manner that produces a smaller angle of attack. This means that a wing operating in ground effect with a given angle of attack will generate less induced drag than a wing out of ground effect. Therefore, it is more efficient. While this may be useful in specific situations, it can also trap the unwary into expecting greater climb performance than the airplane is capable of sustaining. In other words, an airplane can take off, and while in ground effect establish a climb angle and/or rate that cannot be maintained once the airplane reaches an altitude where ground effect can no longer influence performance. Conversely, on a landing, ground effect may produce "floating," and result in overshooting, particularly at fast approach speeds.

Use of Performance Charts

Most airplane manufacturers provide adequate information from which the pilot can determine airplane performance. This information can be found in Airplane Flight Manuals or Pilot's Operating Handbooks. Two commonly used methods of depicting performance data are tables and graphs.

Because all values are not listed on the tables or graphs, interpolation is often required to determine intermediate values for a particular flight condition or performance situation. Interpolation will be discussed later in this chapter.

The information on airplane performance charts is based on flight tests conducted under normal operating conditions, using average piloting skills, with the airplane and engine in good operating condition. Any deviation from the above conditions will affect airplane performance.

The performance data extracted from performance charts is accurate. To attain this accuracy, reasonable care must be exercised when computing performance information. It is important to consider that the performance of an older airplane will be less than that predicted by the performance charts.

Standard atmospheric conditions (temperature 59 °F/15 °C, zero relative humidity, and a pressure of 29.92 in. Hg. at sea level) are used in the development of performance charts. This provides a base from which to evaluate performance when actual atmospheric conditions change.

Interpolation

To interpolate means to compute intermediate values between a series of given values. In many instances when performance is critical, an accurate determination of the performance values is the only acceptable means to enhance safe flight. Guessing to determine these values should be avoided.

Interpolation is simple to perform if the method is understood. The following are examples of how to interpolate or accurately determine the intermediate values between a series of given values.

The numbers in column A range from 10 to 30 and the numbers in column B range from 50 to 100. Determine the intermediate numerical value in column B that would correspond with an intermediate value of 20 placed in column A.

A	B
10	50
20	X = Unknown
30	100

It can be visualized that 20 is halfway between 10 and 30; therefore, the corresponding value of the unknown number in column B would be halfway between 50 and 100, or 75.

Many interpolation problems are more difficult to visualize than the preceding example; therefore, a systematic method must be used to determine the required intermediate value. The following describes one method that can be used.

The numbers in Column A range from 10 to 30 with intermediate values of 15, 20, and 25. Determine the intermediate numerical value in column B that would correspond with 15 in column A.

A	B
10	50
15	
20	
25	
30	100

First, in column A, determine the relationship of 15 to the range between 10 and 30 as follows:

$$\frac{15 - 10}{30 - 10} = \frac{5}{20} \text{ or } 1/4$$

It should be noted that 15 is 1/4 of the range between 10 and 30. Now determine 1/4 of the range of column B between 50 and 100 as follows:

$$100 - 50 = 50$$
$$1/4 \text{ of } 50 = 12.5$$

The answer 12.5 represents the number of units, but to arrive at the correct value, 12.5 must be added to the lower number in column B as follows:

$$50 + 12.5 = 62.5$$

The interpolation has been completed and 62.5 is the actual value which is 1/4 of the range of column B.

Another method of interpolation is shown below:

Using the same numbers as in the previous example, a proportion problem based on the relationship of the number can be set up.

$$\text{Proportion: } \frac{5}{20} = \frac{X}{50}$$
$$20X = 250$$
$$X = 12.5$$

The answer 12.5 must be added to 50 to arrive at the actual value of 62.5.

The following example illustrates the use of interpolation applied to a problem dealing with one aspect of airplane performance:

Temperature (°F)	Takeoff Distance (ft)
70	1,173
80	1,356

If a distance of 1,173 feet is required for takeoff when the temperature is 70 °F and 1,356 feet for 80 °F, what distance is required when the temperature is 75 °F? The solution to the problem can be determined as follows:

$$10\left[5\left[\begin{array}{l}70°\\75°\\80°\end{array}\right.\right. \qquad 50\left[X\left[\begin{array}{l}1,173\\?\\1,356\end{array}\right.\right.$$

$$\frac{5}{10} = \frac{X}{183}$$
$$10X = 915$$
$$X = 91.5$$

Performance Charts

Following are descriptions of various performance charts. The information on these charts is not intended for operational use, but rather for familiarization and study. Because performance charts are developed for each specific make, model, and type of airplane, care must be exercised by the pilot to assure that the chart developed for the specific airplane flown is used when seeking performance data.

Density Altitude Charts

Various methods can be used to determine density altitude, one of which is charts. Figure 4-8 illustrates a typical density altitude chart. The following is an example of a density altitude problem based on figure 4-8.

Given:

Airport Elevation	2,545 ft
Outside Air Temperature	70 °F
Altimeter Setting	29.70 in. Hg.

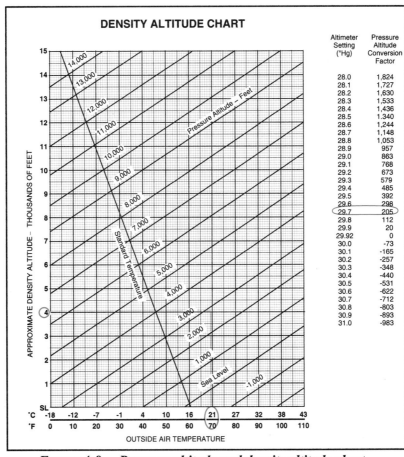

FIGURE 4-8.—*Pressure altitude and density altitude chart.*

Step 1—Find the pressure altitude by locating the altimeter setting of 29.70 in. Hg. and noting the pressure altitude conversion factor. The conversion factor is either added or subtracted from the airport elevation as indicated. In this case, the factor is 205 and should be added. The pressure altitude is 2,750 feet (2,545 + 205 = 2,750).

Step 2—Locate the outside air temperature of 70 °F at the bottom of the chart and draw a vertical line until it intersects with the pressure altitude of 2,750 feet. (The pressure altitude of 2,750 feet is located about three-fourths up between the 2,000 and 3,000-foot lines.)

Step 3—From where the temperature and pressure altitude lines intersect, draw a straight line to the left to determine the density altitude. The density altitude is 4,000 feet.

Takeoff Data Charts

Takeoff data charts are found in many Airplane Flight Manuals or Pilot's Operating Handbooks. From this chart, the pilot can determine (1) the length of the takeoff ground run, and (2) the total distance required to clear a 50-foot obstacle under various airplane weights, headwinds, pressure altitudes, and temperatures. Chart formats will vary with manufacturers. Figure 4-9 shows one such chart.

The following is an example of a problem based on figure 4-9.

Given:

Gross Weight	2,200 lb
Pressure Altitude	1,000 ft
Temperature	20 °C
Headwind	18 kts

Step 1—Locate the gross weight of 2,200 pounds in the first column.

Step 2—Find the pressure altitude of 1,000 feet in the pressure altitude column corresponding to the weight of 2,200 pounds.

Step 3—Determine the ground roll by moving horizontally from the pressure altitude to the ground roll column corresponding to the temperature of 20 °C. The ground roll is 825 feet. To determine the total distance to clear a 50-foot obstacle, move to that column. The total distance would be 1,510 feet.

Step 4—In the notes above the chart, it states to decrease the distance by 10 percent for each 9 knots of headwind. With an 18-knot headwind, the takeoff roll would decrease by 20 percent (825 x 20% = 165; 825 – 165 = 660). The takeoff roll is 660 feet. The same would apply to the distance required to clear a 50-foot obstacle which would be 1,208 feet (1,510 x 20% = 302; 1,510 – 302 = 1,208).

TAKEOFF DISTANCE
MAXIMUM WEIGHT 2400 LB

CONDITIONS:
Flaps 10°
Full Throttle Prior to Brake Release
Paved Level Runway
Zero Wind

SHORT FIELD

NOTES:
1. Prior to takeoff from fields above 3000 feet elevation, the mixture should be leaned to give maximum RPM in a full throttle, static runup.
2. Decrease distances 10% for each 9 knots headwind. For operation with tailwind up to 10 knots, increase distances by 10% for each 2 knots.
3. For operation on a dry, grass runway, increase distances by 15% of the "ground roll" figure.

WEIGHT LB	TAKEOFF SPEED KIAS LIFT OFF	TAKEOFF SPEED KIAS AT 50 FT	PRESS ALT FT	0 °C GRND ROLL FT	0 °C TOTAL FT TO CLEAR 50 FT OBS	10 °C GRND ROLL FT	10 °C TOTAL FT TO CLEAR 50 FT OBS	20 °C GRND ROLL FT	20 °C TOTAL FT TO CLEAR 50 FT OBS	30 °C GRND ROLL FT	30 °C TOTAL FT TO CLEAR 50 FT OBS	40 °C GRND ROLL FT	40 °C TOTAL FT TO CLEAR 50 FT OBS
2400	51	56	S.L.	795	1460	860	1570	925	1685	995	1810	1065	1945
			1000	875	1605	940	1725	1015	1860	1090	2000	1170	2155
			2000	960	1770	1035	1910	1115	2060	1200	2220	1290	2395
			3000	1055	1960	1140	2120	1230	2295	1325	2480	1425	2685
			4000	1165	2185	1260	2365	1355	2570	1465	2790	1575	3030
			5000	1285	2445	1390	2660	1500	2895	1620	3160	1745	3455
			6000	1425	2755	1540	3015	1665	3300	1800	3620	1940	3990
			7000	1580	3140	1710	3450	1850	3805	2000	4220	- - -	- - -
			8000	1755	3615	1905	4015	2060	4480	- - -	- - -	- - -	- - -
2200	49	54	S.L.	650	1195	700	1280	750	1375	805	1470	865	1575
			1000	710	1310	765	1405	825	1510	885	1615	950	1735
			2000	780	1440	840	1545	905	1660	975	1785	1045	1915
			3000	855	1585	925	1705	995	1835	1070	1975	1150	2130
			4000	945	1750	1020	1890	1100	2040	1180	2200	1270	2375
			5000	1040	1945	1125	2105	1210	2275	1305	2465	1405	2665
			6000	1150	2170	1240	2355	1340	2555	1445	2775	1555	3020
			7000	1270	2440	1375	2655	1485	2890	1605	3155	1730	3450
			8000	1410	2760	1525	3015	1650	3305	1785	3630	1925	4005
2000	46	51	S.L.	525	970	565	1035	605	1110	650	1185	695	1265
			1000	570	1060	615	1135	665	1215	710	1295	765	1385
			2000	625	1160	675	1240	725	1330	780	1425	840	1525
			3000	690	1270	740	1365	800	1465	860	1570	920	1685
			4000	755	1400	815	1500	880	1615	945	1735	1015	1865
			5000	830	1545	900	1660	970	1790	2145	1925	1120	2070
			6000	920	1710	990	1845	1070	1990	2405	2145	1235	2315
			7000	1015	1900	1095	2055	1180	2225	2715	2405	1370	2605
			8000	1125	2125	1215	2305	1310	2500	1410	2715	1520	2950

FIGURE 4-9.—Takeoff performance data chart.

Step 5—If the runway is dry grass, the notes state to increase the distance by 15 percent of the ground roll. In this problem, it would require adding 15 percent of 660 feet.

Climb and Cruise Performance Data

Climb and cruise performance are compiled from actual flight tests. This information is helpful in cross-country flight planning. Examples using different types of charts are provided as an example for determining climb performance and cruise performance.

Determine the time, fuel, and distance to climb using figure 4-10.

Given:

Airport Pressure Altitude	5,650 ft
Cruise Altitude	9,500 ft

FIGURE **4-10.**—*Crosswind and headwind component charts.*

Step 1—Locate the airport pressure altitude of 5,650 feet on the chart, and draw a straight line until it intersects the curved line, then draw a line to the bottom of the chart.

Step 2—Using the scale at the bottom of the chart, note the time, fuel, and distance to climb (9 minutes; 1.9 gallons; 12 miles).

Step 3—Repeat steps 1 and 2 using the cruise altitude of 9,500 feet (20 minutes; 3.9 gallons; 27 miles).

Step 4—Subtract the information found in step 2 from that found in step 3 (Time to climb 20 - 9 = 11 minutes; fuel to climb 3.9 - 1.9 = 2 gallons; miles to climb 27 - 12 = 15 miles).

Determine the true airspeed and fuel consumption rate based on figure 4-11.

Given:

Pressure Altitude	4,000 ft
Temperature	Standard
Power	2,400 RPM

CRUISE PERFORMANCE

CONDITIONS:
2400 Pounds
Recommended Lean Mixture
NOTE: Cruise speeds are shown for an airplane equipped with speed fairings which increase the speeds by approximately 2 knots.

PRESSURE ALTITUDE FT	RPM	20° C BELOW STANDARD TEMP			STANDARD TEMPERATURE			20° C ABOVE STANDARD TEMP		
		% BHP	KTAS	GPH	% BHP	KTAS	GPH	% BHP	KTAS	GPH
2000	2500	---	---	---	76	114	8.5	72	114	8.1
	2400	72	110	8.1	69	109	7.7	65	106	7.3
	2300	65	104	7.3	62	103	6.9	59	102	6.6
	2200	58	99	6.6	55	97	6.3	53	96	6.1
	2100	52	92	6.0	50	91	5.8	48	89	5.7
4000	2550	---	---	---	76	117	8.5	72	116	8.1
	2500	77	115	8.6	73	114	8.1	69	113	7.7
	2400	69	109	7.8	65	108	7.3	62	107	7.0
	2300	62	104	7.0	59	102	6.6	57	101	6.4
	2200	56	98	6.3	54	96	6.1	51	94	5.9
	2100	51	91	5.8	48	89	5.7	47	88	5.5
6000	2600	---	---	---	77	119	8.6	72	118	8.1
	2500	73	114	8.2	69	113	7.8	66	112	7.4
	2400	66	108	7.4	63	107	7.0	60	106	6.7
	2300	60	103	6.7	57	101	6.4	55	99	6.2
	2200	54	96	6.1	52	95	5.9	50	92	5.8
	2100	49	90	5.7	47	88	5.5	46	86	5.5
8000	2650	---	---	---	77	121	8.6	73	120	8.1
	2600	77	119	8.7	73	118	8.2	69	117	7.8
	2500	70	113	7.8	66	112	7.4	63	111	7.1
	2400	63	108	7.1	60	106	6.7	58	104	6.5
	2300	57	101	6.4	55	100	6.2	53	97	6.0
	2200	52	95	6.0	50	93	5.8	49	91	5.7
10,000	2600	74	118	8.3	70	117	7.8	66	115	7.4
	2500	67	112	7.5	64	111	7.1	61	109	6.8
	2400	61	106	6.8	58	105	6.5	56	102	6.3
	2300	55	100	6.3	53	98	6.0	51	96	5.9
	2200	50	93	5.8	49	91	5.7	47	89	5.6
12,000	2550	67	114	7.5	64	112	7.1	61	111	6.9
	2500	64	111	7.2	61	109	6.8	59	107	6.6
	2400	59	105	6.6	56	103	6.3	54	100	6.1
	2300	53	98	6.1	51	96	5.9	50	94	5.8

FIGURE **4-11.**—*Cruise performance chart.*

Step 1—Locate the pressure altitude of 4,000 feet on the chart.

Step 2—Locate 2,400 RPM in the proper column.

Step 3—Move across the chart to the standard temperature column, and note the true airspeed and fuel consumption rate (True airspeed, 108 knots; fuel consumption rate, 7.3 gallons per hour).

Takeoffs and landings in certain crosswind conditions are inadvisable or even dangerous. If the crosswind is strong enough to warrant an extreme drift correction, a hazardous landing condition may result. Therefore, always consider the takeoff or landing capabilities with respect to the reported surface wind conditions and the available landing directions.

Before an airplane is type certificated by the FAA, it must be flight tested to meet certain requirements. Among these is the demonstration of being satisfactorily controllable with no exceptional degree of skill or alertness on the part of the pilot in 90° crosswinds up to a velocity equal to 0.2 V_{SO}. This means a windspeed of two-tenths of the airplane's stalling speed with power-off and gear and flaps down. (If the stalling speed is 60 knots, then the airplane must be capable of being landed in a 12 knot 90° crosswind.) To inform the pilot of the airplane's capability, regulations require that the demonstrated crosswind velocity be made available. Certain Airplane Owner's Manuals provide a chart for determining the maximum safe wind velocities for various degrees of crosswind for that particular airplane. The chart, with the example included, will familiarize pilots with a method of determining crosswind components. [Figure 4-12]

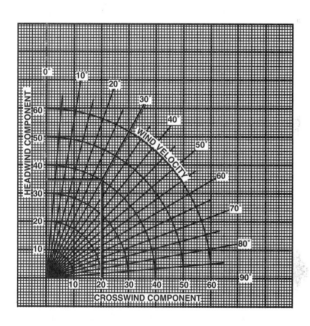

FIGURE 4-12.—Crosswind and headwind component chart.

Determine the headwind and crosswind component based on figure 4-12.

Given:

Runway	36
Wind	330° at 40 kts

Step 1—Subtract the runway heading from the wind direction to determine the wind angle (360-330 = 30).
Step 2—Locate the 30° line and draw a line from that point until it intersects the wind velocity line of 40 knots.
Step 3—From where the wind angle line and wind velocity line intersect, draw a straight line across the chart to determine the headwind component and draw a line straight down the chart to determine the crosswind component (Headwind, 35 knots; crosswind, 20 knots).

Landing Performance Data

Variables similar to those affecting takeoff distance, also affect landing distances, although generally to a lesser extent. Consult your Aircraft Flight Manual or Pilot's Operating Handbook for landing distance data, recommended flap settings, and recommended approach airspeeds.

Combined Graphs

Some aircraft performance charts incorporate two or more graphs into one when an aircraft flight performance involves several conditions. A simple combination of graphs is illustrated in figure 4-13. It requires three functions to solve for takeoff distance with adjustments for air density, gross weight, and headwind conditions. The first function converts pressure altitude to density altitude. The right margin of this portion of the graph, even though it is not numbered, represents density altitude and starts the second function, the effect of gross weight on takeoff distance. The right margin of this section represents takeoff distance with no wind and starts the final phase of correcting for the effect of headwind.

Determine the ground roll and total landing distance to clear a 50-foot obstacle based on figure 4-13.

Given:

OAT	75 °F
Pressure Altitude	4,000 ft
Landing Weight	3,200 lb
Headwind	10 kts

Step 1—Locate the temperature at the bottom of the chart and draw a line up the chart until it intersects the pressure altitude. From where the temperature and pressure altitude lines intersect, draw a line across to the reference line.

Step 2—From the reference line, draw a line which parallels the other lines. Locate the weight at the bottom of the chart and draw a line upward until it intersects the parallel line just drawn. From that point, draw a straight line across to the next reference line.

Step 3—Repeat the same procedure as outlined in step 2 for applying the wind factor. The landing distance is 1,475 feet.

Step 4—The notes on the chart indicate the ground roll is 53 percent of the total landing distance (1,475 x .53 = 781.75 or 782 feet).

NORMAL LANDING

ASSOCIATED CONDITIONS:

POWER	AS REQUIRED TO MAINTAIN 800 FT/MIN DESCENT ON APPROACH
FLAPS	DOWN
RUNWAY	PAVED, LEVEL DRY SURFACE
APPROACH SPEED	IAS AS TABULATED

NOTE: GROUND ROLL IS APPROX. 53% OF TOTAL LANDING DISTANCE OVER A 50 FT OBSTACLE.

EXAMPLE:

OAT	75° F
PRESSURE ALTITUDE	4000 FT
LANDING WEIGHT	3200 LB
HEADWIND	10 KNOTS

TOTAL LANDING DISTANCE OVER A 50 FT OBSTACLE	1475 FT
GROUND ROLL (53% OF 1475)	782 FT
IAS APPROACH SPEED	87 MPH IAS

WEIGHT POUNDS	IAS APPROACH SPEED (ASSUMES ZERO INSTR. ERROR)	
	MPH	KNOTS
3400	90	78
3200	87	76
3000	84	73
2800	81	70
2600	78	68
2400	75	65

FIGURE 4-13.—Landing chart.

CHAPTER 5

WEATHER

INTRODUCTION

Despite all the technological advancements, safety in flight is still subject to weather conditions such as limited visibility, turbulence, and icing.

One may wonder why pilots need more than general information available from the predictions of the meteorologist. The answer is well known to the experienced pilot. Meteorologists' predictions are based upon movements of large air masses and upon local conditions at points where weather stations are located. Air masses at times are unpredictable, and weather stations in some areas are spaced rather widely apart. Therefore, pilots must understand the conditions that could cause unfavorable weather to occur between the stations, as well as the conditions that may be different from those indicated by weather reports.

Furthermore, the meteorologist can only predict the weather conditions; the pilot must decide whether the particular flight may be hazardous, considering the type of aircraft being flown, equipment used, flying ability, experience, and physical limitations.

Weather service to aviation is a combined effort of the National Weather Service (NWS), the Federal Aviation Administration (FAA), the Department of Defense (DOD), and other aviation groups and individuals. Because of the increasing need for worldwide weather services, foreign weather services also have a vital input into our service.

This chapter is designed to help the pilot acquire a general background of weather knowledge and the principles upon which sound judgment can be built as experience is gained and further study is undertaken. There is no substitute for experience in any flight activity, and this is particularly true if good judgment is to be applied to decisions concerning weather.

OBSERVATIONS

Weather observations are measurements and estimates of existing weather both at the surface and aloft. When recorded and transmitted, an observation becomes a report, and these reports are the basis of all weather analyses and forecasts.

Surface Aviation Weather Observations

Surface aviation weather observations include elements pertinent to flying. A network of airport stations provides routine up-to-date surface weather information. Automated surface observing systems (ASOS), automated weather observing systems (AWOS), and other automated weather observing systems are becoming a major part of the surface weather observing network.

Upper Air Observations

Upper air observations are data received from sounding balloons (known as radiosonde observations) and pilot weather reports (PIREPs). Upper air observations are taken twice daily at specified stations. These observations furnish temperature, humidity, pressure, and wind data. In addition, pilots are a vital source of upper air weather observations. In fact, aircraft in flight are the only means of directly observing turbulence, icing, and height of cloud tops.

Radar Observation

Precipitation reflects radar signals which are displayed as echoes on the radar scope. The use of radar is particularly helpful in determining the exact location of storm areas. Except for some mountainous terrain, radar coverage is complete over the contiguous 48 states.

A radar remote weather display system (RRWDS) is specifically designed to provide real-time radar weather information from many different radars. A radar system that uses Doppler technology is being installed across the United States. This radar gives greater detail and enhanced information about thunderstorms and weather systems.

SERVICE OUTLETS

A weather service outlet as used here is any facility, either government or private, that provides aviation weather service to users. Information concerning some of the service outlets provided by the FAA follows.

FAA Flight Service Station (FSS)

The FAA flight service station provides more aviation weather briefing services than any other government service outlet. They provide preflight and inflight briefings, make scheduled and unscheduled weather broadcasts, and furnish weather advisories to flights within the FSS area.

The FAA has modernized its FSS program. Automated flight service stations (AFSS) are becoming abundant, with about one per state, with lines of communications radiating out from it.

Pilot's Automatic Telephone Weather Answering System (PATWAS)

Pilot's automatic telephone weather answering system is a recorded telephone briefing with the forecast for the local area, usually within a 50 nautical mile radius of the station.

Transcribed Information Briefing Service (TIBS)

Transcribed information briefing service is provided by AFSS's and provides continuous telephone recordings of meteorological and/or aeronautical information. Specifically, TIBS provides area and/or route briefings, airspace procedures, and special announcements, if applicable. Other items may be included depending on user demand.

Direct User Access Terminal Service (DUATS)

A direct user access terminal service is an FAA-operated information system which enables pilots and other aviation interests to conduct their own weather briefings. The computer-based system receives and stores a number of NWS and FAA products which are commonly used in weather briefings. Pilots using a personal computer and modem can access the system and request weather and other pertinent data as well as file or amend flight plans.

Transcribed Weather Broadcast (TWEB)

A transcribed weather broadcast is a continuous broadcast on low/medium frequencies (190 to 535 kHz) and selected VORs (108.0 to 117.95 MHz).

WEATHER BRIEFING

Obtaining a good weather briefing is in the interest of safety. It is the pilot's responsibility to ensure all the needed information is obtained to make a safe flight. When requesting a briefing, pilots should identify themselves and provide as much information regarding the proposed flight as possible. The information received will depend on the type of briefing requested. The following would be helpful to the briefer.

- Type of flight, visual flight rule (VFR) or instrument operating rule (IFR).
- Aircraft number or pilot's name.
- Aircraft type.
- Departure point.
- Route of flight.
- Destination.
- Flight altitude(s).
- Estimated time of departure.
- Estimated time en route or estimated time of arrival.

Standard Briefing should include:

- Adverse conditions.
- VFR flight not recommended when conditions warrant.
- Weather synopsis (positions and movements of lows, highs, fronts, and other significant causes of weather).
- Current weather.
- Forecast weather (en route and destination).
- Forecast winds/temperatures aloft.
- Alternate routes (if any).
- Notices to Airmen (NOTAMs).
- Air traffic control (ATC) delays.
- Request for PIREPs.

Abbreviated Briefing

An abbreviated briefing will be provided at the user's request to supplement mass disseminated data, to update a previous briefing, or to request specific information only.

Outlook Briefing

An outlook briefing will be provided when the briefing is 6 or more hours in advance of the proposed departure time. It will be limited to applicable forecast data for the proposed flight.

NATURE OF THE ATMOSPHERE

Life exists at the bottom of an ocean of air called the atmosphere. This ocean extends upward from the Earth's surface for many miles, gradually thinning as it nears the top. Near the surface, the air is relatively warm from contact with the Earth. The temperature in the United States averages about 15 °C (59 °F) the year round. As altitude increases, the temperature decreases by about 2 °C (3.5 °F) for every 1,000 feet (normal lapse rate) until air temperature reaches about –55 °C (–67 °F) at 7 miles above the Earth.

For flight purposes, the atmosphere is divided into two layers: the upper layer, where temperature remains practically constant, is the "stratosphere;" the lower layer, where the temperature changes, is the "troposphere." Although jets routinely fly in the stratosphere, the private pilot usually has no occasion to go that high, but usually remains in the lower layer– the troposphere. This is the region where all weather occurs and practically all light airplane flying is done. The top of the troposphere lies 5 to 10 miles above the Earth's surface. [Figure 5-1]

Obviously, a body of air as deep as the atmosphere has tremendous weight. It is difficult to realize that the normal sea level pressure upon the body is about 15 pounds per square inch, or about 20 tons on the

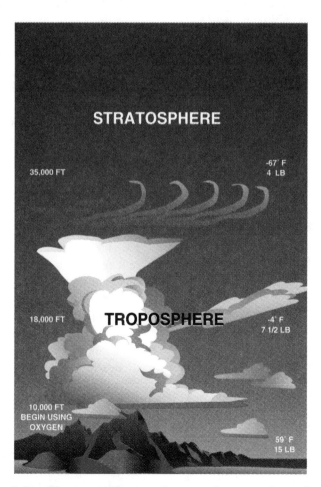

FIGURE 5-1.—The troposphere and stratosphere are the realm of flight.

average person. The body does not collapse because this pressure is equalized by an equal pressure within the body. In fact, if the pressure were suddenly released, the human body would explode. As altitude is gained, the temperature of the air not only decreases (it is usually freezing above 18,000 feet) but the air density also decreases; therefore there is less pressure. Pressure is rapidly reduced up to 18,000 feet where the pressure is only half as great as at sea level.

Oxygen and the Human Body

The atmosphere is composed of about four-fifths nitrogen and one-fifth oxygen, with approximately one percent of various other gases. Oxygen is essential to human life. At 18,000 feet, with only half the normal atmospheric pressure, the body intake of oxygen would be only half the normal amount. Body reactions would be definitely below normal, and unconsciousness might result. In fact, the average person's reactions become affected at 10,000 feet and may be affected at altitudes as low as 5,000 feet.

To overcome these unfavorable conditions at high altitudes, pilots use oxygen-breathing equipment and wear protective clothing, or fly in pressurized cabins in which temperature, pressure, and oxygen content of the air can be maintained within proper range.

Significance of Atmospheric Pressure

The average pressure exerted by the atmosphere is approximately 15 pounds per square inch at sea level. This means that a column of air 1 inch square extending from sea level to the top of the atmosphere would weight about 15 pounds. The actual pressure at a given place and time, however, depends upon several factors. These are altitude, temperature, and density of the air. These conditions definitely affect flight.

Measurement of Atmospheric Pressure

A barometer is generally used to measure the height of a column of mercury in a glass tube. It is sealed at one end and calibrated in inches. An increase in pressure forces the mercury higher in the tube; a decrease allows some of the mercury to drain out, reducing the height of the column. In this way, changes of pressure are registered in inches of mercury (in. Hg.). The standard sea level pressure expressed in these terms is 29.92 inches at a standard temperature of 15 °C (59 °F).

The mercury barometer is cumbersome to move and difficult to read. A more compact, more easily read, and more mobile barometer is the aneroid, although it is not so accurate as the mercurial. The aneroid barometer is a partially evacuated cell sensitive to pressure changes. The cell is linked to an indicator which moves across a scale graduated in pressure units.

If all weather stations were at sea level, the barometer readings would give a correct record of the distribution of atmospheric pressure at a common level. To achieve a common level, each station translates its barometer reading into terms of sea level pressure. A change of 1,000 feet of elevation makes a change of about 1 inch on the barometer reading. Thus, if a station located 5,000 feet above sea level found the mercury to be 25 inches high in the barometer tube, it would translate and report this reading as 30 inches. [Figure 5-2]

Since the rate of decrease in atmospheric pressure is fairly constant in the lower layers of the atmosphere, the approximate altitude can be determined by finding the difference between pressure at sea level and pressure at the given atmospheric level. In fact, the aircraft altimeter is an aneroid barometer with its scale in units of altitude instead of pressure.

Effect of Altitude on Atmospheric Pressure

It can be concluded that atmospheric pressure decreases as altitude increases. It can also be stated that pressure at a given point is a measure of the weight of the column of air above that point. As altitude increases, pressure diminishes as the weight of the air column decreases. This decrease in pressure (increase in density altitude) has a pronounced effect on flight.

Effect of Altitude on Flight

The most noticeable effect of a decrease in pressure, due to an altitude increase, becomes evident in takeoffs, rate of climb, and landings. An airplane that requires a 1,000-foot run for takeoff at a sea level airport will require a run almost twice as long to take off at an airport which is approximately 5,000 feet above sea level. The purpose of a takeoff run is to gain enough speed to generate lift from the passage of air over the wings. If the air is thin, more speed is required to obtain enough lift for takeoff—hence, a longer ground run. It is also true that the engine is less efficient in thin air, and the thrust of the propeller is less effective. The rate of climb is also slower at the higher elevation, requiring a greater distance to gain the altitude necessary to clear any obstructions. In landing, the difference is not so noticeable except that the plane has greater groundspeed when it touches the ground. [Figures 5-3 and 5-4]

FIGURE 5-2.—*Barometric pressure at a weather station is expressed as pressure at sea level.*

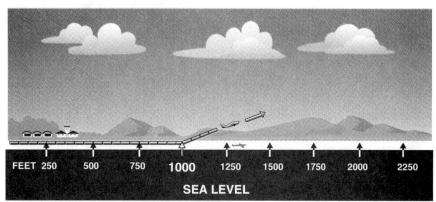

FIGURE 5-3.—*Atmospheric density at sea level enables an airplane to take off in a relatively short distance.*

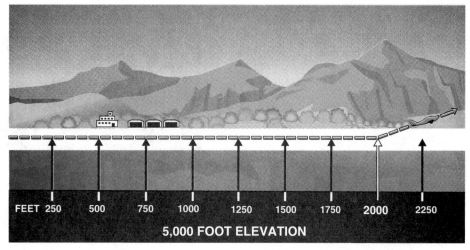

FIGURE 5-4.—*The distance required for takeoff increases with the altitude of the field.*

Effect of Differences in Air Density

Differences in air density caused by changes in temperature result in changes in pressure. This, in turn, creates motion in the atmosphere, both vertically and horizontally (current and winds). This action, when mixed with moisture, produces clouds and precipitation—in fact, these are the phenomena called "weather."

Pressure Recorded in "Millibars"

The mercury barometer reading at the individual weather stations is converted to the equivalent sea level pressure and then translated from terms of inches of mercury to a measure of pressure called millibars. One inch of mercury is equivalent to approximately 34 millibars; hence, the normal atmospheric pressure at sea level (29.92), expressed in millibars, is 1,013.2 or roughly 1,000 millibars. The usual pressure readings range from 950.0 to 1,040.0.

Individually these pressure readings are of no particular value to the pilot; but when pressures at different stations are compared, or when pressures at the same station show changes in successive readings, it is possible to determine many symptoms indicating the trend of weather conditions. In general, a falling pressure indicates the approach of bad weather and a rising pressure indicates a clearing of the weather.

Wind

The pressure and temperature changes discussed in the previous section produce two kinds of motion in the atmosphere—vertical movement of ascending and descending currents, and horizontal flow known as "wind." Both of these motions are of primary interest to the pilot because they affect the flight of aircraft during takeoff, landing, climbing, and cruising flight. These motions also bring about changes in weather, which require a pilot to determine if a flight can be made safely.

Conditions of wind and weather occurring at any specific place and time are the result of the general circulation in the atmosphere. This will be discussed briefly in the following pages.

The atmosphere tends to maintain an equal pressure over the entire Earth, just as the ocean tends to maintain a constant level. When the equilibrium is disturbed, air begins to flow from areas of higher pressure to areas of lower pressure.

THE CAUSE OF ATMOSPHERIC CIRCULATION

The factor that upsets the normal equilibrium is the uneven heating of the Earth. At the Equator, the Earth receives more heat than in areas to the north and south. This heat is transferred to the atmosphere, warming the air and causing it to expand and become less dense. Colder air to the north and south, being more dense, moves toward the Equator forcing the less dense air upward. This air in turn becomes warmer and less dense and is forced upward, thus establishing a constant circulation that might consist of two circular paths; the air rising at the Equator, traveling aloft toward the poles, and returning along the Earth's surface to the Equator, as shown in figure 5-5.

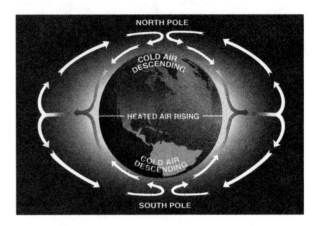

FIGURE 5-5.—Heat at the Equator would cause the air to circulate uniformly, as shown, if the Earth did not rotate.

This theoretical pattern, however, is greatly modified by many forces, a very important one being the rotation of the Earth. In the Northern Hemisphere, this rotation causes air to deflect to the right of its normal path. In the Southern Hemisphere, air is deflected to the left of its normal path. For simplicity, this discussion will be confined to the motion of air in the Northern Hemisphere. [Figure 5-6]

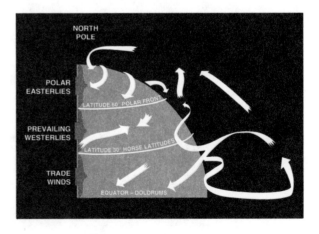

FIGURE 5-6.—Principal air currents in the Northern Hemisphere.

As the air rises and moves northward from the Equator, it is deflected toward the east, and by the time it has traveled about a third of the distance to the pole, it is no longer moving northward, but eastward. This causes the air to accumulate in a belt at about latitude 30°, creating an area of high pressure. Some of this air is then forced down to the Earth's surface, where part flows southwestward, returning to the Equator, and part flows northeastward along the surface.

A portion of the air aloft continues its journey northward, being cooled en route, and finally settles down near the pole, where it begins a return trip toward the Equator. Before it has progressed very far southward, it comes into conflict with the warmer surface air flowing northward from latitude 30°. The warmer air moves up over a wedge of the colder air, and continues northward, producing an accumulation of air in the upper latitudes.

Further complications in the general circulation of the air are brought about by the irregular distribution of oceans and continents, the relative effectiveness of different surfaces in transferring heat to the atmosphere, the daily variation in temperature, the seasonal changes, and many other factors.

Regions of low pressure, called "lows," develop where air lies over land or water surfaces that are warmer than the surrounding areas. In India, for example, a low forms over the hot land during the summer months, but moves out over the warmer ocean when the land cools in winter. Lows of this type are semipermanent, however, and are less significant to the pilot than the "migratory cyclones" or "cyclonic depressions" that form when unlike air masses meet. These lows will be discussed later in this chapter.

Wind Patterns

This is a discussion of wind patterns associated with areas of high and low pressure. As previously stated, air flows from an area of high pressure to an area of low pressure. In the Northern Hemisphere, during this flow, the air is deflected to the right. Therefore, as the air leaves the high pressure area, it is deflected to produce a clockwise circulation. As the air flows toward the low pressure area, it is deflected to produce a counterclockwise flow around the low pressure area.

Another important aspect is that air moving out of a high pressure area depletes the quantity of air. Therefore, highs are areas of descending air. Descending air favors dissipation of cloudiness; hence the association, high pressure—good weather. By similar reasoning, when air converges into a low

pressure area; it cannot go outward against the pressure gradient, nor can it go downward into the ground; it must go upward. Rising air is conducive to cloudiness and precipitation; thus the general association low pressure—bad weather.

A knowledge of these patterns frequently enables a pilot to plan a course to take advantage of favorable winds, particularly during long flights. In flying from east to west, for example, the pilot would find favorable winds to the south of a high, or to the north of a low. It also gives the pilot a general idea of the type of weather to expect relative to the "highs" and "lows." [Figures 5-7 and 5-8]

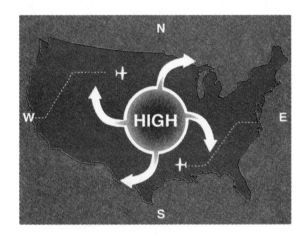

FIGURE 5-7.—Circulation of wind within a "low."

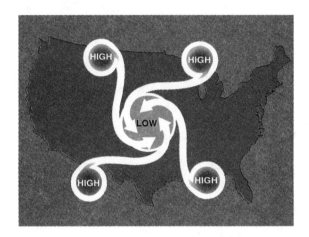

FIGURE 5-8.—Use of favorable winds in flight.

The theory of general circulation in the atmosphere, and the wind patterns formed within areas of high pressure and low pressure have been discussed. These concepts account for the large scale movements of the wind, but do not take into consideration the effects of local conditions that frequently cause drastic modifications in wind direction and speed near the Earth's surface.

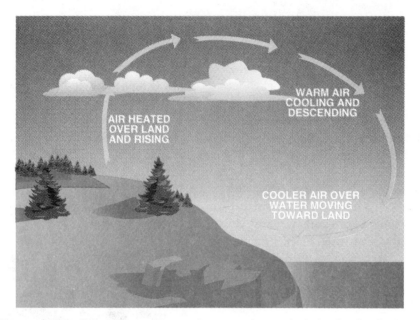

FIGURE 5-9.—Convection currents form on-shore winds in the daytime.

Convection Currents

Certain kinds of surfaces are more effective than others in heating the air directly above them. Plowed ground, sand, rocks, and barren land give off a great deal of heat, whereas water and vegetation tend to absorb and retain heat. The uneven heating of the air causes small local circulations called "convection currents," which are similar to the general circulation just described.

This may be particularly noticeable over land adjacent to a body of water. During the day, air over land becomes heated and less dense; colder air over water moves in to replace it forcing the warm air aloft and causing an on-shore wind. At night, the land cools, and the water is relatively warmer. The cool air over the land, being heavier, then moves toward the water as an off-shore wind, lifting the warmer air and reversing the circulation. [Figures 5-9 and 5-10]

Convection currents cause the bumpiness experienced by pilots flying at low altitudes in warmer weather. On a low flight over varying surfaces, the pilot will encounter updrafts over pavement or barren places and downdraft over vegetation and water. Ordinarily, this can be avoided by flight at higher altitudes. When the larger convection currents form cumulus clouds, the pilot will invariably find smooth air above the cloud level. [Figure 5-11]

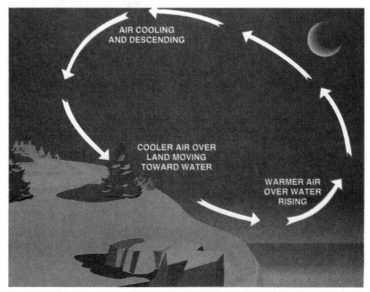

FIGURE 5-10.—Convection currents form off-shore winds at night.

5-8

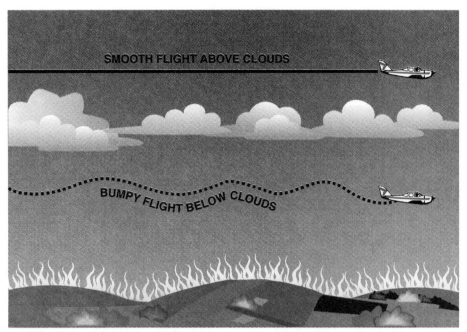

FIGURE 5-11.—Avoiding turbulence caused by convection currents by flying above the cloud level.

Convection currents also cause difficulty in making landings, since they affect the rate of descent. For example, a pilot flying a normal glide frequently tends to land short of or overshoot the intended landing spot, depending upon the presence and severity of convection currents. [Figures 5-12 and 5-13]

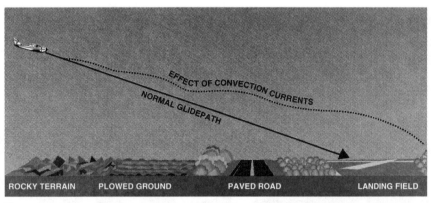

FIGURE 5-12.— Varying surfaces affect the normal glidepath. Some surfaces create rising currents which tend to cause the pilot to overshoot the field.

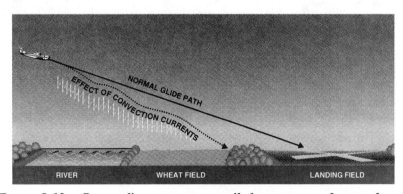

FIGURE 5-13.—Descending currents prevail above some surfaces and tend to cause the pilot to land short of the field.

5-9

The effects of local convection, however, are less dangerous than the turbulence caused when wind is forced to flow around or over obstructions. The only way for the pilot to avoid this invisible hazard is to be forewarned, and to know where to expect unusual conditions.

Effect of Obstructions on Wind

When the wind flows around an obstruction, it breaks into eddies—gusts with sudden changes in speed and direction—which may be carried along some distance from the obstruction. A pilot flying through such turbulence should anticipate the bumpy and unsteady flight that may be encountered. This turbulence—the intensity of which depends upon the size of the obstacle and the velocity of the wind—can present a serious hazard during takeoffs and landings. For example, during landings, it can cause an aircraft to "drop in;" during takeoffs, it could cause the aircraft to fail to gain enough altitude to clear low objects in its path. Any landings or takeoffs attempted under gusty conditions should be made at higher speeds, to maintain adequate control during such conditions. [Figure 5-14]

This same condition is more noticeable where larger obstructions such as bluffs or mountains are involved. As shown in figure 5-15, the wind blowing up the slope on the windward side is relatively smooth, and its upward current helps to carry the aircraft over the peak. The wind on the leeward side, following the terrain contour, flows definitely downward with considerable turbulence and would tend to force an aircraft into the mountain side. The stronger the wind, the greater the downward pressure and the accompanying turbulence. Consequently, in approaching a hill or mountain from the leeward side, a pilot should gain enough altitude well in advance. Because of these downdrafts, it is recommended that mountain ridges and peaks be cleared by at least 2,000 feet. If there is any doubt about having adequate clearance, the pilot should turn away at once and gain more altitude. Between hills or mountains, where there is a canyon or narrow valley, the wind will generally veer from its normal course and flow through the passage with increased velocity and turbulence. A pilot flying over such terrain needs to be alert for wind shifts, and particularly cautious if making a landing.

FIGURE 5-14.—Turbulence caused by obstructions.

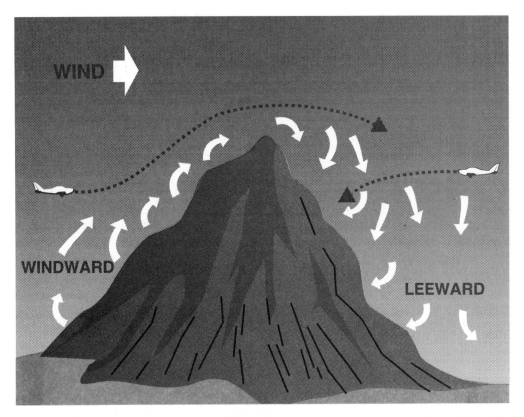

FIGURE 5-15.—Airplanes approaching hills or mountains from windward are helped by rising currents. Those approaching from leeward encounter descending currents.

Low-Level Wind Shear

Wind shear is best described as a change in wind direction and/or speed within a very short distance in the atmosphere. Under certain conditions, the atmosphere is capable of producing some dramatic shears very close to the ground; for example, wind direction changes of 180° and speed changes of 50 knots or more within 200 feet of the ground have been observed. This, however, is not something encountered every day. In fact, it is unusual, which makes it more of a problem. It has been thought that wind cannot affect an aircraft once it is flying except for drift and groundspeed. This is true with steady winds or winds that change gradually. It isn't true, however, if the wind changes faster than the aircraft mass can be accelerated or decelerated.

The most prominent meteorological phenomena that cause significant low-level wind shear problems are thunderstorms and certain frontal systems at or near an airport.

Basically, there are two potentially hazardous shear situations. First, a tailwind may shear to either a calm or headwind component. In this instance, initially the airspeed increases, the aircraft tends to pitch up, and the altitude may increase. Second, a headwind may shear to a calm or tailwind component. In this situation, initially the airspeed decreases, the aircraft pitches down, and the altitude decreases. Aircraft speed, aerodynamic characteristics, power/weight ratio, powerplant response time, and pilot reactions along with other factors have a bearing on wind shear effects. It is important, however, to remember that shear can cause problems for any aircraft and any pilot.

There are two atmospheric conditions that cause the type of low-level wind shear discussed herein. They are thunderstorms and fronts.

The winds around a thunderstorm are complex. Wind shear can be found on all sides of a cell. The wind shift line or gust front associated with thunderstorms can precede the actual storm by up to 15 nautical miles. Consequently, if a thunderstorm is near an airport of intended landing or takeoff, low-level wind shear hazards may exist. At some large airports a low-level wind shear alert system (LLWAS) has been installed which aids in detecting wind shear.

While the direction of the winds above and below a front can be accurately determined, existing procedures do not provide precise and current measurements of the height of the front above an airport. The following is a method of determining the approximate height of the front, with the consideration that wind shear is most critical when it occurs close to the ground.

• A cold front wind shear occurs just after the front passes the airport and for a short period thereafter. If the front is moving 30 knots or more, the frontal surface will usually be 5,000 feet above the airport about 3 hours after the frontal passage.

• With a warm front, the most critical period is before the front passes the airport. Warm front windshear may exist below 5,000 feet for approximately 6 hours; the problem ceases to exist after the front passes the airport. Data compiled on wind shear indicate that the amount of shear in warm fronts is much greater than that found in cold fronts.

• Turbulence may or may not exist in wind shear conditions. If the surface wind under the front is strong and gusty, there will be some turbulence associated with wind shear.

The pilot should be alert to the possibilities of low-level wind shear at any time the conditions stated are present.

Wind and Pressure Representation on Surface Weather Maps

The excerpted portion of a surface weather map provides information about winds at the surface. The wind direction at each station is shown by an arrow. The arrowhead is represented by the station circle, and points in the direction toward which the wind is blowing. Winds are given the name of the direction from which they blow; a northwest wind is a "wind blowing from the northwest." [Figure 5-16]

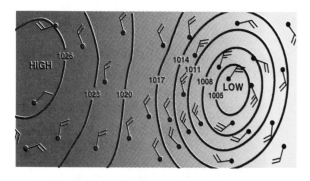

FIGURE 5-16.—Speed and direction of wind are shown on a weather map by wind arrows and isobars.

Windspeed is shown by "barbs" and/or "pennants" placed on the end of the arrow. The speed is indicated by the number of half barbs, full barbs, or pennants. Each half barb represents approximately 5 knots, each full barb indicates approximately 10 knots, and each pennant 50 knots. Thus two and one-half barbs indicate a windspeed of approximately 25 knots; a pennant and two and one-half barbs indicate a windspeed of approximately 75 knots, etc. The pilot can thus tell at a glance, the wind conditions prevailing at map time at any weather station.

Pilots can obtain this information and forecasts of expected winds from all weather reporting stations.

The pressure at each station is recorded on the weather map, and lines (isobars) are drawn to connect points of equal pressure. Many of the lines make complete circles to surround pressure areas marked "H" (high) or "L" (low).

Isobars are quite similar to the contour lines appearing on aeronautical charts. However, instead of indicating altitude of terrain and steepness of slopes, isobars indicate the amount of pressure and steepness of pressure gradients. If the gradient (slope) is steep, the isobars will be close together, and the wind will be strong. If the gradient is gradual, the isobars will be far apart, and the wind gentle. [Figure 5-17]

Isobars furnish valuable information about winds in the first few thousand feet above the surface. Close to the Earth, wind direction is modified by the contours over which it passes, and windspeed is reduced by friction with the surface. At levels 2,000 or 3,000 feet above the surface, however, the speed is greater and the direction is usually parallel to the isobars. Thus, while wind arrows on the weather map excerpt indicate wind near the surface, isobars indicate winds at slightly higher levels. [Figure 5-16]

In the absence of specific information on upper wind conditions, the pilot can often make a fairly reasonable estimate of the wind conditions in the lower few thousand feet on the basis of the observed surface wind. Generally, it will be found that the wind at an altitude of 2,000 feet above the surface will veer about 20° to 40° to the right and almost double in speed. The veering will be greatest over rough terrain and least over flat surfaces. Thus, a north wind of 20 knots at the airport would be likely to change to a northeast wind of 40 knots at 2,000 feet. This subject will be reviewed later in this chapter.

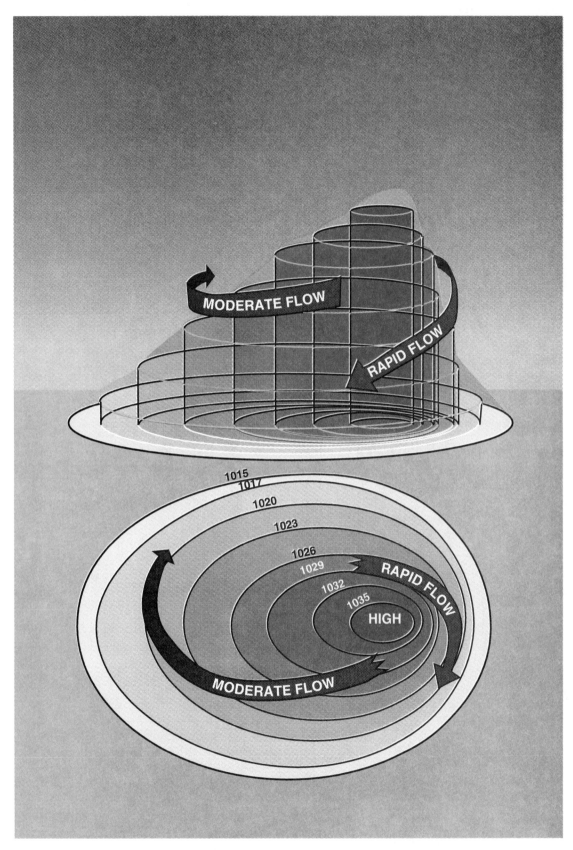

FIGURE 5-17.—Above: Flow of air around a "high." Below: Isobars on a weather map indicate various degrees of pressure within a high.

Moisture and temperature

The atmosphere always contains a certain amount of foreign matter—smoke, dust, salt particles, and particularly moisture in the form of invisible water vapor. The amount of moisture that can be present in the atmosphere depends upon the temperature of the air. For each increase of 20 °F, the capacity of the air to hold moisture is about doubled; conversely, for each decrease of 20 °F, the capacity becomes only half as much.

Relative Humidity

"Humidity" is commonly referred to as the apparent dampness in the air. A similar term used by the National Weather Service, is relative humidity, which is a ratio of the amount of moisture present in any given volume of air to the amount of moisture the air could hold in that volume of air at prevailing temperature and pressure. For instance, "75 percent relative humidity," means that the air contains three-fourths of the water vapor which it is capable of holding at the existing temperature and pressure.

Temperature/Dewpoint Relationship

For the pilot, the relationship discussed under relative humidity is expressed in a slightly different way—as "temperature and dewpoint." It is apparent from the foregoing discussion that if a mass of air at 27 °C (80 °F) has a relative humidity of 50 percent and the temperature is reduced 11 °C (20 °F) to 16 °C (60 °F), the air will then be saturated (100 percent relative humidity). In this case, the original relationship will be stated as "temperature 80 °F, dewpoint 60." In other words, dewpoint is the temperature to which air must be cooled to become saturated.

Dewpoint is of tremendous significance to the pilot because it represents a critical condition of the air. When temperature reaches the dewpoint, water vapor can no longer remain invisible, but is forced to condense, becoming visible on the ground as dew or frost, appearing in the air as fog or clouds, or falling to the Earth as rain, snow, or hail.

NOTE: This is how water can get into the fuel tanks when the tanks are left partially filled overnight. The temperature cools to the dewpoint, and the water vapor contained in the fuel tank air space condenses. This condensed moisture then sinks to the bottom of the fuel tank, since water is heavier than gasoline.

Methods by Which Air Reaches the Saturation Point

It is interesting to note the various ways by which air can reach the saturation point. As previously discussed, this is brought about by a lowering of temperature such as might occur when warm air moves over a cold surface, when cold air mixes with warm air, when air is cooled during the night by contact with the cold ground, or when air is forced upward. Only the fourth method needs any special comment.

When air rises, it uses heat energy in expanding. Consequently, the rising air loses heat rapidly. If the air is unsaturated, the loss will be approximately 3.0 °C (5.4 °F) for every 1,000 feet of altitude.

Warm air can be lifted aloft by three methods; by becoming heated through contact with the Earth's surface, resulting in convective currents; by moving up sloping terrain (as wind blowing up a mountainside); and by being forced to flow over another body of air. For example, when air masses of different temperatures and densities meet. Under the last condition, the warmer, lighter air tends to flow over the cooler, denser air. This will be discussed in greater detail in this chapter under "Air Masses and Fronts."

Air can also become saturated by precipitation. Whatever the cause, when temperature and dewpoint at the ground are close together, there is a good possibility for low clouds and fog to form.

Effect of Temperature on Air Density

Atmospheric pressure not only varies with altitude, it also varies with temperature. When air is heated, it expands and therefore has less density. A cubic foot of warm air is less dense than a cubic foot of cold air. This decrease in air density (increase in density altitude), brought about by an increase in temperature, has a pronounced effect on flight.

Effect of Temperature on Flight

Since an increase in temperature makes the air less dense (increases density altitude), the takeoff run will be longer, the rate of climb slower, and the landing speed (groundspeed) faster on a hot day than on a cold day. Thus, an increase in temperature has the same effect as an increase in altitude. An airplane which requires a ground run of 1,000 feet on a winter day when the temperature is –18 °C (0 °F), will require a much longer run on a summer day when the temperature is 38 °C (100 °F). An airplane that requires the greater portion of a short runway for takeoff on a cold winter day may be unable to take off on this runway during a hot summer day.

Effect of High Humidity on Air Density

A common misconception is that water vapor weighs more than an equal volume of dry air. This is not true. Water vapor weighs approximately five-eighths or 62 percent of an equal volume of perfectly dry air. When the air contains moisture in the form of water vapor, it is not as heavy as dry air and so is less dense.

Assuming that temperature and pressure remain the same, the air density varies inversely with the humidity—that is, as the humidity increases, the air density decreases, (density altitude increases); and, as the humidity decreases, the air density increases (density altitude decreases).

The higher the temperature, the greater the moisture-carrying ability of the air. Therefore, air at a temperature of 38 °C (100 °F) and a relative humidity of 80 percent will contain a greater amount of moisture than air at a temperature of 16 °C (60 °F) and a relative humidity of 80 percent.

Effect of High Humidity on Flight

Since high humidity makes the air less dense (increases density altitude), the takeoff roll will be longer, rate of climb slower, and landing speed higher.

When all three conditions are present, the problem is aggravated. Therefore, beware of "high, hot, and humid" conditions (high density altitudes), and take the necessary precautions, by using performance charts, to assure the runway is long enough for takeoff.

Dew and Frost

When the ground cools at night, the temperature of the air immediately adjacent to the ground is frequently lowered to the saturation point, causing condensation. This condensation takes place directly upon objects on the ground as dew if the temperature is above freezing, or as frost if the temperature is below freezing.

Dew is of no importance to aircraft, but frost creates friction which interferes with the smooth flow of air over the wing surfaces, resulting in a higher stall speed. Frost should always be removed before flight.

Fog

When the air near the ground is four or five degrees above the dewpoint, the water vapor condenses and becomes visible as fog. There are many types of fog, varying in degree of intensity and classified according to the particular phenomena which cause them. One type, "ground fog," which frequently forms at night in low places, is limited to a few feet in height, and is usually dissipated by the heat of the Sun shortly after sunrise. Other types, which can form any time conditions are favorable, may extend to greater heights and persist for days or even weeks. Along seacoasts fog often forms over the ocean and is blown inland. All types of fog produce low visibility and therefore constitute a serious hazard to aircraft.

Clouds

There are two fundamental types of clouds. First, those formed by vertical currents carrying moist air upward to its condensation point are lumpy or billowy and are called "cumulus," which means an "accumulation" or a "pile." Second, those which develop horizontally and lie in sheets or formless layers like fog are called "stratus," which means "spread out." [Figures 5-18 and 5-19]

When clouds are near the Earth's surface, they are generally designated as "cumulus" or "stratus" unless they are producing precipitation, in which case the word "nimbus" (meaning "rain cloud") is added—as "nimbostratus" or "cumulonimbus." [Figure 5-20]

If the clouds are ragged and broken, the word "fracto" (meaning "broken") is added—as "fractostratus" or "fractocumulus."

The word "alto" (meaning "high") is generally added to designate clouds at intermediate heights, usually appearing at levels of 5,000 to 20,000 feet—as "altostratus" or "altocumulus."

Clouds formed in the upper levels of the troposphere (commonly between 20,000 and 50,000 feet) are composed of ice crystals and generally have a delicate, curly appearance, somewhat similar to frost on a windowpane. For these clouds, the word "cirro" (meaning "curly") is added—as "cirrocumulus" or "cirrostratus." At these high altitudes, there is also a fibrous type of cloud appearing as curly wisps, bearing the single name "cirrus."

Under "Air Masses and Fronts" the relationship will be shown between the various types of clouds and the kind of weather expected. At present the chief concern is with the flying conditions directly associated with the different cloud formations.

The ice-crystal clouds (cirrus group) are well above ordinary flight levels of light aircraft and normally do not concern the pilots of these aircraft, except as indications of approaching changes in weather.

FIGURE 5-18.—*Cumulus clouds as they appear at low, intermediate, and high levels.*

FIGURE 5-19.—*Stratus-type clouds at various altitudes.*

STRATOCUMULUS   NIMBOSTRATUS   CUMULONIMBUS   FRACTOCUMULUS

FIGURE 5-20.—Various types of bad weather clouds.

The clouds in the "alto" group are not normally encountered in flights of smaller planes, but they sometimes contain icing conditions important for commercial and military planes. Altostratus clouds usually indicate that unfavorable flying weather is near.

The low clouds are of great importance to the pilot because they create low ceilings and low visibility. They change rapidly, and frequently drop to the ground, forming a complete blanket over landmarks and landing fields. In temperatures near freezing, they are a constant threat because of the probability of icing. The pilot should be constantly alert to any changes in conditions, and be prepared to land before visibility lowers to the point where objects are suddenly obscured.

Cumulus clouds vary in size from light "scud" or fluffy powder puffs to towering masses rising thousands of feet in the sky. Usually they are somewhat scattered, and the pilot can fly around them without difficulty. Under some conditions, particularly in the late afternoon, they are likely to multiply, flatten out, and cover the sky.

Cumulonimbus clouds are very dangerous. When they appear individually or in small groups, they are usually of the type called "air mass thunderstorms" (caused by heating of the air at the Earth's surface) or "orographic thunderstorms" (caused by the upslope motion of air in mountainous regions). On the other hand, when these clouds take the form of a continuous or almost continuous line, they are usually caused by a front or squall line. The most common position for a squall line is in advance of a cold front, but one can form in air far removed from a front.

Since cumulonimbus clouds are formed by rising air currents, they are extremely turbulent; moreover, it is possible for an airplane flying nearby to be drawn into the cloud. Once inside, an airplane may encounter updrafts and downdrafts with velocities of 3,000 feet per minute or greater. Airplanes have been torn apart by the violence of these currents. In addition, the clouds frequently contain large hailstones capable of severely damaging aircraft, lightning, and great quantities of water at temperatures conducive to heavy icing. The only practical procedure for a pilot caught within a thunderstorm is to reduce airspeed. A recommended safe speed for an airplane flying through turbulence is an airspeed which provides a safe margin above the stall speed, but not greater than the maneuvering speed for the particular airplane.

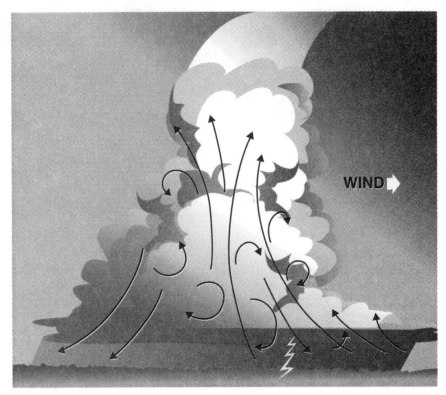

FIGURE 5-21.—Cross-section of a cumulonimbus cloud (thunderhead).

Figure 5-21 shows the important characteristics of a typical cumulonimbus cloud. The top of the cloud flattens into an anvil shape, which points in the direction the cloud is moving, generally with the prevailing wind. Near the base, however, the winds blow directly toward the cloud and increase in speed, becoming violent updrafts as they reach the low rolls at the forward edge.

Within the cloud and directly beneath it are updrafts and downdrafts. In the rear portion is a strong downdraft which becomes a wind blowing away from the cloud.

The cloud is a storm factory. The updrafts quickly lift the moist air to its saturation point, whereupon it condenses and raindrops begin to fall. Before these have reached the bottom of the cloud, updrafts pick them up and carry them aloft, where they may freeze and again start downward, only to repeat the process many times until they have become heavy enough to break through the updrafts and reach the ground as hail or very large raindrops. As the storm develops, more and more drops fall through the turbulence, until the rain becomes fairly steady. The lightning that accompanies such a storm is probably due to the breakup of raindrops. This produces static electricity that discharges as lightning, thus causing sudden expansion of the air in its path, resulting in thunder.

It is impossible for a small plane to fly over these clouds because they frequently extend to 50,000 feet and are usually too low to fly under. If they are close together, there may be violent turbulence in the clear space between them. If they are isolated thunderstorms, it usually is possible to fly around them safely by remaining a good distance from them. If, however, they are "frontal" or squall line storms, they may extend for hundreds of miles, and the only safe procedure is to land as soon as possible and wait until the cumulonimbus cloud formation has passed.

Ceiling

A ceiling for aviation purposes is the lowest broken, overcast layer, or vertical visibility into an obscuration. Clouds are reported as broken when they cover five-eighths to seven-eighths of the sky, and as overcast when they cover eight-eighths of the sky. The latest information on ceilings can be obtained from an aviation routine weather report (METAR). Forecasts of expected changes in ceilings and other conditions also are available at weather stations.

Visibility

Closely related to ceiling and cloud cover is "visibility"—the greatest horizontal distance at which prominent objects can be distinguished with the naked eye. Visibility, like ceiling, is included in hourly weather reports and in aviation forecasts.

Precipitation

In addition to possible damage by hail and the danger of icing, precipitation may be accompanied by low ceilings, and in heavy precipitation visibility may suddenly be reduced to zero.

It should be obvious that aircraft, which may have accumulated snow while on the ground, should never be flown until all traces of snow have been removed, including the hard crust that frequently adheres to the surfaces. An aircraft, which has been exposed to rain, followed by freezing temperatures, should be carefully cleared of ice and checked before takeoff to make certain that the controls operate freely.

AIR MASSES AND FRONTS

Large, high pressure systems frequently stagnate over large areas of land or water with relatively uniform surface conditions. They take on characteristics of these "source regions"—the coldness of polar regions, the heat of the tropics, the moisture of oceans, or the dryness of continents.

As they move away from their source regions and pass over land or sea, the air masses are constantly being modified through heating or cooling from below, lifting or subsiding, absorbing or losing moisture. Actual temperature of the air mass is less important than its temperature in relation to the land or water surface over which it is passing. For example, an air mass moving from polar regions usually is colder than the land and sea surfaces over which it passes. On the other hand, an air mass moving from the Gulf of Mexico in winter usually is warmer than the territory over which it passes.

If the air is colder than the surface, it will be warmed from below and convection currents will be set up, causing turbulence. Dust, smoke, and atmospheric pollution near the ground will be carried upward by these currents and dissipated at higher levels, improving surface visibility. Such air is called "unstable."

Conversely, if the air is warmer than the surface, there is no tendency for convection currents to form, and the air is smooth. Smoke, dust, etc., are concentrated in lower levels, with resulting poor visibility. Such air is called "stable."

From the combination of the source characteristics and the temperature relationship just described, air masses can be associated with certain types of weather.

The following are general characteristics of certain air masses but they may vary considerably.

Characteristics of a Cold (Unstable) Air Mass

- Type of clouds—cumulus and cumulonimbus.
- Ceilings—generally unlimited (except during precipitation).
- Visibility—excellent (except during precipitation).
- Unstable air—pronounced turbulence in lower levels (because of convection currents).
- Type of precipitation—occasional local thunderstorms or showers - hail, sleet, snow flurries.

Characteristics of a Warm (Stable) Air Mass

- Type of clouds—stratus and stratocumulus (fog, haze).
- Ceilings—generally low.
- Visibility—poor (smoke and dust held in lower levels).
- Stable air—smooth, with little or no turbulence.
- Type of precipitation—drizzle.

When two air masses meet, they will not mix readily unless their temperatures, pressures, and relative humidities are very similar. Instead, they set up boundaries called frontal zones, or "fronts," the colder air mass projecting under the warmer air mass in the form of a wedge. This condition is termed a "stationary front," if the boundary is not moving.

Usually, however, the boundary moves along the Earth's surface, and as one air mass withdraws from a given area, it is replaced by another air mass. This action creates a moving front. If warmer air is replacing colder air, the front is called "warm;" if colder air is replacing warmer air, the front is called "cold."

Warm Front

When a warm front moves forward, the warm air slides up over the wedge of colder air lying ahead of it.

Warm air usually has high humidity. As this warm air is lifted, its temperature is lowered. As the lifting process continues, condensation occurs, low nimbostratus and stratus clouds form, and drizzle or rain develops. The rain falls through the colder air below, increasing its moisture content so that it also

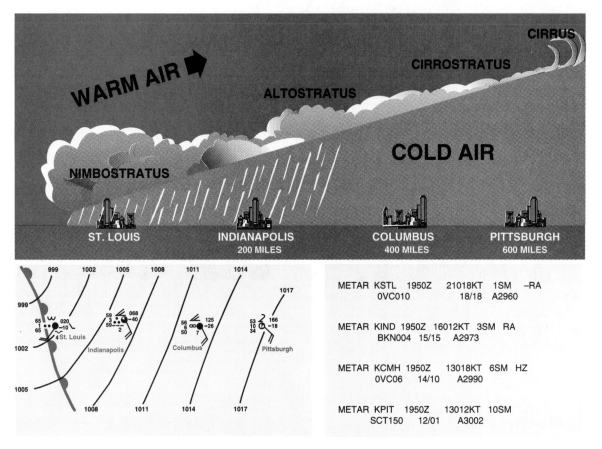

FIGURE 5-22.—A warm front: (upper) cross-section; (lower left) as shown on a weather map; (lower right) as shown in an aviation routine weather report (METAR).

becomes saturated. Any reduction of temperature in the colder air, which might be caused by upslope motion or cooling of the ground after sunset, may result in extensive fog.

As the warm air progresses up the slope, with constantly falling temperatures, clouds appear at increasing heights in the form of altostratus and cirrostratus, if the warm air is stable. If the warm air is unstable, cumulonimbus clouds and altocumulus clouds will form and frequently produce thunderstorms. Finally, the air is forced up near the stratosphere, and in the freezing temperatures at that level, the condensation appears as thin wisps of cirrus clouds. The upslope movement is very gradual, rising about 1,000 feet every 20 miles. Thus, the cirrus clouds, forming at perhaps 25,000 feet altitude, may appear as far as 500 miles in advance of the point on the ground which marks the position of the front. [Figure 5-22]

Flight Toward an Approaching Warm Front

Although no two fronts are exactly alike, a clearer understanding of the general pattern may be gained if the atmospheric conditions which might exist when a warm front is moving eastward from St. Louis, MO,

is considered. [Figure 5-22]

At St. Louis, the weather would be very unpleasant, with drizzle and probably fog.

At Indianapolis, IN, 200 miles in advance of the warm front, the sky would be overcast with nimbostratus clouds, and continuous rain.

At Columbus, OH, 400 miles in advance, the sky would be overcast with stratus and altostratus clouds predominating. The beginning of a steady rain would be probable.

At Pittsburgh, PA, 600 miles ahead of the front, there would probably be high cirrus and cirrostratus clouds.

If a flight was made from Pittsburgh to St. Louis, ceiling and visibility would decrease steadily. Starting under bright skies, with unlimited ceilings and visibilities, lower stratus-type clouds would be noted as Columbus was approached, and soon afterward precipitation would be encountered. After arriving at Indianapolis, the ceilings would be too low for further flight. Precipitation would reduce visibilities to practically zero. Thus, it would be wise to remain in Indianapolis until the warm front had passed, which might require a day or two.

If a return flight to Pittsburgh was made, it would

be recommended to wait until the front had passed beyond Pittsburgh, which might require three or four days. Warm fronts generally move at the rate of 10 to 25 MPH.

On the trip from Pittsburgh to Indianapolis, a gradual increase in temperature would have been noticed, and a much faster increase in dewpoint until the two coincided. Also the atmospheric pressure would gradually lessen because the warmer air aloft would have less weight than the colder air it was replacing. This condition illustrates the general principle that a falling barometer indicates the approach of stormy weather.

Cold Front

When a cold front moves forward, it acts like a snow plow, sliding under the warmer air and forcing it aloft. This causes the warm air to cool suddenly and form cloud types that depend on the stability of the warm air.

Fast-Moving Cold Fronts

In fast-moving cold fronts, friction retards the front near the ground, which brings about a steeper frontal surface. This steep frontal surface results in a narrower band of weather concentrated along the forward edge of the front. If the warm air is stable, an overcast sky may occur for some distance ahead of the front, accompanied by general rain. If the warm air is conditionally unstable, scattered thunderstorms and showers may form in the warm air. At times an almost continuous line of thunderstorms may form along the front or ahead of it. These lines of thunderstorms (squall lines) contain some of the most turbulent weather experienced by pilots.

Behind the fast-moving cold front, there is usually rapid clearing, with gusty and turbulent surface winds, and colder temperatures.

Flight Toward an Approaching Cold Front

If a flight was made from Pittsburgh toward St. Louis when a cold front was approaching from St. Louis, weather conditions quite different from those associated with a warm front would be experienced. The sky in Pittsburgh would probably be somewhat overcast with stratocumulus clouds typical of a warm air mass, the air smooth, and the ceilings and visibilities relatively low, although suitable for flight. [Figure 5-23]

As the flight proceeded, these conditions would prevail until reaching Indianapolis. At this point, it

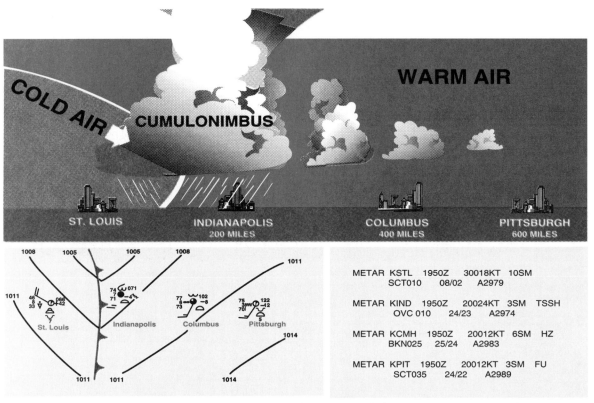

FIGURE 5-23.—A cold front: (upper) cross section; (lower left) as shown on a weather map; (lower right) as shown in an aviation routine weather report (METAR).

would be wise to check the position of the cold front by reviewing current weather charts and reports. It would probably be found that the front was now about 75 miles west of Indianapolis. A pilot with sound judgment, based on knowledge of frontal conditions, would remain in Indianapolis until the front had passed—a matter of a few hours—and then continue to the destination under near perfect flying conditions.

If, however, through the lack of better judgment the flight was continued toward the approaching cold front, a few altostratus clouds and a dark layer of nimbostratus lying low on the horizon, with perhaps cumulonimbus in the background would be noted. Two courses would now be open: (1) either turn around and outdistance the storm, or (2) make an immediate landing which might be extremely dangerous because of gusty wind and sudden wind shifts.

If flight was continued, entrapment in a line of squalls and cumulonimbus clouds could occur. It may be unsafe to fly beneath these clouds; impossible, in a small plane, to fly above them. At low altitudes, there are no safe passages through them. Usually there is no possibility of flying around them because they often extend in a line for 300 to 500 miles.

Comparison of Cold Fronts with Warm Fronts

The slope of a cold front is much steeper than that of a warm front and the progress is generally more rapid—usually from 20 to 35 MPH—although in extreme cases, cold fronts have been known to move at 60 MPH. Weather activity is more violent and usually takes place directly at the front instead of in advance of the front. In late afternoon during the warm season, however, squall lines frequently develop as much as 50 to 200 miles in advance of the actual cold front. Whereas warm front dangers are low ceilings and visibilities, and cold front dangers are chiefly sudden storms, high and gusty winds, and turbulence.

Unlike the warm front, the cold front rushes in almost unannounced, makes a complete change in the weather within a period of a few hours, and then continues. Altostratus clouds sometimes form slightly ahead of the front, but these are seldom more than 100 miles in advance. After the front has passed, the weather often clears rapidly and cooler, drier air with usually unlimited ceilings and visibilities prevail.

Wind Shifts

Wind shifts perhaps require further explanation. The wind in a "high" blows in a clockwise spiral. When two highs are adjacent, the winds are in almost direct opposition at the point of contact as illustrated

in figure 5-24. Since fronts normally lie between two areas of higher pressure, wind shifts occur in all types of fronts, but they usually are more pronounced in cold fronts.

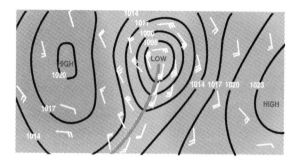

FIGURE 5-24.—Weather map indication of wind shift line (center line leading to low).

Occluded Front

One other form of front with which the pilot should become familiar is the "exclusion" or "occluded front." This is a condition in which a warm air mass is trapped between two colder air masses and forced aloft to higher and higher levels until it finally spreads out and loses its identity.

Meteorologists subdivide occlusions into two types, but as far as the pilot is concerned, the weather in any occlusion is a combination of warm front and cold front conditions. As the occlusion approaches, the usual warm front indications prevail—lowering ceilings, lowering visibilities, and precipitation. Generally, the warm front weather is then followed almost immediately by the cold front type, with squalls, turbulence, and thunderstorms.

Figure 5-25 is a vertical cross section of an occlusion. Figure 5-26 shows the various stages as they might occur during development of a typical occlusion. Usually the development requires three or four days, during which the air mass may progress as indicated on the map.

The first stage (A) represents a boundary between two air masses, the cold and warm air moving in opposite directions along a front. Soon, however, the cooler air, being more aggressive, thrusts a wedge under the warm air, breaking the continuity of the boundary, as shown in (B). Once begun, the process continues rapidly to the complete occlusion as shown in (C). As the warmer air is forced aloft, it cools quickly and its moisture condenses, often causing heavy precipitation. The air becomes extremely turbulent, with sudden changes in pressure and temperature.

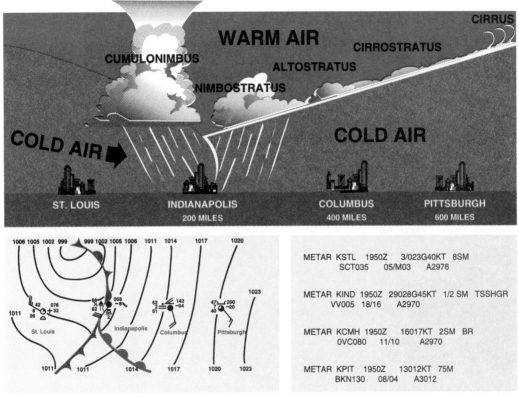

FIGURE 5-25.—An occluded front: (upper) cross section; (lower left) as shown on a weather map; (lower right) as shown in an aviation routine weather report (METAR).

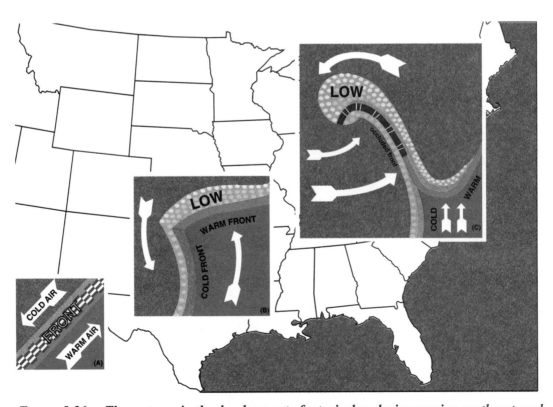

FIGURE 5-26.—Three stages in the development of a typical occlusion moving northeastward.

(A) Air flowing along a front in equilibrium.

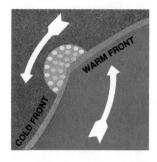

(B) Increased cold-air pressure causes "bend."

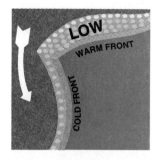

(C) Cold air begins to surround warm air.

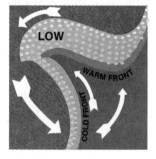

(D) Precipitation becomes heavier.

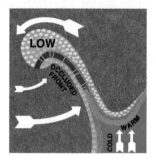

(E) Warm air completely surrounded.

(F) Warm-air sector ends in mild whirl.

FIGURE 5-27.—Development of an occlusion. If warm air were red and cold air were blue, this is how various stages of an occlusion would appear to a person aloft looking toward the Earth. (Precipitation is green.)

Figure 5-27 shows the development of the occluded front in greater detail.

Figure 5-28 is an enlarged view of (C) in Figure 5-26, showing the cloud formations and the areas of precipitation.

In figures 5-22, 5-23, and 5-25, a panel representing a surface weather map is placed below each cross-sectional view. These panels represent a bird's eye or plan view, and show how the weather conditions are recorded. A warm front is indicated by a red line, a cold front by a blue line, an occluded front by a purple line, and a stationary front by alternating red and blue dashes. The rounded and pointed projections are generally omitted from manuscript maps, but are placed on facsimile, printed, or duplicated maps to distinguish the different fronts.

A frontal line on the weather map represents the position of the frontal surface on the Earth's surface. A pilot flying west at an altitude of 6,500 feet would pass through the frontal boundary about 100 miles in advance of the point where the warm front is shown, or about 25 to 50 miles to the rear of the line on the map representing the cold front.

Figure 5-29 is a section of a surface weather map as transmitted on facsimile. It shows a low pressure center with warm, cold, and occluded fronts.

The preceding discussion categorizes weather with types of fronts. However, weather with a front depends more on the characteristics of the conflicting air masses than on the type of front. A pilot should not attempt to determine expected weather from fronts and pressure centers on the surface chart alone. The pilot must rely heavily on other charts, reports, and forecasts which are discussed in the next section of this chapter.

AVIATION WEATHER REPORTS, FORECASTS, AND WEATHER CHARTS

A few reports and forecasts that are available to pilots were discussed briefly in previous portions of this chapter. This section will discuss these reports and forecasts in greater detail along with weather charts. Although pilots may often receive a telephone briefing, they should be able to read and interpret these reports, forecasts, and charts. Printed aviation data may be found at the National Weather Service Office, flight service stations, as well as reports generated through a direct user access terminal (DUAT) system.

Although this section contains a great deal of

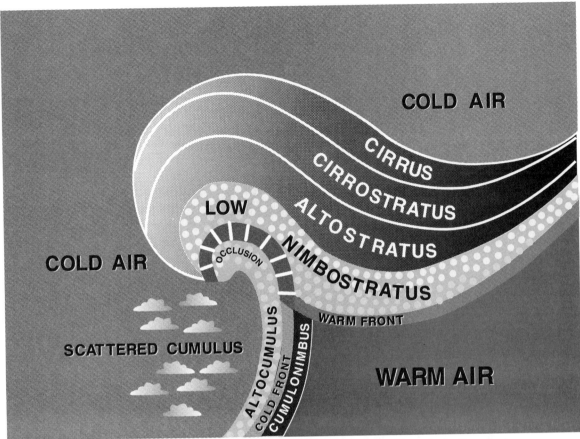

FIGURE 5-28.—Cloud formations and precipitation accompanying a typical occlusion.

information about reports, forecasts, and charts, for further information, reference should be made to AC 00-45 (latest revision), Aviation Weather Services, which is for sale by the Superintendent of Documents, U.S. Government Printing Office, Washington, DC 20402.

Aviation Weather Reports

These reports provide information on existing conditions at the time the report was generated. The aviation routine weather report (METAR) provides surface weather conditions at a specified location and is presented in a coded format which is standard internationally. A pilot weather report (PIREP) is generated from information received from a pilot in flight. A RADAR weather report contains information on thunderstorms and precipitation as observed by radar.

Aviation Routine Weather Report (METAR)
The aviation routine weather report contains various weather elements in a coded form. The elements of the report are: [Figure 5-30]

- Type of Report
- Station Designator
- Time of Report
- Wind
- Visibility
- Weather and Obstructions to Visibility
- Sky Conditions
- Temperature and Dewpoint
- Altimeter Setting
- Remarks

Example:
METAR KBNA 1250Z 33018KT 290V360 1/2SM R31/2700FT +SN BLSN FG VV008 00/M03 A2991 RMK RAE42SNB42

Explanation:
- This is an aviation routine weather report.
- It is for Nashville, Tennessee.
- The observation was taken at 1250 universal coordinated time (UTC).
- The wind is from 330° at 18 knots, with the direction varying from 290 to 360°.

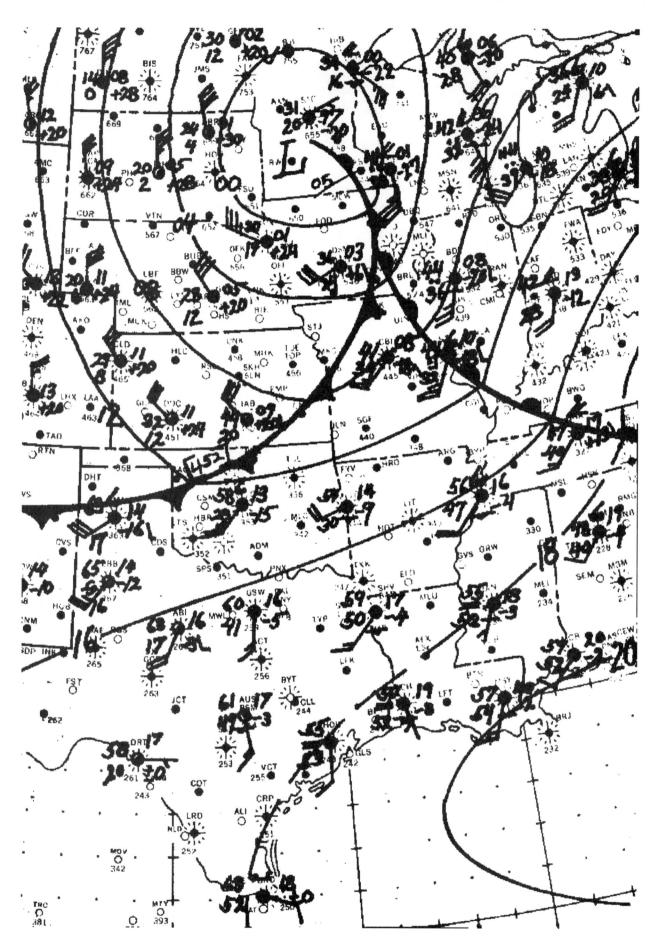

FIGURE 5-29.—Section of a surface weather map.

KEY TO METAR (NEW AVIATION ROUTINE WEATHER REPORT) OBSERVATIONS

TYPE OF REPORT:

There are two types of report—the METAR which is a routine observation report and SPECI which is a Special METAR weather observation. The type of report, METAR or SPECI, will always appear in the report header or lead element of the report.

STATION DESIGNATOR:

The METAR code uses ICAO 4-letter station identifiers. In the contiguous 48 states, the 3-letter domestic station identifier is prefixed with a "K." Elsewhere, the first two letters of the ICAO identifier indicate what region of the world and country (or state) the station is in. For Alaska, all station identifiers start with "PA;" for Hawaii, all station identifiers start with "PH."

TIME:

The time the observation is taken is transmitted as a four-digit time group appended with a Z to denote Coordinated Universal Time (UTC).

WIND:

The wind is reported as a five-digit group (six digits if speed is over 99 knots). The first three digits is the direction the wind is blowing from in ten's of degrees, or "VRB" if the direction is variable. The next two digits is the speed in knots, or if over 99 knots, the next three digits. If the wind is gusty, it is reported as a "G" after the speed followed by the highest gust reported.

VISIBILITY:

Visibility is reported in statute miles with "SM" appended to it. Runway Visual Range (RVR), when reported, is in the format: R(runway)/(visual range)FT. The "R" identifies the group followed by the runway heading, a "/", and the visual range in feet (meters in other countries).

WEATHER:

The weather as reported in the METAR code represents a significant change in the way weather is currently reported. In METAR, weather is reported in the format: Intensity, Proximity, Descriptor, Precipitation, Obstructions to visibility, or Other.

Intensity—applies only to the first type of precipitation reported. A "–" denotes light, no symbol denotes moderate, and a "+" denotes heavy.

Proximity—applies to and reported only for weather occurring in the vicinity of the airport (between 5 and 10 miles of the center of the airport runway complex). It is denoted by the letters "VC."

Descriptor—these seven descriptors apply to the following precipitation or obstructions to visibility:

TS – thunderstorm	DR – low drifting
SH – shower(s)	MI – shallow
FZ – freezing	
BC – patches	
BL – blowing	

Precipitation—there are eight types of precipitation in the METAR code:

RA – rain	GR – hail(>1/4 in.)
DZ – drizzle	GS – small hail/snow pellets
SN – snow	PE – ice pellets
SG – snow grains	IC – ice crystals

Obstructions to visibility—there are eight types of obstructing phenomena in the METAR code:

BR – mist (vsby 5/8–6 mi)	FG – fog
SA – sand	PY – spray
FU – smoke	
DU – dust	
HZ – haze	
VA – volcanic ash	

Note: Fog (FG) is reported only when the visibility is less than five eighths of a mile otherwise mist (BR) is reported.

Other—there are five categories of other weather phenomena which are reported when they occur:

SQ-squall	SS-sandstorm
DS-duststorm	PO-dust/sand whirls
FC-funnel cloud/tornado/waterspout	

SKY CONDITION:

The sky condition as reported in METAR represents a significant change from the way sky condition is currently reported. In METAR, sky condition is reported in the format:

Amount, Height, (Type), or Vertical Visibility

Amount—the amount of sky cover is reported in eighths of sky cover, using the contractions:

SKC-clear (no clouds)
SCT-scattered (1/8 to 4/8's of clouds)
BKN-broken (5/8's to 7/8's of clouds)
OVC-overcast (8/8's of clouds)

Note: A ceiling layer is not designated in the METAR code. For aviation purposes, the ceiling is the lowest broken or overcast layer, or vertical visibility into an obscuration. Also, there is no provision for reporting thin layers in the METAR code.

Height—cloud bases are reported with three digits in hundreds of feet.

(Type)—if towering cumulus clouds (TCU) or cumulonimbus clouds (CB) are present, they are reported after the height which represents their base.

Vertical Visibility—total obscurations are reported in the format "VVhhh" where VV denotes vertical visibility and "hhh" is the vertical visibility in hundreds of feet. There is no provision in the METAR code to report partial obscurations.

TEMPERATURE/DEWPOINT:

Temperature and dewpoint are reported in a two-digit form in degrees Celsius. Temperatures below zero are prefixed with an "M."

ALTIMETER:

Altimeter settings are reported in a four-digit format in inches of mercury prefixed with an "A" to denote the units of pressure.

REMARKS:

Remarks are limited to reporting significant weather, the beginning and ending times of certain weather phenomena, and low-level wind shear of significance to aircraft landing and taking off. The contraction "RMK" precedes remarks. Wind shear information is denoted by "WS" followed by "TKO" for takeoff or "LDG" for landing, and the runway "RW" affected.

FIGURE 5-30.—Key to aviation routine weather report observations.

ENCODING PILOT WEATHER REPORTS (PIREPS)

1. UA		Routine PIREP, UUA-Urgent PIREP.
2. /OV	Location:	Use 3-letter NAVAID idents only. a. Fix: /OV ABC, /OV ABC 090025. b. Fix: /OV ABC 045020-DEF, /OV ABC-DEF-GHI.
3. /TM	Time:	4 digits in UTC: /TM 0915.
4. /FL	Altitude/Flight Level:	3 digits for hundreds of feet. If not known use UNKN: /FL095, /FL310, /FLUKN.
5. /TP	Type Aircraft:	4 digits maximum, if not known use UNKN: /TP L329, /TP B727, /TP UNKN.
6. /SK	Cloud Layers:	Describe as follows: a. Height of cloud base in hundreds of feet. If unknown, use UNKN. b. Cloud cover symbol. c. Height of cloud tops in hundreds of feet.
7. /WX	Weather:	Flight visibility reported first: Use standard weather symbols, Intensity is not reported: /WX FV02 R H, /WX FV01 TRW.
8. /TA	Air Temperature in Celsius:	If below zero, prefix with a hyphen: /TA 15, /TA -06.
9. /WV	Wind:	Direction and speed in six digits: /WV 270045, /WV 280110.
10. /TB	Turbulence:	Use standard contractions for intensity and type (use CAT or CHOP when appropriate). Include altitude only if different from /FL, /TB EXTREME, /TB LGT-MDT BLO 090.
11. /IC	Icing:	Describe using standard intensity and type contractions. Include altitude only if different than /FL: /IC LGT-MDT RIME, /IC SVR CLR 028-045.
12. /RM	Remarks:	Use free form to clarify the report and type hazardous elements first: /RM LLWS -15 KT SFC-030 DURC RNWY 22 JFK.

FIGURE 5-31.—Encoding pilot weather reports.

- The visibility is one-half statute mile.
- The runway visual range for runway 31 is 2,700 feet and the visibility is obstructed by heavy blowing snow and fog.
- The sky is obscure with a vertical visibility of 800 feet.
- The temperature is 0 °C and the dewpoint is -3 °C.
- The altimeter setting is 29.91 inches.
- The rain ended at 42 past the hour and snow began at 42 past the hour.

Pilot Weather Reports (PIREPs)

The pilot weather reports are a timely and helpful observation to fill in the gap between reporting stations. Aircraft in flight are the only means of directly observing cloud tops, icing, and turbulence.

A pilot weather report is usually transmitted as an individual report, but can be appended to a surface report. Figure 5-31 shows the format, and how to decode the information contained in a PIREP. Most of the contractions in a PIREP are self-explanatory to use standard terminology.

Example:

UA /OV OKC 063064/TM 1522/FL080/TP C172/
TA -04/WV 245040/TB LGT/RM IN CLR

Explanation:

- This is a routine pilot weather report.
- The location is 64 nautical miles (NM) on the 63° radial from Oklahoma City VOR.
- The time of the report is 1522 UTC.
- The aircraft altitude is 8,000 feet.
- The type of aircraft is a Cessna 172.
- The temperature is -4 °C.
- The wind is from 245° at 40 knots. There is light turbulence.
- The aircraft is in clear skies.

Radar Weather Reports (RAREPs)

The radar weather reports provide information on thunderstorms and areas of precipitation as observed by radar. These reports include the type, intensity, intensity trend, and location of precipitation.

Also included is the echo top of the precipitation, and if significant, the base echo. All heights are reported in above mean sea level (MSL).

The contents of a radar weather report include:

• Location identifier and time of radar observation.
• Echo patterns which can be identified as:
• Line (LN)—a line of precipitation echoes at least 30 miles long, is at least five times as long as it is wide, and is at least 30 percent coverage within the line.
• Fine Line (FINE LN)—a unique, clear air echo (usually precipitation and cloud free) in the form of a thin or fine line in the planned position indicator (PPI) scope. It represents a strong temperature/moisture boundary such as an advancing cold front.
• Area (AREA)—a group of echoes of similar type and not classified as a line.
• Spiral Band Area (SPRL BAND AREA)—an area of precipitation associated with a hurricane that takes on a spiral band configuration around the center.
• Single Cell (CELL)—a single, isolated convective echo such as a rain shower.
• Layer (LYR)—an elevated layer of stratiform precipitation not reaching the ground.
• Coverage in tenths.
• Type, intensity, and trend of weather. [Figure 5-32]
• Azimuth, referenced to true north, and range in nautical miles (NM), of points defining the echo pattern.
• Dimension of the echo pattern. The dimension is given when the azimuth and range define only the center line of the pattern.
• Pattern movement. The movement of individual storms or cells "C" and area movement "A" may also be indicated.
• Maximum top land location.
• Remarks which are normally self-explanatory and use plain language contractions.
• Digital section used for preparing a radar summary chart.

Intensity		Intensity Trend	
Symbol	Intensity	Symbol	Trend
–	Light	+	Increasing
(none)	Moderate		
+	Heavy	–	Decreasing
++	Very Heavy		
X	Intense	NC	No Change
XX	Extreme		
U	Unknown	NEW	New Echo

FIGURE 5-32.—Precipitation intensity and trend.

Example:
FAR 1133 AREA 4TRW+/+ 22/100 88/170 196/180 220/115 C2425 MT 310 AT 162/110

Explanation:
Fargo, ND radar weather observation at 1133 UTC. An area of echoes, four-tenths coverage, containing thunderstorms and heavy rain showers, increasing in intensity. Area is defined by points at 22°, 100 NM; 88°, 170 NM; 196°, 180 NM and 220°, 115 NM. These points, plotted on a map with straight lines, outline the area of echoes. The thunderstorm cells are moving from 240° at 25 knots. Maximum top (MT) is 31,000 feet MSL located at 162° and 110 NM from Fargo.

Aviation Forecasts

Forecasts especially prepared for aviation include terminal aerodrome forecast (TAF), area forecasts (FA), winds and temperatures aloft forecasts (FD), AIRMET (WA), SIGMET (WS), and CONVECTIVE SIGMET (WST). These forecasts help a pilot in flight planning and alert the pilot to any significant weather which is forecast for the intended flight.

Terminal Aerodrome Forecasts (TAF)
The terminal aerodrome forecasts are prepared to give a description of expected conditions at an airport and within a 5 nautical mile radius of a runway complex. A terminal aerodrome forecast is a concise statement of the expected meteorological conditions over a specified time period, usually 24 hours. Figure 5-33 provides information on the format and information contained in the TAF. The descriptors and abbreviations used in the TAF are the same as those used in the METAR report. [Figure 5-30]

Explanation of figure 5-34:
1. The terminal aerodrome forecast was issued for Memphis, TN on the 12th of the month at 1720 UTC and is valid from 1800 UTC to 1800 UTC (24 hours).
2. The forecast from 1800Z to 2200Z is wind from 200° at 12 knots, visibility 5 statute miles in haze, broken clouds at 3,000 feet. A 40-49 percent chance of thunderstorms with moderate rain, visibility 1 statute mile, and overcast sky at 800 feet by cumulonimbus cloud.
3. Forecast from 2200Z to 0200Z, wind from 330° at 15 knots with gusts to 20 knots, visibility greater than 6 statute miles, broken clouds at 1,500 feet, overcast clouds at 2,500 feet. Between the hours of 2200Z and 0200Z, there is a 40-49 percent chance of visibility 3 statute miles in moderate rain showers.

TYPE	Routine (TAF) Amended (TAF AMD)
LOCATION	ICAO four-letter location identifier (contiguous) 48 states, the 3-letter domestic identifier prefixed with a "K;" elsewhere the first two letters of the ICAO identifier indicate what region of world and country (or state) the station is in.
ISSUANCE DATE/TIME	A six-digit group giving the date (first two digits) the time (last four digits) in UTC.
VALID PERIOD	A four-digit group which gives the valid period, usually 24 hours, of the forecast in UTC. Where airports or terminals operate part time, the TAF will have the abbreviated statement "AMD NOT SKED AFT (closing time) UTC" added to their forecast. For a TAF issued after these locations are closed, the word "NIL" will appear in place of forecast text.
FORECAST	Body of the TAF has a basic format: WIND/VISIBILITY/WEATHER/SKY CONDITION
WIND	Five or six digits followed by "KT" wind speed in knots. The first three are direction and last two speed unless 100 knots or greater than three digits. Wind gust denoted by the letter "G" appended to the wind speed followed highest gust. Variable wind direction noted by "VRB" where direction usually appears. A calm wind (3 knots less) is shown as 00000KT.
VISIBILITY	Prevailing visibility up to and including 6 statute miles (SM follows miles) including fractions of miles. Visibility greater than 6 miles is forecast as P6SM.
WEATHER	Weather phenomena significant to aviation are included and follow a format which is: Intensity or Proximity/Descriptor/Precipitation/Obstruction/Visibility/Other.
SKY CONDITION	Sky condition is presented in a format which includes Amount/Height (Type) or Vertical Visibility.
OTHER	Probability - A PROB40 HHhh group in a TAF indicates the probability of occurrence of thunderstorms or other precipitation. PROB40 indicates a 40-49% chance and PROB30 indicates a 30-39% chance. The HHhh is a four-digit beginning and ending time.
TEMPORARY CONDITIONS	Changes usually lasting less than an hour. TEMPO HHhh (beginning and ending time).
FORECAST CHANGE GROUPS	Used when a significant or permanent change is expected. The change is indicated by the group FMHH (from) and BECMG (becoming) followed by HHhh (times).

FIGURE 5-33.—Terminal aerodrome forecast (TAF) format.

4.   From 0200Z to 0600Z, wind from 350° at 12 knots, overcast clouds at 800 feet. Between 0200Z and 0500Z, a 40-49 percent chance of visibility 2 statute miles in light rain and snow mixed. (Since the visibility is not included, it is not expected to change from the 6 statute miles.)

5.   Between 0600Z and 0800Z, conditions forecast to become wind from 020° at 8 knots, no significant weather, broken clouds at 1,200 feet with conditions continuing until 1000Z.

6.   Between 1000Z and 1200Z, conditions forecast to be wind calm, visibility 3 statute miles in mist with clear skies. Between 1200 and 1400Z, visibility temporarily 1/2 statute mile in fog. Conditions continuing until 1600Z.

7.   From 1600Z until the end of the forecast, wind variable in direction at 4 knots, visibility greater than 6 statute miles, no significant weather, and sky clear.

Area Forecast (FA)

An area forecast contains general weather conditions over an area the size of several states. It is used to determine forecast en route weather and to help in determining weather at airports for which TAF's are not issued. Area forecasts are issued three times a day by the National Aviation Weather Advisory Unit in Kansas City, MO for each of the six areas in the contiguous 48 states. Alaska uses a different format for their respective reports which are issued for the areas of Anchorage, Fairbanks, and Juneau. There is also a specialized FA for the Gulf of Mexico which combines both aviation and marine

information, and is intended to support offshore helicopter operations. The format of an FA is:

• Communication and product headers.
• Precautionary statements.
• Synopsis (brief summary of location and movement of fronts, pressure systems, and circulation patterns for an 18-hour period).
• VFR clouds and weather (contains a 12-hour specific forecast followed by a 6-hour, 18-hour in Alaska, categorical outlook giving a total forecast period of 18-hours, 30 in Alaska).

Example:
SLCC FA 141045
SYNOPSIS AND VFR CLDS/WX
SYNOPSIS VALID UNTIL 150500
CLDS/WX VALID UNTIL 142300...OTLK VALID 142300-150500
ID MT NV UT WY CO AZ NM

SEE AIRMET SIERRA FOR IFR CONDS AND MTN OBSCN. TSTMS IMPLY PSBL SVR OR GTR TURBC SVR ICG LLWS AND IFR CONDS.

NON MSL HEIGHTS HGTS ARE DENOTED BY AGL OR CIG.

SYNOPOSIS...HIGH PRES OR NERN MT CONTG EWD GRDLY. LOW PRES OVR AZ NM AND WRN TX RMNG GENLY STNRY. ALF...TROF EXTDS FROM WRN MT INTO SRN AZ RMNG STNRY.

```
KMEM 121720Z 1818   20012KT 5SM HZ BKN030 PROB40 2022 1SM TRSA OVC008CB
1                   2


FM 22 33015G20KT P6SM BKN015 OVC025 PROB40 2202 3SM SHRA
3


FM02 35012 KT OVC008 PROB440 0205 2SM -RASN   BECMG 0608 02008KT P6SM NSW SKC
4                                             5


BECMG 1012 00000KT 3SM BR SKC TEMPO 1214 1/2SM FG   FM16 VRB04KT P6SM NSW SKC
6                                                   7
```

FIGURE 5-34.—Example of terminal aerodrome forecast (TAF).

ID MT
FROM YXH TO SHR TO 30SE BZN TO 60SE PIH TO LKT TO YXC TO YXH.
70-90 SCT-BKN 120-150. WDLY SCT RW-. TOPS SHWRS 180.OTKL...VFR.
RMNDR AREA...100-120. ISOLD RW-MNLY ERN PTNS AREA. OTKL...VFR.

UT NV NM AZ
80 SCT-BKN 150-200. WDLY SCT RW-/TRW-. CB TOPS 450.
OTKL...VFR.

WY CO
FROM BZN TO GCC TO LBL TO DVC TO RKS TO BZN. 70-90 BKN-OVC 200. OCLN VSBY 3R-F. AFT 20Z WDLY SCT TRW-. CB TOPS 450. OTKL...MVFR CIG RW.

In-Flight Weather Advisories

In-flight weather advisories are unscheduled forecasts to advise aircraft in flight of the development of potentially hazardous weather. There are three types of in-flight weather advisories: SIGMET, AIRMET, and convective SIGMET.

The format of these advisories consists of a heading and text. The heading identifies the issuing Weather Service Forecast Office (WSFO), type of advisory, and the valid period. The text of the advisory contains a message identifier, a flight precautions statement, and further details if necessary. Figure 5-35 shows an example of these advisories.

Significant Meteorological Information (SIGMET)

A SIGMET is issued to advise pilots of weather considered potentially hazardous to ALL categories of aircraft, and is valid for the period stated in the advisory. SIGMETs are based specifically on forecasts of:

- Severe icing not associated with thunderstorms.
- Severe or extreme turbulence or clear air turbulence (CAT) not associated with thunderstorms.
- Dust storms, sandstorms, or volcanic ash lowering surface visibility to below 3 miles.
- Volcanic eruption.

```
ZCZC MKCWA4T ALL 242000
WAUS1 KDFW 241650
DFWT WA 241650 AMD
AIRMET TANGO UPDT 3 FOR TURBC...STG SFC WINDS AND
LLWS VALID UNTIL 242000

AIRMET TURBC...OK TX...UPDT
FROM OSW TO LRD TO PEQ TO 40W LBL TO OSW
OCNL MDT TURBC BLO 60 DUE TO STG AND GUSTY LOW
LVL WINDS. CONDS CONTG BYD 2000Z.

AIRMET STG SFC WINDS...TX
FROM CDS TO DFW TO SAT TO MAF TO CDS
AFT 18Z...SUSTAINED SFC WINDS GTR THAN 30 KTS XPCD.
COND CONTG BYD 2000Z.

LLWS BLO 20 AGL DUE TO STG WINDS DMSHG BY 18Z.

OTLK VALID 2000-0200Z...OK TX AR
MDT TURBC BLO 60 CONTG OVR OK/TX AND SPRDG INTO
AR BY 2200-0200Z. CONTG ENTR AREA BYD 0200Z.
```

```
MKCC WST 221855
CONVECTIVE SIGMET 20C
VALID UNTIL 2055Z
ND SD
FROM 90W MOT-GFK-ABR-90 MOT
INTSFYG AREA SVR TSTMS MOVG FROM 2445. TOP ABV
450. WIND GUSTS TO 60 KTS RPRTD. TORNADOES...HAIL TO
2 IN...WIND GUSTS TO 65 KTS PSBL ND PTN.
```

```
DFWP UWS 051710
SIGMET PAPA 1 VALID UNTIL 052110
AR LA MS
FROM STL TO 30N MEI TO BTR TO MLU TO STL
OCNL SVR ICING 90 TO 130 EXPCD.
FRZLVL 80 E TO 120 W. CONDS CONTG BYD 2100Z.

SFOR WS 100130
SIGMET ROMEO 2 VALID UNTIL 100530
OR WA
FROM SEA TO PDT TO EUG TO SEA
OCNL MOGR CAT BTN 280 AND 350 EXPCD DUE TO JTSTR.
CONDS BGNG AFT 0200Z CONTG BYD 0530Z AND SPRDG
OVR CNTRL ID BY 0400Z.
```

FIGURE 5-35.—Example of in-flight weather advisories.

Airmen's Meteorological Information (AIRMET)

An AIRMET is issued to advise pilots of significant weather, but describes conditions at intensities lower than those which trigger SIGMETs. AIRMETs are issued on forecast conditions such as:

- Moderate icing.
- Moderate turbulence.
- Sustained surface winds of 30 knots or more.
- Ceiling less than 1,000 feet and/or visibility less than 3 miles affecting over 50 percent of the area at one time.
- Extensive mountain obscurement.

Convective Significant Meteorological Information

A convective SIGMET implies severe or greater turbulence, severe icing, and low-level wind shear. A convective SIGMET may be issued for any situation which the forecaster feels is hazardous to all categories of aircraft. Convective SIGMETs are specifically based on:

- Severe turbulence due to:
  - surface winds greater than or equal to 50 knots.
  - hail at the surface greater than or equal to three-fourths inches in diameter.
  - tornadoes.
- Embedded thunderstorms.
- A line of thunderstorms.
- Thunderstorms greater than or equal to video integrator processor (VIP) level 4 affecting 40 percent or more of an area at least 3,000 square miles.

Winds and Temperatures Aloft Forecast (FD)

The winds and temperatures aloft forecast is for specific locations in the contiguous United States. These forecasts are also prepared for a network of locations in Alaska and Hawaii. Forecasts are made twice daily based on 00Z and 12Z data for use during specified time intervals. Figure 5-36 is an example of a winds and temperature aloft forecast.

In figure 5-36, the first line of the heading "FD KWBC 151640," the FD identifies this forecast as a winds and temperatures aloft forecast. "KWBC" indicates that the forecast is prepared at the National Meteorological Center. The other information indicates the data the forecast was based on, and the valid time for the forecast. The forecast levels line labeled "FT" shows the 9 standard levels in feet for which the winds and temperatures apply. The levels through 12,000 feet are based on true altitude, and

the levels at 18,000 feet and above are based on pressure altitude. The station identifiers denoting the location for which the forecast applies are arranged in alphabetical order in a column along the left side of the data sheet. The coded wind and temperature information in digits is found in columns under each level and in the line to the right of the station identifier.

Note that at some of the lower levels the wind and temperature information is omitted. The reason for the omission is that winds aloft are not forecast for levels within 1,500 feet of the station elevation. Also, note that no temperatures are forecast for the 3,000-foot level or for a level within 2,500 feet of the station elevation.

Decoding: A 4-digit group shows the wind direction in reference to true north, and the windspeed in knots. Refer to the St. Louis' (STL) forecast for the 3,000-foot level. The group "2113" means the wind is forecast to be from 210° true north at a speed of 13 knots. To decode, a zero is added to the end of the first two digits giving the direction in increments of 10°, and the second two digits give speed in knots.

A 6-digit group includes the forecast temperature aloft. Refer to the Denver (DEN) forecast for the 9,000-foot level. The group 2321-04 means the wind is forecast to be from 230° at 21 knots with a temperature of -04 °C.

If the windspeed is forecast to be 100 to 199 knots, the forecaster adds 50 to the direction and subtracts 100 from the speed. To decode, the reverse must be done; i.e., subtract 50 from the direction and add 100 to the speed. For example, if the forecast for the 39,000-foot level appears as "731960," subtract 50 from 73, and add 100 to 19, and the wind would be 230° at 119 knots with a temperature of -60 °C.

It is quite simple to recognize when the coded direction has been increased by 50. Coded direction (in tens of degrees) ranges from 01 (010°) to 36 (360°). Thus any coded direction with a numerical value greater than "36" indicates a wind of 100 knots or greater. The coded direction for winds of 100 to 199 knots ranges from 51 through 86.

If the windspeed is forecast to be 200 knots or greater, the wind group is coded as 199 knots, i.e., "7799" is decoded 270 degrees at 199 knots or GREATER.

When the forecast speed is less than 5 knots, the coded group is "9900" which means "LIGHT AND VARIABLE."

Weather Charts

There are various graphic charts which depict weather conditions at a specified time. These charts

FD KWBC 151640
BASED ON 151200Z DATA
VALID 151800Z FOR USE 1700-2100Z TEMPS NEG ABV 24000

FT	3000	6000	9000	12000	18000	24000	30000	34000	39000
ALA			2420	2635-08	2535-18	2444-30	245945	246755	246862
AMA		2714	2725+00	2625-04	2531-15	2542-27	265842	256352	256762
DEN			2321-04	2532-08	2434-19	2441-31	235347	236056	236262
HLC		1707-01	2113-03	2219-07	2330-17	2435-30	244145	244854	245561
MKC	0507	2006+03	2215-01	2322-06	2338-17	2348-29	236143	237252	238160
STL	2113	2325+07	2332+02	2339-04	2356-16	2373-27	239440	730649	731960

FIGURE 5-36.—Winds and temperature aloft forecast.

allow a pilot to get a picture of weather conditions and an idea on the movement of weather systems and fronts.

Surface Analysis Chart

The surface analysis chart, often referred to as a surface weather map, is the basic weather chart. The chart is transmitted every 3 hours. The valid time of the map corresponds to the time of the plotted observations. A date and time group in universal coordinated time (UTC) informs the user of when the conditions portrayed on the map were actually occurring. The surface analysis chart displays weather information such as surface wind direction and speed, temperature, dewpoint, and various other weather data. It also includes the position of fronts, and areas of high or low pressure. [Figure 5-37]

Each reporting station is depicted on the chart by a small circle. The weather information pertaining to the station is placed in a standard pattern around this circle, and is called a station model.

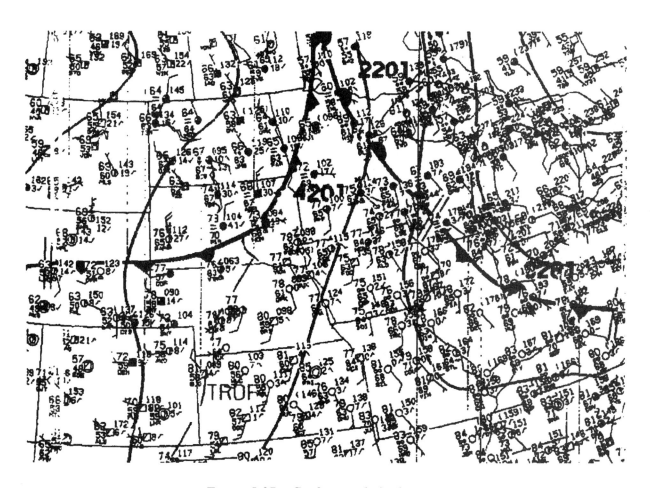

FIGURE 5-37.—Surface analysis chart.

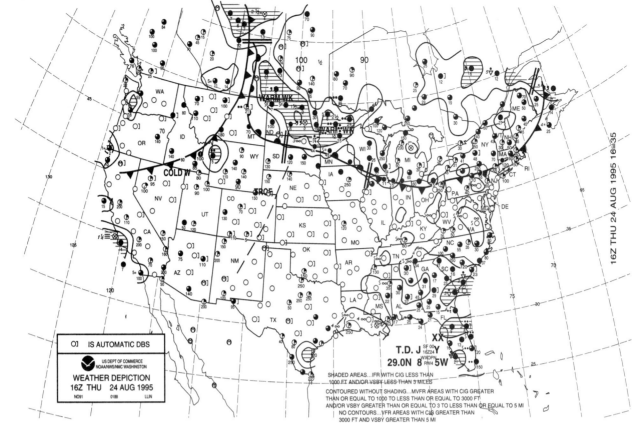

FIGURE 5-38.—Weather depiction chart.

Weather Depiction Chart

The weather depiction chart is prepared from surface aviation observations and gives a quick picture of the weather conditions as of the valid time stated on the chart. This chart is abbreviated to a certain extent and contains only a portion of the surface weather information. However, areas where clouds and weather may be a factor can be seen at a glance. The chart also shows major fronts and high and low pressure centers, and is considered to be a good place to begin a weather briefing for flight planning. [Figure 5-38]

An abbreviated station model is used to plot data consisting of total sky cover, cloud height or ceiling, weather and obstructions to vision, visibility, and an analysis.

Cloud height is the lowest ceiling shown in hundreds of feet; or if there is no ceiling, it is the height of the lowest layer. Weather and obstructions to vision are shown using the same symbol designators as the surface analysis. When visibility is less than 7 miles, it is entered in miles and fractions of miles.

The chart shows ceilings and visibilities at reporting stations and categorizes areas as IFR (outlined with smooth lines), MVFR (outlined with scalloped lines), and VFR (not outlined).

For information which will assist in interpreting information on both the surface analysis and weather depiction chart, refer to figures 5-39, 5-40, 5-41, 5-42, 5-43.

Radar Summary Chart

The radar summary chart aids in preflight planning by identifying general areas and movement of precipitation and/or thunderstorms. Weather radar generally detects precipitation only; it does not ordinarily detect small water droplets such as found in fog and nonprecipitating clouds; therefore, the absence of echoes does not guarantee clear weather.

Significant Weather Prognostic Charts

Significant weather prognostic charts, called progs, portray forecast weather to assist in flight planning. There are low-level and high-level prognostic charts. Our discussion will focus on the low-level chart.

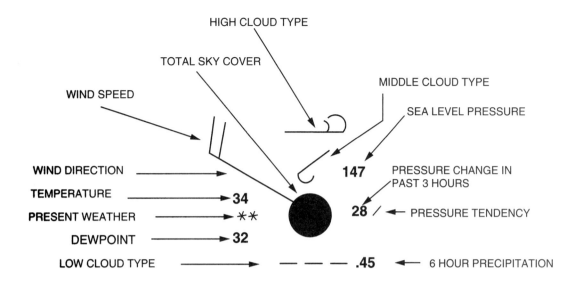

1. **Total sky** cover: OVERCAST
2. **Temperature**:   34 DEGREES F, Dewpoint: 32 DEGREES F.
3. **Wind: FROM THE NORTHWEST AT 20 KNOTS** (relative to True North).

Examples of wind direction and speed

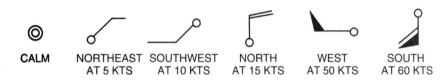

| CALM | NORTHEAST AT 5 KTS | SOUTHWEST AT 10 KTS | NORTH AT 15 KTS | WEST AT 50 KTS | SOUTH AT 60 KTS |

4. **Present weather: CONTINUOUS LIGHT SNOW**
5. **Predominant** low, middle, high cloud reported: STRATO FRACTUS OR CUMULUS
   FRACTUS OF BAD WEATHER, ALTOCUMULUS IN PATCHES, AND DENSE CIRRUS
6. **Sea level** pressure: 1014.7 MILLIBARS (mbs).
   NOTE: Pressure is always shown in 3 digits to the nearest tenth of a millibar.
   _____   For 1000 mbs or greater, prefix a "10" to the 3 digits. For less than
   1000 mbs, prefix a "9" to the 3 digits.
7. **Pressure** change in past 3 hours: INCREASED STEADILY OR UNSTEADILY BY 2.8 mbs.
   The actual change is in tenths of a millibar.
8. **6-hour** precipitation: 45 hundredths of an inch.
   The amount is given to the nearest hundredth of an inch.

FIGURE 5-39.—Weather chart station model.

Code Figure	Description
0	Quasi-stationary at surface
1	Quasi-stationary above surface
2	Warm front at surface
3	Warm front above surface
4	Cold front at surface
5	Cold front above surface
6	Occlusion
7	Instability line
8	Intertropical front
9	Coverage line

Code Figure	Description
0	No specification
1	Weak, decreasing
2	Weak, little, or no change
3	Weak, increasing
4	Moderate, decreasing
5	Moderate, little, or no change
6	Moderate, increasing
7	Strong, decreasing
8	Strong, little, or no change
9	Strong, increasing

Code Figure	Description
0	No specification
1	Frontal area activity, decreasing
2	Frontal area activity, little change
3	Frontal area activity, increasing
4	Intertropical
5	Forming or existence expected
6	Quasi-stationary
7	With waves
8	Diffuse
9	Position doubtful

Symbol	Total Sky Cover
◯	Sky clear (less than 1/10)
◔	1/10 to 5/10 inclusive (Scattered)
◕	6/10 to 9/10 inclusive (Broken)
●	10/10 (Overcast)
⊗	Sky obscured or partially obscured

Description of Characteristic		Graphic
Primary Unqualified Requirement	Additional Requirements	
HIGHER Atmospheric pressure now higher than 3 hours ago	Increasing then decreasing	 ⌢
	Increasing then steady; or	
	Increasing then increasing more slowly	⌐
	Increasing Steadily / Unsteadily	/
	Decreasing or steady then increasing; or	
	Increasing then increasing more rapidly	✓
SAME Atmospheric pressure now same as 3 hours ago	Decreasing then increasing	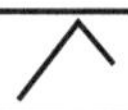 ⌃
	Steady	 —
	Decreasing then decreasing more slowly	 ⌄
LOWER Atmospheric pressure now lower than 3 hours ago	Decreasing then increasing	 ⌄
	Decreasing then steady or	
	Decreasing then decreasing more slowly	⟍
	Decreasing Steadily / Unsteadily	\
	Steady or increasing then decreasing; or	
	Decreasing then decreasing more rapidly	⌍

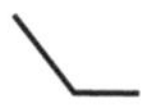

FIGURE 5-40.—Weather chart symbols.

FIGURE 5-41.—Cloud symbols.

CLOUD ABBREVIATION	C_L	DESCRIPTION (Abridged from W.M.O. Code)	C_M	DESCRIPTION (Abridged from W.M.O. Code)	C_H	DESCRIPTION (Abridged from W.M.O. Code)
St or Fs – Stratus or Fractostratus	1	Cu. fair weather, little vertical development & flattened	1	Thin As (most of cloud layer semitransparent)	1	Filaments of Ci, or "mares tails", scattered and not increasing
Ci – Cirrus	2	Cu, considerable development, towering with or without other Cu or SC bases at same level	2	Thick As, greater part sufficiently dense to hide sun (or moon), or Ns	2	Dense Ci in patches or twisted sheaves, usually not increasing, sometimes like remains of Cb; or towers tufts
Cs – Cirrostratus	3	Cb with tops lacking clear-cut outlines, but distinctly not cirriform or anvil shaped; with or without Cu, Sc, St	3	Thin Ac, mostly semi-transparent; cloud elements not changing much at a single level	3	Dense Ci, often anvil-shaped derived from associated Cb
Ac – Altocumulus	4	Sc formed by spreading out of Cu; Cu often present also	4	Thin Ac in patches; cloud elements continually changing and/or occurring at more than one level	4	Ci, often hook-shaped gradually spreading over the sky and usually thickening as a whole
As – Altostratus	5	Sc not formed by spreading out of Cu	5	Thin Ac in bands or in a layer gradually spreading over sky and usually thickening as a whole	5	Ci and Cs, often in converging bands or Cs alone; generally overspreading and growing denser; the continuous layer not reaching 45 altitude
Sc–Stratocumulus	6	St or Fs or both, but no Fs of bad weather	6	Ac formed by the spreading out of Cu	6	Ci and Cs, often in converging bands or Cs alone; generally overspreading and growing denser; the continuous layer exceeding 45 altitude
Ns–Nimbostraus	7	Fs and/or Fc of bad weather (scud)	7	Double-layered Ac, or a thick layer of Ac, not increasing; or Ac with As and/or Ns	7	Veil of Cs covering the entire sky
Cu or Fc–Cumulus or Fractocumulus	8	Cu and Sc (not formed by spreading out of Cu) with bases at different levels	8	Ac in the form of Cu-shaped tufts or Ac with turrets	8	Cs not increasing and not covering entire sky
Cb-Cumulonimbus	9	Cb having a clearly fibrous (cirriform) top, often anvil-shaped, with or without Cu, Sc, ST or scud	9	Ac of a chaotic sky, usually at different levels; patches of dense Ci are usually present	9	Cc alone or Cc with some Ci or Cs but the Cc being the main cirriform cloud

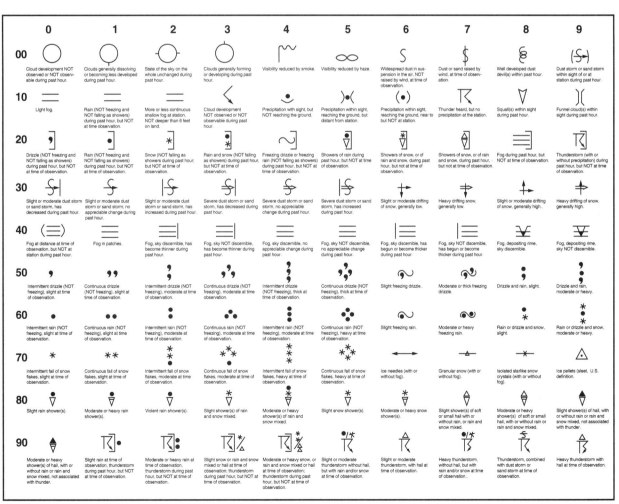

FIGURE 5-42.—Weather chart symbols.

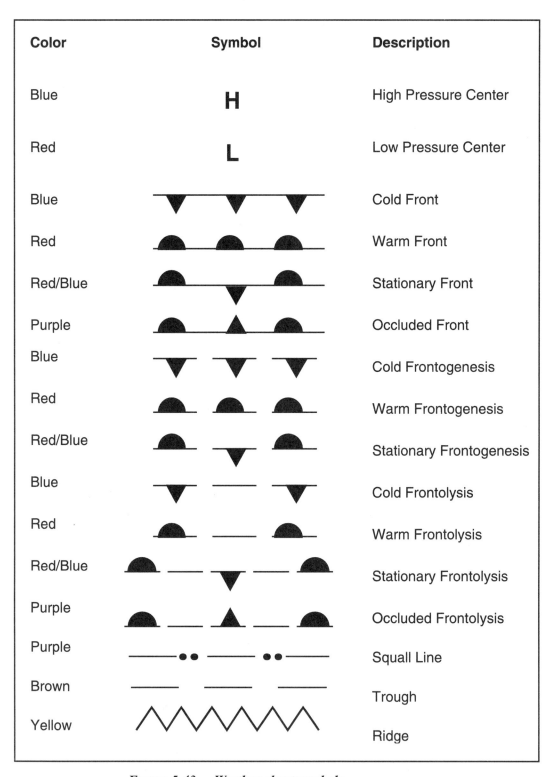

Color	Symbol	Description
Blue	**H**	High Pressure Center
Red	**L**	Low Pressure Center
Blue		Cold Front
Red		Warm Front
Red/Blue		Stationary Front
Purple		Occluded Front
Blue		Cold Frontogenesis
Red		Warm Frontogenesis
Red/Blue		Stationary Frontogenesis
Blue		Cold Frontolysis
Red		Warm Frontolysis
Red/Blue		Stationary Frontolysis
Purple		Occluded Frontolysis
Purple		Squall Line
Brown		Trough
Yellow		Ridge

FIGURE 5-43.—Weather chart symbols.

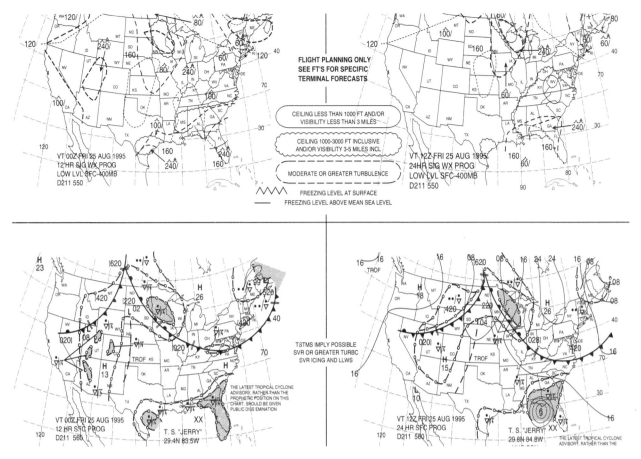

FIGURE 5-44.—Low-level prognostic chart.

The low-level prog is a four panel chart as shown in figure 5-44. The two lower panels are the 12-and 24-hour surface progs. The two upper panels are the 12-and 24-hour progs and portray significant weather from the surface up to 400 millibars (24,000 feet MSL). These charts show conditions as they are forecast to be at the valid time of the chart.

The two surface prog panels use the standard symbols to depict fronts and pressure centers. The movement of each pressure center is indicated by an arrow showing the direction and a number indicating speed in knots. Isobars depicting forecast pressure patterns are included on some 24-hour surface progs.

The surface progs outline areas in which precipitation and/or thunderstorms are forecast. Smooth lines enclose areas of expected precipitation, either continuous or intermittent; dashed lines enclose areas of expected showers or thunderstorms. The symbols indicate the type and character of the precipitation. The area is shaded if the precipitation is expected to cover half or more of the area, and unshaded if less than half.

The upper panels depict forecasts of significant weather such as ceiling, visibility, turbulence, and freezing level. A legend is placed between the panels which explains methods of depicting weather information on the Significant Weather Prog.

In summarizing this chapter on weather, pilots are encouraged to use the wealth of information made available for aviation purposes. Although some airports do not have all weather services mentioned in this chapter, a phone call or radio transmission to the nearest facility equipped with weather services will inform the pilot about weather conditions and add much to the safety of the flight.

CHAPTER 6

AIRPORT OPERATIONS

INTRODUCTION

Each time a pilot operates an airplane, the flight normally begins and ends at an airport. An airport may be a small sod field or a large complex utilized by air carriers. In this chapter we will discuss airport operations and identify features of an airport complex, as well as provide information on operating on or in the vicinity of an airport.

TYPES OF AIRPORTS

There are two types of airports.

- Controlled Airport
- Uncontrolled Airport

Controlled Airport

A controlled airport has an operating control tower. Air traffic control (ATC) is responsible for providing for the safe, orderly, and expeditious flow of air traffic at airports where the type of operations and/or volume of traffic requires such a service. Pilots operating from a controlled airport are required to maintain two-way radio communication with air traffic controllers, and to acknowledge and comply with their instructions.

Pilots must advise ATC if they cannot comply with the instructions issued and request amended instructions. A pilot may deviate from an air traffic instruction in an emergency, but must advise air traffic of the deviation as soon as possible.

Uncontrolled Airport

An uncontrolled airport does not have an operating control tower. Two-way radio communications are not required, although it is a good operating practice for pilots to transmit their intentions on the specified frequency for the benefit of other traffic in the area. Figure 6-1 lists recommended communication procedures. More information on radio communications will be discussed later in this chapter.

SOURCES FOR AIRPORT DATA

When a pilot flys into a different airport, it is important to review the current data for that airport. This data can provide the pilot with information such as communication frequencies, services available, closed runways, or airport construction, etc. Three common sources of information are:

- Aeronautical Charts
- Airport/Facility Directory (A/FD)
- Notices to Airmen (NOTAMs)

Aeronautical Charts

Aeronautical charts provide specific information on airports. Chapter 8 contains an excerpt from an aeronautical chart and an aeronautical chart legend which provides guidance on interpreting the information on the chart. Refer to Chapter 8, figures 8-1 and 8-22 for chart information.

Airport/Facility Directory (A/FD)

The Airport/Facility Directory provides the most comprehensive information on a given airport. It contains information on airports, heliports, and seaplane bases which are open to the public. The A/FD's are contained in seven books which are organized by regions. These A/FD's are revised every 8 weeks. Figure 6-2 contains an excerpt from a directory. For a complete listing of information provided in an A/FD and how the information may be decoded, a pilot should refer to the "Directory Legend Sample" located in the front of each A/FD.

FACILITY AT AIRPORT	FREQUENCY USE	COMMUNICATION/BROADCAST PROCEDURES		
		OUTBOUND	INBOUND	PRACTICE INSTRUMENT APPROACH
UNICOM (No Tower or FSS)	Communicate with UNICOM station on published CTAF frequency (122.7, 122.8, 122.725, 122.975, or 123.0). If unable to contact UNICOM station, use self-announce procedures on CTAF.	Before taxiing and before taxiing on the runway for departure.	10 miles out. Entering downwind, base, final. Leaving the runway.	
No Tower, FSS, or UNICOM	Self-announce on MULTICOM frequency 122.9.	Before taxiing and before taxiing on the runway for departure.	10 miles out. Entering downwind, base, and final. Leaving the runway.	Departing final approach fix (name) or on final approach segment inbound.
No Tower in operation, FSS open	Communicate with FSS on CTAF frequency.	Before taxiing and before taxiing on the runway for departure.	10 miles out. Entering downwind, base, final. Leaving the runway.	Approach completed/ terminated.
FSS closed (No Tower)	Self-announce on CTAF.	Before taxiing and before taxiing on the runway for departure.	10 miles out. Entering downwind, base, and final. Leaving the runway.	
Tower or FSS not in operation	Self-announce on CTAF.	Before taxiing and before taxiing on the runway for departure.	10 miles out. Entering downwind, base, and final. Leaving the runway.	

FIGURE 6-1.—Recommended communication procedures.

ARKANSAS

FORT SMITH REGIONAL   (FSM) 3 SE UTC-6(-5DT) N35°20.20'W94°22.05'   **MEMPHIS**
   469 B S4 FUEL 100LL, JET A ARFF Index A   **H-4G, L-6H, 13D**
  RWY 07-25: H8000X150 (ASPH-GRVD) S-75, D-175, DT-295 HIRL 0.6% up W   **IAP**
    RWY 07: MALSR. VASI(V4R)—GA 3.0° TCH 52'. Water tower. Arresting device.
    RWY 25: MALSR. VASI(V4L)—GA 2.9° TCH 60'. Ground. Arresting device.
  RWY 01-19: H5002X150 (ASPH-GRVD) S-55, D-70, DT-120 MIRL
    RWY 01: Railroad.   **RWY 19:** Fence.
  AIRPORT REMARKS: Attended continuously. Rwy 01-19 CLOSED indef. Rwy 01-19 restricted to prop acft
   unless crosswinds on Rwy 07-25 exceed acft safe operating capability. 180' AGL crane 1/2 NM N Rwy 01-19 Mon-Fri 1400-
   2300Z•. Mounds of dirt 700' NE of Rwy 25 thld. Acft training on Rwy 01-19 (including practice approaches, touch and go
   landings and practice instrument approaches) prohibited between 0100-1500Z•. Flock of migratory birds on and in vicinity of
   arpt. Landing fee for all FAR 121 and FAR 135 ops. PPR for all U.S. govt acft (including civilian contract) above 100,000
   lbs. Contact arpt manager 1400-2300Z• Mon-Fri 501-646-1681 minimum 24 hrs in advance. PAEW adjacent Rwy 01-19,
   open trenches. Personnel, equipment and open trenches in Rwy 07-25 safety area indef. Twy A between Twy D and Twy E
   non-movement area. Twy A at Twy C non-movement area. Twy B N of Twy G has PAEW and open trenches adjacent to twy.
   Twy C clsd indef. Twy B, Twy D and Twy H clsd indef. Twy D to Twy A; Twy D to Twy G, and Twy G to Twy B marked as
   main timing cockpit over centerline. Acft with wingspans of 118 ft or greater should not follow centerline. When twr clsd
   ACTIVATE HIRL Rwy 07-25, MIRL Rwy 01-19, MALSR Rwy 07 and Rwy 25—CTAF. NOTE: See Land and Hold Short
   Operations Section.
  WEATHER DATA SOURCES: ASOS (501) 646-2504. LLWAS.
  COMMUNICATIONS: CTAF 118.3 **ATIS** 126.3 (1130-0500Z•) **UNICOM** 122.95
    JONESBORO FSS   (JBR) TF 1-800-WX-BRIEF. NOTAM FILE FSM.
    RCO   122.2 (JONESBORO FSS)
   ®**RAZORBACK APP CON** 120.9 (256°-074°) 125.4 (075°-255°) 124.55 (1130-0500Z•)
   RAZORBACK DEP CON   120.9 (256°-074°) 125.4 (075°-255°) (1130-0500Z•)
   ®**MEMPHIS CENTER APP/DEP CON** 119.25 (0500-1130Z•)
    TOWER 118.3 (1130-0500Z•) **GND CON** 121.9 **CLNC DEL** 133.85
  AIRSPACE: CLASS D svc effective 1130-0500Z• other times CLASS E.
   TRSA svc ctc   **APP CON** within 25 NM. Service not provided within R2401 and R2402 when activated.
  RADIO AIDS TO NAVIGATION: NOTAM FILE FSM.
   (L) VORTACW   110.4 FSM Chan 41 N35°23.30'W94°16.29' 230° 5.6 NM to fld. 430/7E. **HIWAS.**
     WIZER NDB (MHW/LOM) 223 FS N35°21.25' W94°13.03' 257° 7.5 NM to fld.
      Unmonitored when tower closed.
     PENO BOTTOMS NDB (MHW) 311 AFT N35°19.37'W94°28.45' 076° 5.3 NM to fld. NOTAM FILE JBR.
      Unmonitored when tower closed.
  ILS 111.3 I-FSM Rwy 25 LOM WIZER NDB. Unmonitored when tower closed.
  ASR (1130-0500Z•)

FRANK FEDERER MEM (See BRINKLEY)

GASTONS (See LAKEVIEW)

GILMORE N35°20.82'W90°28.69' NOTAM FILE JBR.   **MEMPHIS**
  (L) VORW/DME 113.0 GQE Chan 77 132° 17.4 NM to West Memphis Muni. 211/04E.   **H-4G, L-14F**

GOSNELL N35°57.07'W89°56.43' NOTAM FILE JBR.   **MEMPHIS**
  (L)VORW 111.8 GOJ at Arkansas Intl.   **L-14F**

GRIDER FLD (See PINE BLUFF)

GURDON MUNI   (5M8) 1 NW UTC-6(-5DT) N33°55.51'W93°09.76'   **MEMPHIS**
  229 B FUEL 100LL   **L-14E**
  RWY 08-26: H4600X30 (ASPH) S-12.5 MIRL
    RWY 26: Trees. Rgt tfc.
  AIRPORT REMARKS: Unattended. ACTIVATE MIRL Rwy 08-26-122.7.
  COMMUNICATIONS: CTAF 122.9
    JONESBORO FSS (JBR) TF 1-800-WX-BRIEF. NOTAM FILE JBR.
  RADIO AIDS TO NAVIGATION: NOTAM FILE ELD.
   EL DORADO (H) VORTACW 115.5 ELD Chan 102 N33°15.37'W92°44.64' 325° 45.2 NM to fld. 230/07E.

FIGURE 6-2.—Airport facility directory excerpt.

In the back of each A/FD, there is information such as special notices, parachute jumping areas, and facility telephone numbers, etc. It would be helpful to review an A/FD to become familiar with the information they contain.

Notices to Airmen (NOTAMs)

Notices to Airmen provide the most current information available. They provide information on airports and changes which affect the national airspace system that are time-critical and in particular are of concern to instrument flight rule (IFR) operations. NOTAM information is classified into three categories. These are NOTAM-D or distant, NOTAM-L or local, and flight data center (FDC) NOTAMs. NOTAM-Ds are attached to hourly weather reports and are available at flight service stations (AFSS/FSS). NOTAM-Ls include items of a local nature such as taxiway closures, construction near a runway, etc. These NOTAMs are maintained at the FSS nearest the airport affected. NOTAM-Ls must be requested from an FSS other than the one nearest the local airport for which the NOTAM was issued. FDC NOTAMs are issued by the National Flight Data Center and contain regulatory information such as temporary flight restrictions or an amendment to instrument approach procedure. The NOTAM-Ds and FDC NOTAMs are contained in the Notices to Airmen publication which is issued every 14 days. Prior to any flight, pilots should check for any NOTAMs which could affect their intended flight.

AIRPORT MARKINGS AND SIGNS

There are markings and signs used at airports which provide directions and assist the pilot in airport operations. We will discuss some of the most common markings and signs. Additional information may be found in the Aeronautical Information Manual (AIM).

Runway Markings

Runway markings vary depending on the type of operations conducted at the airport. Figure 6-3 shows a runway which is approved as a precision instrument approach runway and also shows some other common runway markings. A basic VFR runway may only have centerline markings and runway numbers.

Since aircraft are affected by the wind during takeoffs and landings, runways are laid out according to the local prevailing winds. Runway numbers are in reference to magnetic north. Certain airports have two or even three runways laid out in the same direction. These are referred to as parallel runways and are distinguished by a letter being added to the runway number. Examples are runway 36L (left), 36C (center), and 36R (right).

Another feature of some runways is a displaced threshold. A threshold may be displaced because of an obstruction near the end of the runway. Although this portion of the runway is not to be used for landing, it may be available for taxiing, takeoff, or landing rollout.

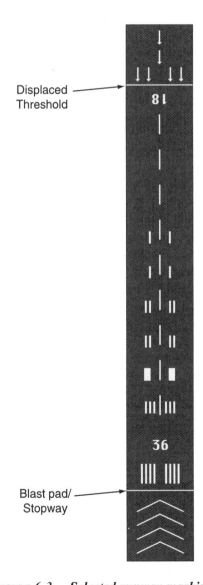

FIGURE 6-3.—Selected runway markings.

Some airports may have a blast pad/stopway area. The blast pad is an area where a propeller or jet blast can dissipate without creating a hazard. The stopway area is paved in order to provide space for an aircraft to decelerate and stop in the event of an aborted takeoff. These areas cannot be used for takeoff or landing.

Taxiway Markings

Airplanes use taxiways to transition from parking areas to the runway. Taxiways are identified by a continuous yellow centerline stripe. A taxiway may include edge markings to define the edge of the taxiway. This is usually done when the taxiway edge does not correspond with the edge of the pavement. If an edge marking is a continuous line, the paved shoulder is not intended to be used by aircraft. If it is a dashed marking, an aircraft may use that portion of the pavement. Where a taxiway approaches a runway, there may be a holding position marker. These consist of four yellow lines (two solid and two dashed). The solid lines are where the aircraft is to hold. At some controlled airports, holding position markings may be found on a runway. They are used when there are intersecting runways, and air traffic control issues instructions such as "cleared to land — hold short of runway 30."

Other Markings

Some of the other markings found on the airport include vehicle roadway markings, VOR receiver checkpoint markings, and non-movement area boundary markings.

Vehicle roadway markings are used when necessary to define a pathway for vehicle crossing areas that are also intended for aircraft. These markings usually consist of a solid white line to delineate each edge of the roadway and a dashed line to separate lanes within the edges of the roadway.

A VOR receiver checkpoint marking consists of a painted circle with an arrow in the middle. The arrow is aligned in the direction of the checkpoint azimuth. This allows a pilot to check aircraft instruments with navigational aid signals.

A non-movement area boundary marking delineates a movement area under air traffic control. These markings are yellow and located on the boundary between the movement and non-movement area. They normally consist of two yellow lines (one solid and one dashed).

Airport Signs

There are six types of signs that may be found at airports. The more complex the layout of an airport, the more important the signs become to pilots. Figure 6-4 shows examples of signs, their purpose, and appropriate pilot action. The six types of signs are:

• **Mandatory Instruction Signs**—have a red background with a white inscription. These signs denote an entrance to a runway, a critical area, or a prohibited area.
• **Location Signs**—are black with yellow inscription and a yellow border and do not have arrows. They are used to identify a taxiway or runway location, to identify the boundary of the runway, or identify an instrument landing system (ILS) critical area.
• **Direction Signs**—have a yellow background with black inscription. The inscription identifies the designation of the intersecting taxiway(s) leading out of an intersection.
• **Destination Signs**—have a yellow background with black inscription and also contain arrows. These signs provide information on locating things such as runways, terminals, cargo areas, and civil aviation areas, etc.
• **Information Signs**—have a yellow background with black inscription. These signs are used to provide the pilot with information on such things as areas that cannot be seen from the control tower, applicable radio frequencies, and noise abatement procedures. The airport operator determines the need, size, and location of these signs.
• **Runway Distance Remaining Signs**—have a black background with white numbers. The numbers indicate the distance of the remaining runway in thousands of feet.

Airport Lighting

The majority of airports have some type of lighting for night operations. The variety and type of lighting systems depends on the volume and complexity of operations at a given airport. Airport lighting is standardized so that airports use the same light colors for runways, taxiways, etc.

U.S. Airport Signs

Sign & Location	Pilot Action/Sign Purpose	Sign & Location	Pilot Action/Sign Purpose
4-22 — On taxiways at Intersection with Runway and at Runway/Runway Intersection	Do not cross unless clearance has been received (towered airport) or until clear (nontowered airport). At runway/runway intersections, hold short if land and hold-short clearance has been accepted.	**Edge of ILS Critical Area**	These sign are used on controlled airports to identify the boundary of the ILS critical area. It is intended that pilots exiting this area would use this sign as a guide to judge when the aircraft is clear of the ILS critical area.
4-APCH — Hold Position on Taxiway Located in Runway Approach or Departure Area Hold	**Controlled Airport** — Hold when instructed by ATC. **Noncontrolled Airport** — Proceed when no traffic conflict exists.	**B→** — Taxiways and Runways	**On Taxiways**— Provides direction to turn at next intersection to maneuver aircraft onto named taxiway. **On Runways**— Provides direction to turn to exit runway onto named taxiway.
ILS — ILS Critical Area	Hold when instructed by ATC when approaches are being made with visibility less than 2 miles or ceiling less than 800 feet.	**22→** — Taxiway	Provides general taxiing direction to named runway.
⊖ — Areas where Aircraft are Forbidden to Enter	Do not enter. Identifies paved areas where aircraft entry is prohibited.	**TERM→** — Taxiways and Runways	Provides general taxiing direction to identified destination. Other destination signs include directions to taxiway, runway.
B — Taxiway	Identifies taxiway on which aircraft is located.	**4** — Runway	Provides remaining runway length in 1,000 feet increments.
22 — Runway	Identifies runway on which aircraft is located.	**HS-1** — HS-1	Land and Hold Short point for other than intersecting runways as instructed by ATC.
Edge of Protected Area for Runway	These signs are used on controlled airports to identify the boundary of the runway protected area. It is intended that pilots exiting this area would use this sign as a guide to judge when the aircraft is clear of the protected area.	**Taxiway Ending Marker**	Indicates taxiway does not continue.

FIGURE 6-4.—Airport signs.

Airport Beacon

Airport beacons help a pilot identify an airport at night. The beacons are operated from dusk till dawn and sometimes they are turned on if the ceiling is less than 1,000 feet and/or the ground visibility is less than 3 statute miles (SM) (visual flight rules minimums). However, there is no requirement for this so a pilot has the responsibility of determining if the weather is VFR. The beacon has a vertical light distribution to make it most effective from 1-10° above the horizon, although it can be seen well above or below this spread. The beacon may be an omnidirectional capacitor-discharge device or it may rotate at a constant speed which produces the visual effect of flashes a regular intervals. The combination of light colors from an airport beacon indicates the type of airport. [Figure 6-5]

FIGURE 6-5.—Airport rotating beacons.

Some of the most common beacons are:

- Flashing white and green for civilian land airports.
- Flashing white and yellow for a water airport.
- Flashing white, yellow, and green, for a heliport.
- Two quick, white flashes followed by a green flash identifies a military airport.

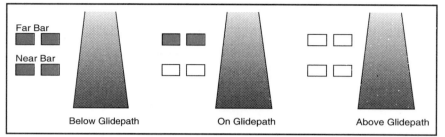

FIGURE 6-6.—2-Bar VASI system.

Approach Light Systems

Approach light systems are primarily intended to provide a means to transition from instrument flight to visual flight for landing. The system configuration depends on whether the runway is a precision or nonprecision instrument runway. Some systems include sequenced flashing lights which appear to the pilot as a ball of light traveling toward the runway at high speed. Approach lights can also aid pilots operating under visual flight rules at night.

Visual Glideslope Indicators

Visual glideslope indicators provide the pilot with glidepath information which can be used for day or night approaches. By maintaining the proper glidepath as provided by the system, a pilot should have adequate obstacle clearance and should touch down within a specified portion of the runway.

Visual Approach Slope Indicator (VASI)

Visual approach slope indicator installations are the most common visual glidepath systems in use. The VASI provides obstruction clearance within 10° of the runway extended runway centerline, and to 4 nautical miles (NM) from the runway threshold.

A VASI consists of light units arranged in bars. There are 2-bar and 3-bar VASIs. The 2-bar VASI has near and far light bars and the 3-bar VASI has near, middle, and far light bars. Two-bar VASI installations provide one visual glidepath which is normally set at 3°. The 3-bar system provides two glidepaths with the lower glidepath normally set at 3° and the upper glidepath one-fourth degree above the lower glidepath.

The basic principle of the VASI is that of color differentiation between red and white. Each light unit projects a beam of light having a white segment in the upper part of the beam and a red segment in the lower part of the beam. The lights are arranged so the pilot will see the combination of lights shown in figure 6-6 to indicate below, on, or above the glidepath.

Other Glidepath Systems

A precision approach path indicator (PAPI) uses lights similar to the VASI system except they are installed in a single row, normally on the left side of the runway. [Figure 6-7]

A tri-color system consists of a single light unit projecting a three-color visual approach path. A below the glidepath indication is red, on the glidepath color is green, and above the glidepath is indicated by amber. [Figure 6-8]

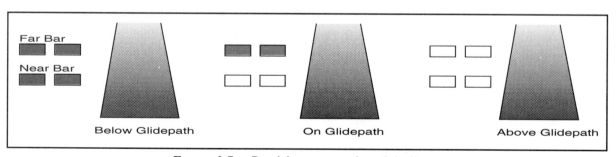

FIGURE 6-7.—Precision approach path indicator.

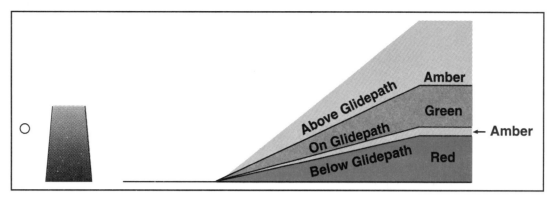

FIGURE 6-8.—Tri-color visual approach slope indicator.

There are also pulsating systems which consist of a single light unit projecting a two-color visual approach path. A below the glidepath indication is shown by the color red, slightly below is indicated by pulsating red, on the glidepath is indicated by a steady white light, and a pulsating white light indicates above the glidepath. [Figure 6-9]

Runway Lighting

There are various lights that identify parts of the runway complex. These assist a pilot in safely making a takeoff or landing during night operations.

Runway End Identifier Lights (REIL)
Runway end identifier lights are installed at many airfields to provide rapid and positive identification of the approach end of a particular runway. The system consists of a pair of synchronized flashing lights located laterally on each side of the runway threshold. REILs may be either omnidirectional or unidirectional facing the approach area.

Runway Edge Lights
Runway edge lights are used to outline the edges of runways at night or during low visibility conditions. These lights are classified according to the intensity they are capable of producing. They are classified as high intensity runway lights (HIRL), medium intensity runway lights (MIRL), or low intensity runway lights (LIRL). The HIRL and MIRL have variable intensity settings. These lights are white except, on instrument runways where amber lights are used on the last 2,000 feet or half the length of the runway, whichever is less. The lights marking the end of the runway are red.

In-Runway Lighting
Touchdown zone lights (TDZL), runway centerline lights (RCLS), and taxiway turnoff lights are installed on some precision runways to facilitate landing under adverse visibility conditions. TZDLs are two rows of transverse light bars disposed symmetrically about the runway centerline in the runway touchdown zone. RCLS consists of flush

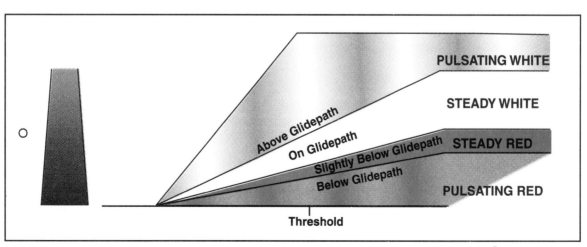

FIGURE 6-9.—Pulsating visual approach slope indicator.

centerline lights spaced at 50-foot intervals beginning 75 feet from the landing threshold. Taxiway turnoff lights are flush lights which emit a steady green color.

Control of Airport Lighting

Airport lighting is controlled by air traffic controllers at controlled airports. At uncontrolled airports, the lights may be on a timer, or where an FSS is located at an airport, the FSS personnel may control the lighting. A pilot may request various light systems be turned on or off and also request a specified intensity, if available, from ATC or FSS personnel. At selected uncontrolled airports, the pilot may control the lighting by using the radio. This is done by selecting a specified frequency and clicking the radio microphone. For information on pilot controlled lighting at various airports, the pilot should refer to the Airport/Facility Directory. [Figure 6-10]

Key Mike	Function
7 times within 5 seconds	Highest intensity available
5 times within 5 seconds	Medium or lower intensity (Lower REIL or REIL-off)
3 times within 5 seconds	Lowest intensity available (Lower REIL or REIL-off)

FIGURE 6-10.—Radio control runway lighting.

Taxiway Lights

Taxiway lights outline the edges of the taxiway and are blue in color. At many airports, these edge lights may have variable intensity settings that may be adjusted by an air traffic controller when deemed necessary or when requested by the pilot. Some airports also have taxiway centerline lights which are green in color.

Obstruction Lights

Obstructions are marked or lighted to warn pilots of their presence during daytime and nighttime conditions. Obstruction lighting can be found both on and off an airport to identify obstructions. They may be marked or lighted in any of the following conditions.

• **Red Obstruction Lights**—either flash or emit a steady red color during nighttime operations, and the obstructions are painted orange and white for daytime operations.
• **High Intensity White Obstruction Light**—flash high intensity white lights during the daytime with the intensity reduced for nighttime.
• **Dual Lighting**—is a combination of flashing red beacons and steady red lights for nighttime operation, and high intensity white lights for daytime operations.

WIND DIRECTION INDICATORS

It is important for a pilot to know the direction of the wind. At facilities with an operating control tower, this information is provided by ATC. Information may also be provided by FSS personnel located at a particular airport or by requesting information on a common air traffic frequency (CTAF) at airports which have the capacity to receive and broadcast on this frequency.

When none of these services are available, it is possible to determine wind direction and runway in use by visual wind indicators. A pilot should check these wind indicators even when information is provided on the CTAF at a given airport because there is no assurance that the information provided is accurate.

Wind direction indicators include a wind sock, wind tee, or tetrahedron. These are usually located in a central location near the runway and may be placed in the center of a segmented circle which will identify the traffic pattern direction if it is other than the standard left-hand pattern. [Figures 6-11 and 6-12]

The wind sock is a good source of information since it not only indicates wind direction, but allows the pilot to estimate the wind velocity and gust. The wind sock extends out straighter in strong winds and will tend to move back and forth when the wind is gusty. Wind tees and tetrahedrons can swing freely, and will align themselves with the wind direction. The wind tee and tetrahedron can also be manually set to align with the runway in use, therefore a pilot should also look at the wind sock if available.

RADIO COMMUNICATIONS

Operating in and out of a controlled airport, as well as in a good portion of the airspace system, requires that an aircraft have two-way radio communication capability. For this reason, a pilot should be knowledgeable of radio station license requirements and radio communications equipment and procedures.

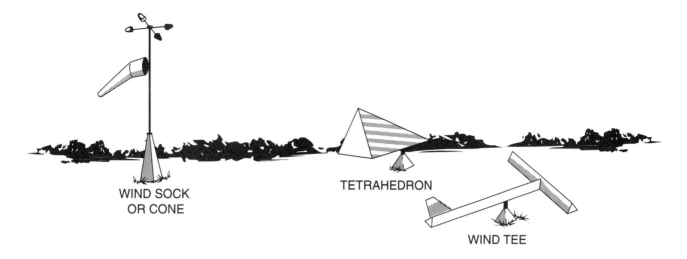

FIGURE 6-11.—Wind direction indicators.

Radio License

There is no license requirement for a pilot operating in the United States; however, a pilot who operates internationally is required to hold a restricted radiotelephone permit issued by the Federal Communications Commission (FCC). There is also no station license requirement for most general aviation aircraft operating in the United States. A station license is required however for an aircraft which is operating internationally, which uses other than a very high frequency (VHF) radio, and which meets other criteria.

Radio Equipment

In general aviation, the most common types of radios are VHF. A VHF radio operates on frequencies between 118.0 and 136.975 and is classified as 720 or 760 depending on the number of channels it can accommodate. The 720 and 760 uses .025 spacing (118.025, 118.050, etc.) with the 720 having a frequency range up to 135.975 and the 760 going up to 136.975. VHF radios are limited to line of sight transmissions; therefore, aircraft at higher altitudes are able to transmit and receive at greater distances.

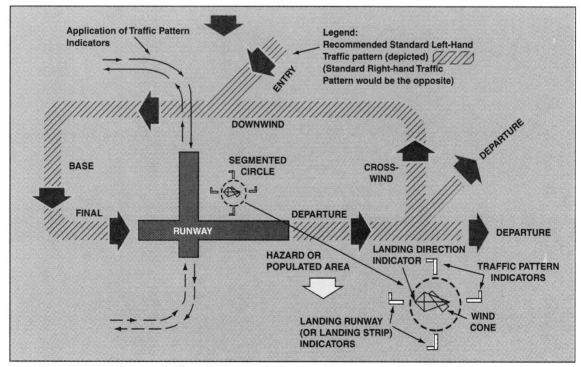

FIGURE 6-12.—Segmented circle and airport traffic pattern.

CHARACTER	MORSE CODE	TELEPHONY	PHONIC (PRONUNCIATION)
A	•−	Alfa	(AL-FAH)
B	−•••	Bravo	(BRAH-VOH)
C	−•−•	Charlie	(CHAR-LEE) OR (SHAR-LEE)
D	−••	Delta	(DELL-TAH)
E	•	Echo	(ECK-OH)
F	••−•	Foxtrot	(FOKS-TROT)
G	−−•	Golf	(GOLF)
H	••••	Hotel	(HOH-TEL)
I	••	India	(IN-DEE-AH)
J	•−−−	Juliett	(JEW-LEE-ETT)
K	−•−	Kilo	(KEY-LOH)
L	•−••	Lima	(LEE-MAH)
M	−−	Mike	(MIKE)
N	−•	November	(NO-VEM-BER)
O	−−−	Oscar	(OSS-CAH)
P	•−−•	Papa	(PAH-PAH)
Q	−−•−	Quebec	(KEH-BECK)
R	•−•	Romeo	(ROW-ME-OH)
S	•••	Sierra	(SEE-AIR-RAH)
T	−	Tango	(TANG-GO)
U	••−	Uniform	(YOU-NEE-FORM) OR (OO-NEE-FORM)
V	•••−	Victor	(VIK-TAH)
W	•−−	Whiskey	(WISS-KEY)
X	−••−	Xray	(ECKS-RAY)
Y	−•−−	Yankee	(YANG-KEY)
Z	−−••	Zulu	(ZOO-LOO)
1	•−−−−	One	(WUN)
2	••−−−	Two	(TOO)
3	•••−−	Three	(TREE)
4	••••−	Four	(FOW-ER)
5	•••••	Five	(FIFE)
6	−••••	Six	(SIX)
7	−−•••	Seven	(SEV-EN)
8	−−−••	Eight	(AIT)
9	−−−−•	Nine	(NIN-ER)
0	−−−−−	Zero	(ZEE-RO)

FIGURE 6-13.—Phonetic alphabet.

Radio Procedures

Using proper radio phraseology and procedures will contribute to a pilot's ability to operate safely and efficiently in the airspace system. A review of the Pilot/Controller Glossary contained in the Aeronautical Information Manual (AIM) will assist a pilot in the use and understanding of standard terminology. The AIM also contains many examples of radio communications which should be helpful.

The International Civil Aviation Organization (ICAO) has adopted a phonetic alphabet which should be used in radio communications. When communicating with ATC, pilots should use this alphabet to identify their aircraft. [Figure 6-13]

Lost Communication Procedures

It is possible that a pilot might experience a malfunction of the radio. This might cause the transmitter, receiver, or both to become inoperative. If a receiver becomes inoperative and a pilot needs to land at a controlled airport, it is advisable to remain outside or above Class D airspace until the direction and flow of traffic is determined. A pilot should then advise the tower of the aircraft type, position, altitude, and intention to land. The pilot should then continue and enter the pattern, report his or her position as appropriate, and watch for light signals from the tower. Light signal colors and their meaning are contained in figure 6-14.

LIGHT GUN SIGNALS			
COLOR AND TYPE OF SIGNAL	MOVEMENT OF VEHICLES, EQUIPMENT AND PERSONNEL	AIRCRAFT ON THE GROUND	AIRCRAFT IN FLIGHT
STEADY GREEN	Cleared to cross, proceed or go	Cleared for takeoff	Cleared to land
FLASHING GREEN	Not applicable	Cleared for taxi	Return for landing (to be followed by steady green at the proper time)
STEADY RED	STOP	STOP	Give way to other aircraft and continue circling
FLASHING RED	Clear the taxiway/runway	Taxi clear of the runway in use	Airport unsafe, do not land
FLASHING WHITE	Return to starting point on airport	Return to starting point on airport	Not applicable
ALTERNATING RED AND GREEN	Exercise Extreme Caution!!!!	Exercise Extreme Caution!!!!	Exercise Extreme Caution!!!!

FIGURE 6-14.—Light gun signals.

If the transmitter becomes inoperative, a pilot should follow the previously stated procedures and also monitor the appropriate air traffic frequency. During daylight hours air traffic transmissions may be acknowledged by rocking the wings, and at night by blinking the landing light.

When both receiver and transmitter are inoperative, the pilot should remain outside of Class D airspace until the flow of traffic has been determined and then enter the pattern and watch for light signals.

If a radio malfunctions prior to departure, it is advisable to have it repaired if possible. If this is not possible, a call should be made to air traffic and the pilot should request authorization to depart without two-way radio communications. If authorization is given to depart, the pilot will be advised to monitor the appropriate frequency and/or watch for light signals as appropriate.

AIR TRAFFIC SERVICES

Besides the services provided by FSS as discussed in Chapter 5, there are numerous other services provided by air traffic. In many instances a pilot is required to have contact with air traffic, but even when not required a pilot will find it helpful to request their services.

Primary Radar

Radar is a method whereby radio waves are transmitted into the air and are then received when they have been reflected by an object in the path of the beam. Range is determined by measuring the time it takes (at the speed of light) for the radio wave to go out to the object and then return to the receiving antenna. The direction of a detected object from a radar site is determined by the position of the rotating antenna when the reflected portion of the radio wave is received.

Modern radar is very reliable and there are seldom outages. This is due to reliable maintenance and improved equipment. There are, however, some limitations which may affect air traffic services and prevent a controller from issuing advisories concerning aircraft which are not under their control and cannot be seen on radar.

The characteristics of radio waves are such that they normally travel in a continuous straight line unless they are "bent" by atmospheric phenomena such as temperature inversions, reflected or attenuated by dense objects such as heavy clouds, precipitation, etc., or screened by high terrain features.

RADAR BEACON PHRASEOLOGY

SQUAWK (number)	Operate radar beacon transponder on designated code in MODE A/3/
IDENT	Engage the "IDENT" feature (military I/P) of the transponder.
SQUAWK (number) and IDENT	Operate transponder on specified code in MODE A/3 and engage the "IDENT" (military I/P) feature.
SQUAWK STANDBY	Switch transponder to standby position.
SQUAWK LOW/NORMAL	Operate transponder on low or normal sensitivity as specified. Transponder is operated in "NORMAL" position unless ATC specifies "LOW," ("ON" is used instead of "NORMAL" as a master control label on some types of transponders.
SQUAWK ALTITUDE	Activate MODE C with automatic altitude reporting.
STOP ALTITUDE SQUAWK	Turn off altitude reporting switch and continue transmitting MODE C framing pulses. If your equipment does not have this capability, turn off MODE C.
STOP SQUAWK (mode in use)	Switch off specified mode. (Used for military aircraft when the controller is unaware of military service requirements for the aircraft to continue operation on another MODE.)
STOP SQUAWK	Switch off transponder.
SQUAWK MAYDAY	Operate transponder in the emergency position (MODE A Code 7700 for civil transponder. MODE 3 Code 7700 and emergency feature for military transponder.)
SQUAWK VFR	Operate radar beacon transponder on Code 1200 in the MODE A/3, or other appropriate VFR code.

FIGURE 6-15.—Transponder phraseology.

Air Traffic Control Radar Beacon System (ATCRBS)

The air traffic control radar beacon system is often referred to as "secondary surveillance radar." This system consists of three components and helps in alleviating some of the limitations associated with primary radar. The three components are an interrogator, transponder, and radarscope. The advantages of ATCRBS are the reinforcement of radar targets, rapid target identification, and a unique display of selected codes.

Transponder

The transponder is the airborne portion of the secondary surveillance radar system and a system with which a pilot should be familiar. The ATCRBS cannot display the secondary information unless an aircraft is equipped with a transponder. A transponder is also required to operate in certain controlled airspace. Airspace is discussed in chapter 7.

A transponder code consists of four numbers from zero to seven (4,096 possible codes). There are some standard codes, or air traffic may issue a four-digit code to an aircraft. When a controller requests a code

or function on the transponder, he or she may use the word "squawk." Figure 6-15 lists some standard transponder phraseology.

Radar Traffic Information Service

Radar equipped air traffic facilities provide radar assistance to VFR aircraft provided the aircraft can communicate with the facility and are within radar coverage. This basic service includes safety alerts, traffic advisories, limited vectoring when requested, and sequencing at locations where this procedure has been established. In addition to basic radar service, terminal radar service area (TRSA) has been implemented at certain terminal locations. The purpose of this service is to provide separation between all participating VFR aircraft and all IFR aircraft operating within the TRSA. Class C service provides approved separation between IFR and VFR aircraft, and sequencing of VFR aircraft to the primary airport. Class B service provides approved separation of aircraft based on IFR, VFR, and/or weight, and sequencing of VFR arrivals to the primary airport(s).

ATC issues traffic information based on observed

radar targets. The traffic is referenced by azimuth from the aircraft in terms of the 12-hour clock. Also the distance in nautical miles, direction in which the target is moving, and the type and altitude of the aircraft, if know, are given. An example would be: "Traffic 10 o'clock 5 miles east bound, Cessna 152, 3,000 feet." The pilot should note that traffic position is based on the aircraft track, and that wind correction can affect the clock position at which a pilot locates traffic. [Figure 6-16]

FIGURE 6-16.—*Traffic advisories.*

WAKE TURBULENCE

All aircraft generate a wake while in flight. This disturbance is caused by a pair of counter-rotating vortices trailing from the wingtips. The vortices from larger aircraft pose problems to encountering aircraft. The wake of these aircraft can impose rolling moments exceeding the roll-control authority of the encountering aircraft. Also, the turbulence generated within the vortices can damage aircraft components and equipment if encountered at close range. For this reason, a pilot must envision the location of the vortex wake and adjust the flightpath accordingly.

During ground operations and during takeoff, jet-engine blast (thrust stream turbulence) can cause damage and upsets at close range. For this reason, pilots of small aircraft should consider the effects of jet-engine blast and maintain adequate separation. Also, pilots of larger aircraft should consider the effects of their aircraft's jet-engine blast on other aircraft and equipment on the ground.

Vortex Generation

Lift is generated by the creation of a pressure differential over the wing surface. The lowest pressure occurs over the upper wing surface, and the highest pressure under the wing. This pressure differential triggers the rollup of the airflow aft of the wing resulting in swirling air masses trailing downstream of the wingtips. After the rollup is completed, the wake consists of two counter-rotating cylindrical vortices. Most of the energy is within a few feet of

the center of each vortex, but pilots should avoid a region within about 100 feet of the vortex core. [Figure 6-17]

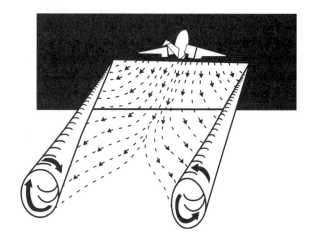

FIGURE 6-17.—*Vortex generation.*

Vortex Strength

The strength of the vortex is governed by the weight, speed, and shape of the wing of the generating aircraft. The vortex characteristics of any given aircraft can also be changed by the extension of flaps or other wing configuration devices as well as by a change in speed. The greatest vortex strength occurs when the generating aircraft is heavy, clean, and slow.

Vortex Behavior

Trailing vortices have certain behavioral characteristics that can help a pilot visualize the wake location and take avoidance precautions.

Vortices are generated from the moment an aircraft leaves the ground, since trailing vortices are the by-product of wing lift. The vortex circulation is outward, upward, and around the wingtips when viewed from either ahead or behind the aircraft. Tests have shown that vortices remain spaced a bit less than a wingspan apart, drifting with the wind, at altitudes greater than a wingspan from the ground. Tests have also shown that the vortices sink at a rate of several hundred feet per minute, slowing their descent and diminishing in strength with time and distance behind the generating aircraft. [Figure 6-18]

When the vortices of larger aircraft sink close to the ground (within 100 to 200 feet), they tend to move laterally over the ground at a speed of 2 or 3 knots. A crosswind will decrease the lateral movement of the upwind vortex and increase the movement of the

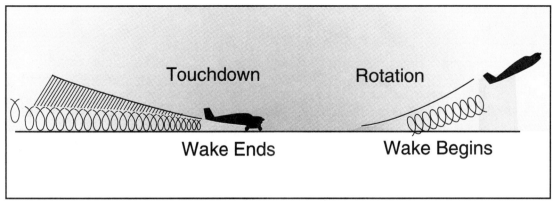

FIGURE 6-18.—Vortex behavior.

downwind vortex. A tailwind condition can move the vortices of the preceding aircraft forward into the touchdown zone.

Vortex Avoidance Procedures

• Landing behind a larger aircraft on the same runway—stay at or above the larger aircraft's approach flightpath and land beyond its touchdown point.

• Landing behind a larger aircraft on a parallel runway closer than 2,500 feet—consider the possibility of drift and stay at or above the larger aircraft's final approach flightpath and note its touchdown point.

• Landing behind a larger aircraft on crossing runway—cross above the larger aircraft's flightpath.

• Landing behind a departing aircraft on the same runway—land prior to the departing aircraft's rotating point.

• Landing behind a larger aircraft on a crossing runway—note the aircraft's rotation point and if past the intersection continue and land prior to the intersection. If the larger aircraft rotates prior to the intersection, avoid flight below its flightpath. Abandon the approach unless a landing is ensured well before reaching the intersection.

• Departing behind a large aircraft, rotate prior to the large aircraft's rotation point and climb above its climb path until turning clear of the wake.

• For intersection takeoffs on the same runway, be alert to adjacent larger aircraft operations, particularly upwind of your runway. An intersection takeoff clearance is received, avoid headings that will cross below the larger aircraft's path.

• If departing or landing after a large aircraft executing a low approach, missed approach, or touch and go landing (since vortices settle and move laterally near the ground, the vortex hazard may exist along the runway and in your flightpath, particularly in a quartering tailwind), it is prudent to wait 2 minutes prior to a takeoff or landing.

• En route it is advisable to avoid a path below and behind a large aircraft and if a large aircraft is observed above on the same track, adjust your position laterally and preferably upwind.

COLLISION AVOIDANCE

14 CFR part 91 has established right-of-way rules, minimum safe altitudes, and VFR cruising altitudes to enhance flight safety. The pilot can contribute to collision avoidance by being alert and scanning for other aircraft. This is particularly important in the vicinity of an airport.

Effective scanning is accomplished with a series of short, regularly spaced eye movements that bring successive areas of the sky into the central visual field. Each movement should not exceed 10°, and each should be observed for at least 1 second to enable detection. Although back and forth eye movements seem preferred by most pilots, each pilot should develop a scanning pattern that is most comfortable and then adhere to it to assure optimum scanning.

If you think another aircraft is too close to you, give way instead of waiting for the other pilot to respect the right-of-way to which you may be entitled.

Clearing Procedures

The following procedures and considerations should assist a pilot in collision avoidance under various situations.

- **Before Takeoff**—Prior to taxiing onto a runway or landing area in preparation for takeoff, pilots should scan the approach area for possible landing traffic, executing appropriate maneuvers to provide a clear view of the approach areas.
- **Climbs and Descents**—During climbs and descents in flight conditions which permit visual detection of other traffic, pilots should execute gentle banks left and right at a frequency which permits continuous visual scanning of the airspace.
- **Straight and Level**—During sustained periods of straight-and-level flight, a pilot should execute appropriate clearing procedures at periodic intervals.
- **Traffic Patterns**—Entries into traffic patterns while descending should be avoided.
- **Traffic at VOR Sites**—Due to converging traffic, sustained vigilance should be maintained in the vicinity of VOR's and intersections.
- **Training Operations**—Vigilance should be maintained and clearing turns should be made prior to a practice maneuver. During instruction, the pilot should be asked to verbalize the clearing procedures (call out clear "left, right, above, and below").

High-wing and low-wing aircraft have their respective blind spots. High-wing aircraft should momentarily raise their wing in the direction of the intended turn and look for traffic prior to commencing the turn. Low-wing aircraft should momentarily lower the wing.

CHAPTER 7

AIRSPACE

INTRODUCTION

This chapter introduces the various classifications of airspace and provides information on the requirements to operate in such airspace. Further information can be found in the Aeronautical Information Manual.

The two categories of airspace are: regulatory and nonregulatory. Within these two categories there are four types: controlled, uncontrolled, special use, and other airspace.

Figure 7-1 presents a profile view of the dimensions of various classes of airspace. Figure 7-2 gives the basic weather minimums for operating in the different classes of airspace. Figure 7-3 lists the operational and equipment requirements. It will be helpful to refer to these figures as this chapter is studied. Also there are excerpts from sectional charts in Chapter 8, Navigation, that will show how airspace is depicted.

CONTROLLED AIRSPACE

Controlled airspace is a generic term that covers the different classifications of airspace and defined dimensions within which air traffic control service is provided in accordance with the airspace classification. Controlled airspace consists of:

- Class A
- Class B
- Class C
- Class D
- Class E

Class A Airspace

Class A airspace is generally the airspace from 18,000 feet mean sea level (MSL) up to and including FL600, including the airspace overlying the waters within 12 nautical miles (NM) of the coast of the 48 contiguous United States and Alaska. Unless otherwise authorized, all operation in Class A airspace will be conducted under instrument flight rules (IFR).

Class B Airspace

Class B airspace is generally the airspace from the surface to 10,000 feet MSL surrounding the nation's busiest airports. The configuration of Class B airspace is individually tailored to the needs of a particular area and consists of a surface area and two or more layers. Some Class B airspace resembles an upside-down wedding cake. At least a private pilot certificate is required to operate in Class B airspace; however, there is an exception to this requirement. Student pilots or recreational pilots seeking private pilot certification may operate in the airspace and land at other than specified primary airports within the airspace if they have received training and had their logbook endorsed by a certified flight instructor in accordance with 14 CFR part 61.

Class C Airspace

Class C airspace generally extends from the surface to 4,000 feet above the airport elevation surrounding those airports having an operational control tower, that are serviced by a radar approach control, and with a certain number of IFR operations or passenger enplanements. This airspace is charted in feet MSL, and is generally of a 5 NM radius surface area that extends from the surface to 4,000 feet above the airport elevation, and a 10 NM radius area that extends from 1,200 feet to 4,000 feet above the airport elevation. There is also an outer area with a 20 NM radius which extends from the surface to 4,000 feet above the primary airport and this area may include one or more satellite airports.

Class D Airspace

Class D airspace generally extends from the surface to 2,500 feet above the airport elevation surrounding those airports that have an operational control tower. The configuration of Class D airspace

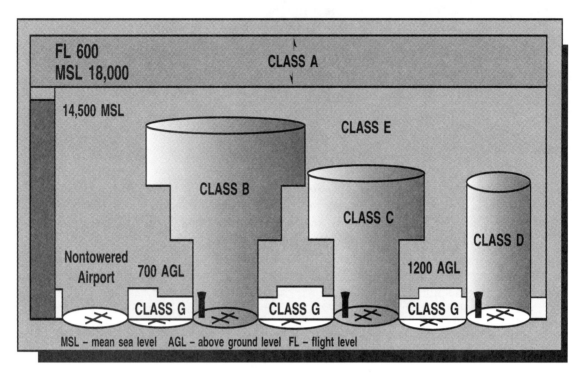

FIGURE 7-1.—Airspace profile.

BASIC VFR WEATHER MINIMUMS		
Airspace	Flight Visibility	Distance from Clouds
Class A	Not Applicable	Not Applicable
Class B	3 statute miles	Clear of Clouds
Class C	3 statute miles	500 feet below 1,000 feet above 2,000 feet horizontal
Class D	3 statute miles	500 feet below 1,000 feet above 2,000 feet horizontal
Class E Less than 10,000 feet MSL	3 statute miles	500 feet below 1,000 feet above 2,000 feet horizontal
At or above 10,000 feet MSL	5 statute miles	1,000 feet below 1,000 feet above 1 statute mile horizontal
Class G 1,200 feet or less above the surface (regardless of MSL altitude).. Day, except as provided in section 91.155(b).	1 statute mile	Clear of clouds
Night, except as provided in section 91.155(b).	3 statute miles	500 feet below 1,000 feet above 2,000 feet horizontal
More than 1,200 feet above the surface but less than 10,000 feet MSL.. Day	1 statute mile	500 feet below 1,000 feet above 2,000 feet horizontal
Night	3 statute miles	500 feet below 1,000 feet above 2,000 feet horizontal
More than 1,200 feet above the surface and at or above 10,000 feet MSL..	5 statute miles	1,000 feet below 1,000 feet above 1 statute mile horizontal

FIGURE 7-2.—Visual flight rule weather minimums.

Class Airspace	Entry Requirements	Equipment	Minimum Pilot Certificate
A	ATC Clearance	IFR Equipped	Instrument Rating
B	ATC Clearance	Two-Way Radio Transponder with Altitude Reporting Capability	Private—Except a student or recreational pilot may operate at other than the primary airport if seeking private pilot certification and if regulatory requirements are met.
C	Two-Way Radio Communications Prior to Entry	Two-Way Radio Transponder with Altitude Reporting Capability	No Specific Requirement
D	Two-Way Radio Communications Prior to Entry	Two-Way Radio	No Specific Requirement
E	None for VFR	No Specific Requirements	No Specific Requirement
G	None	No Specific Requirements	No Specific Requirement

Figure 7-3.—Requirements for airspace operations.

will be tailored to meet the operational needs of the area.

Class E Airspace

Class E airspace is generally controlled airspace that is not designated A, B, C, or D. Except for 18,000 feet MSL, Class E airspace has no defined vertical limit, but rather it extends upward from either the surface or a designated altitude to the overlying or adjacent controlled airspace.

UNCONTROLLED AIRSPACE

Class G Airspace

Uncontrolled airspace or Class G airspace is the portion of the airspace that has not been designated as Class A, B, C, D, or E. It is therefore designated uncontrolled airspace. Class G airspace extends from the surface to the base of the overlying Class E airspace. Although air traffic control (ATC) has no authority or responsibility to control air traffic, pilots should remember there are VFR minimums which apply to Class G airspace.

SPECIAL USE AIRSPACE

Special use airspace exists where activities must be confined because of their nature. In special use airspace, limitations may be placed on aircraft that are not a part of the activities. Special use airspace usually consists of:

- Prohibited Areas
- Restricted Areas
- Warning Areas
- Military Operation Areas
- Alert Areas
- Controlled Firing Areas
- National Securtity Areas

Prohibited Areas

Prohibited areas are established for security or other reasons associated with the national welfare. Prohibited areas are published in the Federal Register and are depicted on aeronautical charts.

Restricted Areas

Restricted areas denote the existence of unusual, often invisible hazards to aircraft such as artillery firing, aerial gunnery, or guided missiles. An aircraft may not enter a restricted area unless permission has been obtained from the controlling agency. Restricted areas are depicted on aeronautical charts and are published in the Federal Register.

Warning Areas

Warning areas consist of airspace which may contain hazards to nonparticipating aircraft in international airspace. The activities may be much the same as those for a restricted area. Warning areas are established beyond the 3-mile limit. Warning areas are depicted on aeronautical charts.

Military Operation Areas

Military operation areas (MOA) consist of airspace of defined vertical and lateral limits established for the purpose of separating certain military training activity from IFR traffic. There is no restriction against a pilot operating VFR in these areas; however, a pilot should be alert since training activities may include acrobatic and abrupt maneuvers. MOAs are depicted on aeronautical charts.

Alert Areas

Alert areas are depicted on aeronautical charts and are to advise pilots that a high volume of pilot training or unusual aerial activity is taking place.

Controlled Firing Areas

Controlled firing areas contain activities, which, if not conducted in a controlled environment, could be hazardous to nonparticipating aircraft. The difference between controlled firing areas and other special use airspace is that activities must be suspended when a spotter aircraft, radar, or ground lookout position indicates an aircraft might be approaching the area.

National Security Areas

National security areas consist of airspace of defined vertical and lateral dimensions established at locations where there is a requirement for increased security and safety of ground facilities. Pilots are requested to voluntarily avoid flying through these depicted areas. When necessary, flight may be temporarily prohibited.

OTHER AIRSPACE AREAS

"Other airspace areas" is a general term referring to the majority of the remaining airspace. It includes:

- Airport Advisory Areas
- Military Training Routes (MTR)
- Temporary Flight Restrictions
- Parachute Jump Areas
- Published VFR Routes

Airport Advisory Areas

An airport advisory area is an area within 10 SM of an airport where a control tower is not operating, but where a flight service station (FSS) is located. At these locations, the FSS provides advisory service to arriving and departing aircraft.

Military Training Routes

Military training routes (MTR) are developed to allow the military to conduct low-altitude, high-speed training. The routes above 1,500 feet AGL are developed to be flown primarily under IFR, and the routes 1,500 feet and less are for VFR flight. The routes are identified on sectional charts by the designation "instrument (IR) or visual (VR)."

Temporary Flight Restrictions

Temporary flight restrictions are established, when required, to protect persons and property in the air or on the surface. The intent of these restrictions is to provide a safe environment for relief or rescue aircraft, eliminate congestion which might occur in airspace over special events, protect airspace in the vicinity of presidential flights, etc. Many times the FSS coordinates temporary flight restrictions, and when necessary, a Notice to Airmen is issued.

Parachute Jump Areas

Parachute jump areas are published in the Airport/Facility Directory. Sites that are used frequently are depicted on sectional charts.

Published VFR Routes

Published VFR routes are for transitioning around, under, or through some complex airspace. Terms such as VFR flyway, VFR corridor, Class B airspace, VFR transition route, and terminal area VFR route have been applied to such routes. These routes are generally found on VFR terminal area planning charts.

CHAPTER 8

NAVIGATION

INTRODUCTION

This chapter provides an introduction to cross-country flying under visual flight rules (VFR). It contains practical information for planning and executing cross-country flights for the beginning pilot.

Air navigation is simply the process of piloting an airplane from one geographic position to another while monitoring one's position as the flight progresses. It introduces the need for planning, which includes plotting the course on an aeronautical chart, selecting checkpoints, measuring distances, obtaining pertinent weather information, and computing flight time, headings, and fuel requirements. The methods used in this chapter include pilotage—navigating by reference to visible landmarks, dead reckoning—computations of direction and distance from a known position, and radio navigation—by use of radio aids.

AERONAUTICAL CHARTS

An aeronautical chart is the road map for a pilot flying under VFR. The chart provides information which allows pilots to track their position and provides available information which enhances safety. The three aeronautical charts used by VFR pilots are:

- Sectional Charts
- VFR Terminal Area Charts
- World Aeronautical Charts

A free catalog listing aeronautical charts and related publications including prices and instructions for ordering is available upon request from:

NOAA Distribution Branch (N/CG33)
National Ocean Survey
Riverdale, MD 20737-1199
Telephone: (301) 436-6990

Sectional Charts

Sectional charts are the most common charts used by pilots today. The charts have a scale of 1:500,000 (1 inch = 6.86 nautical miles or 8 statute miles) which allows for more detailed information to be included on the chart.

The charts provide an abundance of information, including airport data, navigational aids, airspace, and topography etc. Figure 8-1 is an excerpt from the legend of a sectional chart. By referring to the chart legend, a pilot can interpret most of the information on the chart. A pilot should also check the chart for other legend information which includes air traffic control frequencies and information on airspace. These charts are revised semiannually except for some areas outside the contiguous United States where they are revised annually.

Visual Flight Rule (VFR) Terminal Area Charts

Visual flight rule terminal area charts are helpful when flying in or near Class B airspace. They have a scale of 1:250,000 (1 inch =3.43 nautical miles or 4 statute miles). These charts provide a more detailed display of topographical information and are revised semiannually, except for several Alaskan and Caribbean charts.

World Aeronautical Charts

World aeronautical charts are designed to provide a standard series of aeronautical charts, covering land areas of the world, at a size and scale convenient for navigation by moderate speed aircraft. They are produced at a scale of 1:1,000,000 (1 inch = 13.7 nautical miles (NM) or 16 statute miles). These charts are similar to sectional charts and the symbols are the same except there is less detail due to the smaller scale. These charts are revised annually except several Alaskan charts and the Mexican/Caribbean charts which are revised every 2 years.

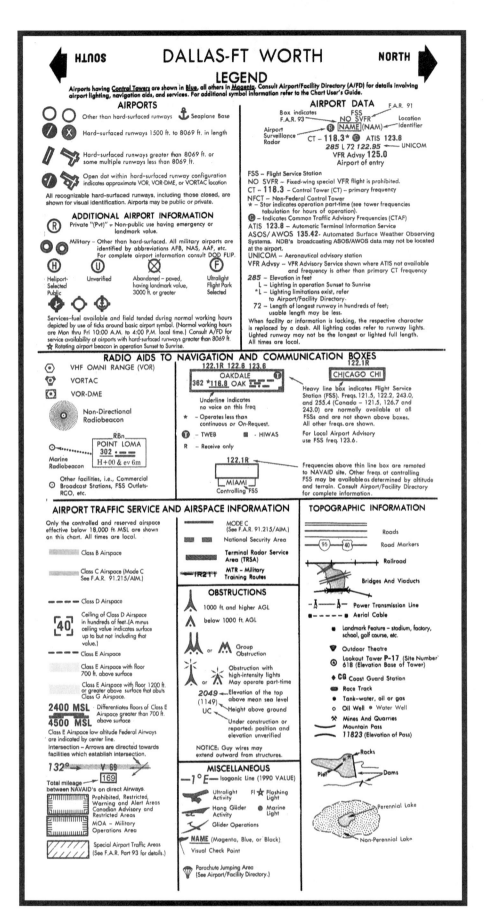

FIGURE 8-1.—Sectional chart legend.

LATITUDE AND LONGITUDE (MERIDIANS AND PARALLELS)

The Equator is an imaginary circle equidistant from the poles of the Earth. Circles parallel to the Equator (lines running east and west) are parallels of latitude. They are used to measure degrees of latitude north or south of the Equator. The angular distance from the Equator to the pole is one-fourth of a circle or 90°. The 48 conterminous states of the United States are located between 25° and 49° N. latitude. The arrows in figure 8-2 labeled "LATITUDE" point to lines of latitude.

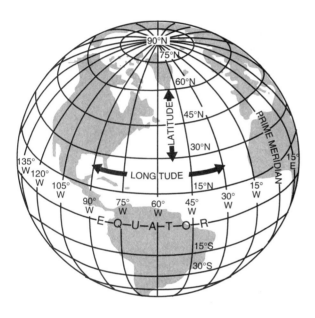

FIGURE 8-2.—Meridians and parallels—the basis of measuring time, distance, and direction.

Meridians of longitude are drawn from the North Pole to the South Pole and are at right angles to the Equator. The "Prime Meridian" which passes through Greenwich, England, is used as the zero line from which measurements are made in degrees east and west to 180°. The 48 conterminous states of the United States are between 67° and 125° W. Longitude. The arrows in figure 8-2 labeled "LONGITUDE" point to lines of longitude.

Any specific geographical point can thus be located by reference to its longitude and latitude. Washington, DC for example, is approximately 39° N. latitude, 77° W. longitude. Chicago is approximately 42° N. latitude, 88° W. longitude.

Time Zones

The meridians are also useful for designating time zones. A day is defined as the time required for the Earth to make one complete revolution of 360°. Since the day is divided into 24 hours, the Earth revolves at the rate of 15° an hour. Noon is the time when the Sun is directly above a meridian; to the west of that meridian is forenoon, to the east is afternoon.

The standard practice is to establish a time zone for each 15° of longitude. This makes a difference of exactly 1 hour between each zone. In the United States, there are four time zones. The time zones are Eastern (75°), Central (90°), Mountain (105°), and Pacific (120°). The dividing lines are somewhat irregular because communities near the boundaries often find it more convenient to use time designations of neighboring communities or trade centers.

Figure 8-3 shows the time zones in the United States. When the Sun is directly above the 90th meridian, it is noon Central Standard Time. At the same time, it will be 1 p.m. Eastern Standard Time, 11 a.m. Mountain Standard Time, and 10 a.m. Pacific Standard Time. When "daylight saving" time is in effect, generally between the last Sunday in April and the last Sunday in October, the Sun is directly above the 75th meridian at noon, Central Daylight Time.

These time zone differences must be taken into account during long flights eastward—especially if the flight must be completed before dark. Remember, an hour is lost when flying eastward from one time zone to another, or perhaps even when flying from the western edge to the eastern edge of the same time zone. Determine the time of sunset at the destination by consulting the flight service stations (AFSS/FSS) or National Weather Service and take this into account when planning an eastbound flight.

FIGURE 8-3.—Time zones.

In most aviation operations, time is expressed in terms of the 24-hour clock. Air traffic control instructions, weather reports and broadcasts, and estimated times of arrival are all based on this system. For example: 9 a.m. is expressed as 0900; 1 p.m. is 1300; 10 p.m. is 2200 etc.

Because a pilot may cross several time zones during a flight, a standard time system has been adopted. It is called Universal Coordinated Time (UTC) and is often referred to as Zulu time. UTC is the time at the 0° line of longitude which passes through Greenwich, England. All of the time zones around the world are based on this reference. To convert to this time, a pilot should do the following:

- Eastern Standard Time   Add 5 hours
- Central Standard Time   Add 6 hours
- Mountain Standard Time   Add 7 hours
- Pacific Standard Time   Add 8 hours

For daylight saving time, 1 hour should be subtracted from the calculated times.

Measurement of Direction

By using the meridians, direction from one point to another can be measured in degrees, in a clockwise direction from true north. To indicate a course to be followed in flight, draw a line on the chart from the point of departure to the destination and measure the angle which this line forms with a meridian. Direction is expressed in degrees, as shown by the compass rose in figure 8-4.

FIGURE 8-4.—Compass rose.

Because meridians converge toward the poles, course measurement should be taken at a meridian near the midpoint of the course rather than at the point of departure. The course measured on the chart is known as the true course. This is the direction measured by reference to a meridian or true north. It is the direction of intended flight as measured in degrees clockwise from true north. As shown in figure 8-5, the direction from A to B would be a true course of 065°, whereas the return trip (called the reciprocal) would be a true course of 245°.

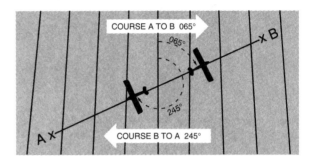

FIGURE 8-5.—Courses are determined by reference to meridians on aeronautical charts.

The true heading is the direction in which the nose of the airplane points during a flight when measured in degrees clockwise from true north. Usually, it is necessary to head the airplane in a direction slightly different from the true course to offset the effect of wind. Consequently, numerical value of the true heading may not correspond with that of the true course. This will be discussed more fully in subsequent sections in this chapter. For the purpose of this discussion, assume a no-wind condition exists under which heading and course would coincide. Thus, for a true course of 065°, the true heading would be 065°. To use the compass accurately, however, corrections must be made for magnetic variation and compass deviation.

Variation

Variation is the angle between true north and magnetic north. It is expressed as east variation or west variation depending upon whether magnetic north (MN) is to the east or west of true north (TN), respectively.

The north magnetic pole is located close to 71° N. latitude, 96° W. longitude and is about 1,300 miles from the geographic or true north pole, as indicated in figure 8-6. If the Earth were uniformly magnetized, the compass needle would point toward the magnetic pole, in which case the variation between true north (as shown by the geographical meridians) and such magnetic north (as shown by the magnetic meridians) could be measured at any intersection of the meridians.

Actually, the Earth is not uniformly magnetized. In the United States the needle usually points in the general direction of the magnetic pole, but it may vary in certain geographical localities by many degrees. Consequently, the exact amount of variation at thousands of selected locations in the United States has been carefully determined. The amount and the direction of variation, which change slightly from time to time, are shown on most aeronautical charts as broken magenta lines, called isogonic lines, which connects points of equal magnetic variation. (The line connecting points at which there is no variation between true north and magnetic north is the agonic line.) An isogonic chart is shown in figure 8-6. Minor bends and turns in the isogonic and agonic lines are caused by unusual geological conditions affecting magnetic forces in these areas.

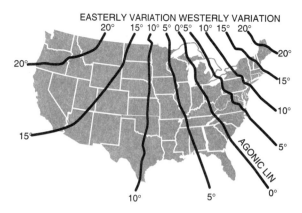

Figure 8-7.—A typical isogonic chart. The black lines are isogonic lines which connect geographic points with identical magnetic variation.

Because courses are measured in reference to geographical meridians which point toward true north, and these courses are maintained by reference to the compass which points along a magnetic meridian in the general direction of magnetic north, the true direction must be converted into magnetic direction for the purpose of flight. This conversion is made by adding or subtracting the variation which is indicated by the nearest isogonic line on the chart. The true heading, when corrected for variation, is known as magnetic heading.

If the variation is shown as "9 °E," this means that magnetic north is 9° east of true north. If a true heading of 360° is to be flown, 9° must be subtracted from 360°, which results in a magnetic heading of 351°. To fly east, a magnetic heading of 081° (090° - 9°) would be flown. To fly south, the magnetic heading would be 171° (180° - 9°). To fly west, it would be 261° (270° - 9°). To fly a true heading of 060°, a magnetic heading of 051° (060° - 9°) would be flown.

Remember, to convert true course or heading to magnetic course or heading, note the variation shown by the nearest isogonic line. If variation is west, add; if east, subtract. One method for remembering whether to add or subtract variation is the phrase "east is least (subtract) and west is best (add)."

Deviation

Determining the magnetic heading is an intermediate step necessary to obtain the correct compass reading for the flight. To determine compass heading, a correction for deviation must be made. Because of magnetic influences within the airplane such as electrical circuits, radio, lights, tools, engine, magnetized metal parts, etc., the compass needle is frequently deflected from its normal reading. This

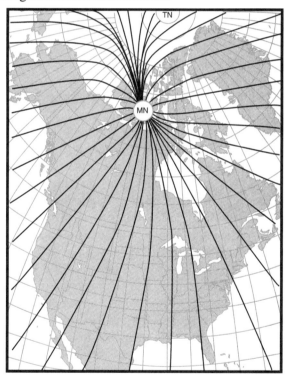

Figure 8-6.—Isogonic chart. Magnetic meridians are in black, geographic meridians and parallels are in blue. Variation is the angle between a magnetic and geographic meridian.

On the west coast of the United States, the compass needle points to the east of true north; on the east coast, the compass needle points to the west of true north. Zero degree variation exists on the agonic line which runs roughly through Lake Michigan, the Appalachian Mountains, and off the coast of Florida, where magnetic north and true north coincide. [Compare figures 8-7 and 8-8]

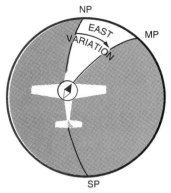
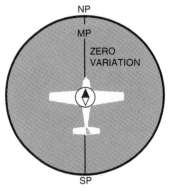
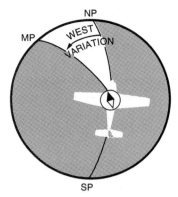

Compass needle pointing east of true north | Compass needle pointing to true north (along agonic line) | Compass needle pointing west of true north

FIGURE 8-8.—*Effect of variation on the compass.*

deflection is deviation. The deviation is different for each airplane, and it also may vary for different headings in the same airplane. For instance, if magnetism in the engine attracts the north end of the compass, there would be no effect when the plane is on a heading of magnetic north. On easterly or westerly headings, however, the compass indications would be in error, as shown in figure 8-9. Magnetic attraction can come from many other parts of the airplane; the assumption of attraction in the engine is merely used for the purpose of illustration.

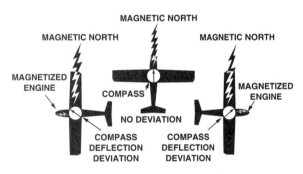

FIGURE 8-9.—*Magnetized portions of the airplane cause the compass to deviate from its normal indications.*

Some adjustment of the compass, referred to as compensation, can be made to reduce this error, but the remaining correction must be applied by the pilot.

Proper compensation of the compass is best performed by a competent technician. Since the magnetic forces within the airplane change, because of landing shocks, vibration, mechanical work, or changes in equipment, the pilot should occasionally have the deviation of the compass checked. The procedure used to check the deviation (called "swinging the compass") is briefly outlined.

The airplane is placed on a magnetic compass rose, the engine started, and electrical devices normally used (such as radio) are turned on. Tailwheel-type airplanes should be jacked up into flying position. The airplane is aligned with magnetic north indicated on the compass rose and the reading shown on the compass is recorded on a deviation card. The airplane is then aligned at 30° intervals and each reading is recorded. If the airplane is to be flown at night, the lights are turned on and any significant changes in the readings are noted. If so, additional entries are made for use at night.

The accuracy of the compass can also be checked by comparing the compass reading with the known runway headings.

On the compass card, the letters, N, E, S, and W, are used for north, east, south, and west. The final zero is omitted from the degree markings so that figures will be larger and more easily seen.

A deviation card, similar to figure 8-10, is mounted near the compass, showing the addition or subtraction required to correct for deviation on various headings, usually at intervals of 30°. For intermediate readings, the pilot should be able to interpolate mentally with sufficient accuracy. For example, if the pilot needed the correction for 195° and noted the correction for 180° to be 0° and for 210° to be +2°, it could be assumed that the correction for 195° would be +1°. The magnetic heading, when corrected for deviation, is known as compass heading.

FOR (MAGNETIC)..........	N	30	60	E	120	150
STEER (COMPASS).......	0	28	57	86	117	148
FOR (MAGNETIC)..........	S	210	240	W	300	330
STEER (COMPASS).......	180	212	243	274	303	332

FIGURE 8-10.—*Compass deviation card.*

The following method is used by many pilots to determine compass heading:

After the true course (TC) is measured, and wind

correction applied resulting in a true heading (TH), the sequence $TH \pm V = MH \pm D = C_H$ is followed to arrive at compass heading. [Figure 8-11]

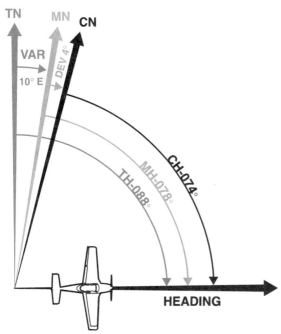

FIGURE 8-11.—Relationship between true, magnetic, and compass headings for a particular instance.

EFFECT OF WIND

The preceding discussion explained how to measure a true course on the aeronautical chart and how to make corrections for variation and deviation, but one important factor has not been considered—wind. As discussed in the study of the atmosphere, wind is a mass of air moving over the surface of the Earth in a definite direction. When the wind is blowing from the north at 25 knots, it simply means that air is moving southward over the Earth's surface at the rate of 25 NM in 1 hour.

Under these conditions, any inert object free from contact with the Earth will be carried 25 NM southward in 1 hour. This effect becomes apparent when clouds, dust, toy balloons, etc., are observed being blown along by the wind. Obviously, an airplane flying within the moving mass of air will be similarly affected. Even though the airplane does not float freely with the wind, it moves through the air at the same time the air is moving over the ground, thus is affected by wind. Consequently, at the end of 1 hour of flight, the airplane will be in a position which results from a combination of these two motions:

• the movement of the air mass in reference to the ground, and

• the forward movement of the airplane through the air mass.

Actually, these two motions are independent. So far as the airplane's flight through the air is concerned, it makes no difference whether the mass of air though which the airplane is flying is moving or is stationary. A pilot flying in a 70-knot gale would be totally unaware of any wind (except for possible turbulence) unless the ground were observed. In reference to the ground, however, the airplane would appear to fly faster with a tailwind or slower with a headwind, or to drift right or left with a crosswind.

As shown in figure 8-12, an airplane flying eastward at an airspeed of 120 knots in calm wind, will have a groundspeed exactly the same—120 knots. If the mass of air is moving eastward at 20 knots, the airspeed of the airplane will not be affected, but the progress of the airplane over the ground will be 120 plus 20, or a groundspeed of 140 knots. On the other hand, if the mass of air is moving westward at 20 knots, the airspeed of the airplane still remains the same, but groundspeed becomes 120 minus 20 or 100 knots.

Assuming no correction is made for wind effect, if the airplane is heading eastward at 120 knots, and

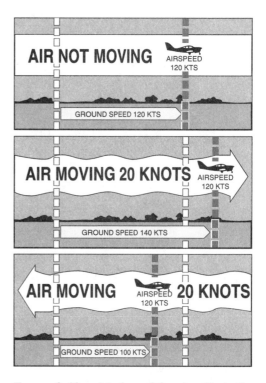

FIGURE 8-12.—Motion of the air affects the speed with which airplanes move over the Earth's surface. Airspeed, the rate at which an airplane moves through the air, is not affected by air motion.

the air mass moving southward at 20 knots, and the airplane at the end of 1 hour will be 120 miles east of its point of departure because of its progress through the air. It will be 20 miles south because of the motion of the air. Under these circumstances, the airspeed remains 120 knots, but the groundspeed is determined by combining the movement of the airplane with that of the air mass. Groundspeed can be measured as the distance from the point of departure to the position of the airplane at the end of 1 hour. The groundspeed can be computed by the time required to fly between two points a known distance apart. It also can be determined before flight by constructing a wind triangle, which will be explained later in this chapter. [Figure 8-13]

FIGURE 8-13.—Airplane flightpath resulting from its airspeed and direction, and the windspeed and direction.

The direction in which the plane is pointing as it flies is heading. Its actual path over the ground, which is a combination of the motion of the airplane and the motion of the air, is track. The angle between the heading and the track is drift angle. If the airplane's heading coincides with the true course and the wind is blowing from the left, the track will not coincide with the true course. The wind will drift the airplane to the right, so the track will fall to the right of the desired course or true course. [Figure 8-14]

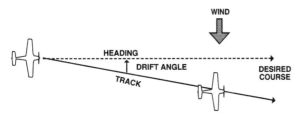

FIGURE 8-14.—Effects of wind drift on maintaining desired course.

By determining the amount of drift, the pilot can counteract the effect of the wind and make the track of the airplane coincide with the desired course. If the mass of air is moving across the course from the left, the airplane will drift to the right, and a correction must be made by heading the airplane sufficiently to the left to offset this drift. To state in another way, if the wind is from the left, the correction will be made

by pointing the airplane to the left a certain number of degrees, therefore correcting for wind drift. This is wind correction angle and is expressed in term of degrees right or left of the true course. [Figure 8-15]

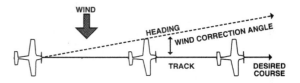

FIGURE 8-15.—Establishing a wind correction angle that will counteract wind drift and maintain the desired course.

To summarize:
• **COURSE**— is the intended path of an aircraft over the Earth; or the direction of a line drawn on a chart representing the intended aircraft path, expressed as the angle measured from a specific reference datum clockwise from 0° through 360° to the line.
• **HEADING**— is the direction in which the nose of the airplane points during flight.
• **TRACK**—is the actual path made over the ground in flight. (If proper correction has been made for the wind, track and course will be identical.)
• **DRIFT ANGLE**—is the angle between heading and track.
• **WIND CORRECTION ANGLE**—is correction applied to the course to establish a heading so that track will coincide with course.
• **AIRSPEED**—is the rate of the airplane's progress through the air.
• **GROUNDSPEED**—is the rate of the airplane's in-flight progress over the ground.

BASIC CALCULATIONS

Before a cross-country flight, a pilot should make common calculations for time, speed, and distance, and the amount of fuel required. These calculations should present no difficulty.

Converting Minutes to Equivalent Hours

It frequently is necessary to convert minutes into equivalent hours when solving speed, time, and distance problems. To convert minutes to hours, divide by 60 (60 minutes = 1 hour). Thus, 30 minutes 30/60 = 0.5 hour. To convert hours to minutes, multiply by 60. Thus, 0.75 hour equals 0.75 x 60 = 45 minutes.

Time T = D/GS

To find the **time** (T) in flight, divide the **distance** (D) by the **groundspeed** (GS). The time to fly 210 nautical miles at a groundspeed of 140 knots is 210 divided by 140, or 1.5 hours. (The 0.5 hour multiplied by 60 minutes equal 30 minutes.) Answer: 1:30.

Distance D = GS X T

To find the distance flown in a given time, multiply groundspeed by time. The distance flown in 1 hour 45 minutes at a groundspeed of 120 knots is 120 x 1.75, or 210 nautical miles.

Groundspeed GS = D/T

To find the groundspeed, divide the distance flown by the time required. If an airplane flies 270 NM in 3 hours, the groundspeed is 270 divided by 3 = 90 knots.

Converting Knots to Miles Per Hour

Another conversion is that of changing knots to miles per hour. The aviation industry is using knots more frequently than miles per hour, but it might be well to discuss the conversion for those who do use miles per hour when working with speed problems. The National Weather Service reports both surface winds and winds aloft in knots. However, airspeed indicators in some airplanes are calibrated in miles per hour (although many are now calibrated in both miles per hour and knots). Pilots, therefore, should learn to convert windspeeds in knots to miles per hour.

A knot is 1 nautical mile per hour. Because there are 6,076.1 feet in a nautical mile and 5,280 feet in a statute mile, the conversion factor is 1.15. To convert knots to miles per hour, multiply knots by 1.15. For example: a windspeed of 20 knots is equivalent to 23 MPH.

Most flight computers or electronic calculators have a means of making this conversion. Another quick method of conversion is to use the scales of nautical miles and statute miles at the bottom of aeronautical charts.

Fuel Consumption

Airplane fuel consumption rate is computed in gallons per hour. Consequently, to determine the fuel required for a given flight, the time required for the flight must be known. Time in flight multiplied by rate of consumption gives the quantity of fuel required. For example, a flight of 400 NM at a groundspeed of 100 knots requires 4 hours. If the plane consumes 5 gallons an hour, the total consumption will be 4 x 5, or 20 gallons.

The rate of fuel consumption depends on many factors: condition of the engine, propeller pitch, propeller RPM, richness of the mixture, and particularly the percentage of horsepower used for flight at cruising speed. The pilot should know the approximate consumption rate from cruise performance charts, or from experience. In addition to the amount of fuel required for the flight, there should be sufficient fuel for reserve.

Flight Computers

Up to this point, only mathematical formulas have been used to determine time, distance, speed, fuel consumption, etc. In reality, most pilots will use a mechanical or electronic flight computer. These devices can compute numerous problems associated with flight planning and navigation. The mechanical or electronic computer will have an instruction book and most likely sample problems so the pilot can become familiar with its functions and operation. [Figure 8-16]

Plotter

Another aid in flight planning is a plotter, which is a protractor and ruler. The pilot can use this when determining true course and measuring distance. Most plotters have a ruler which measures in both nautical and statute miles and has a scale for a sectional chart on one side and a world aeronautical chart on the other. [Figure 8-16]

PILOTAGE

Pilotage is navigation by reference to landmarks or checkpoints. It is a method of navigation that can be used on any course that has adequate checkpoints, but it is more commonly used in conjunction with dead reckoning and VFR radio navigation.

The checkpoints selected should be prominent features common to the area of the flight. Choose checkpoints that can be readily identified by other features such as roads, rivers, railroad tracks, lakes, power lines, etc. If possible, select features that will make useful boundaries or brackets on each side of the course, such as highways, rivers, railroads, mountains, etc. A pilot can keep from drifting too far off course by referring to and not crossing the selected brackets. Never place complete reliance on any single checkpoint. Choose ample checkpoints. If one is missed, look for the next one while maintaining the heading. When determining position from

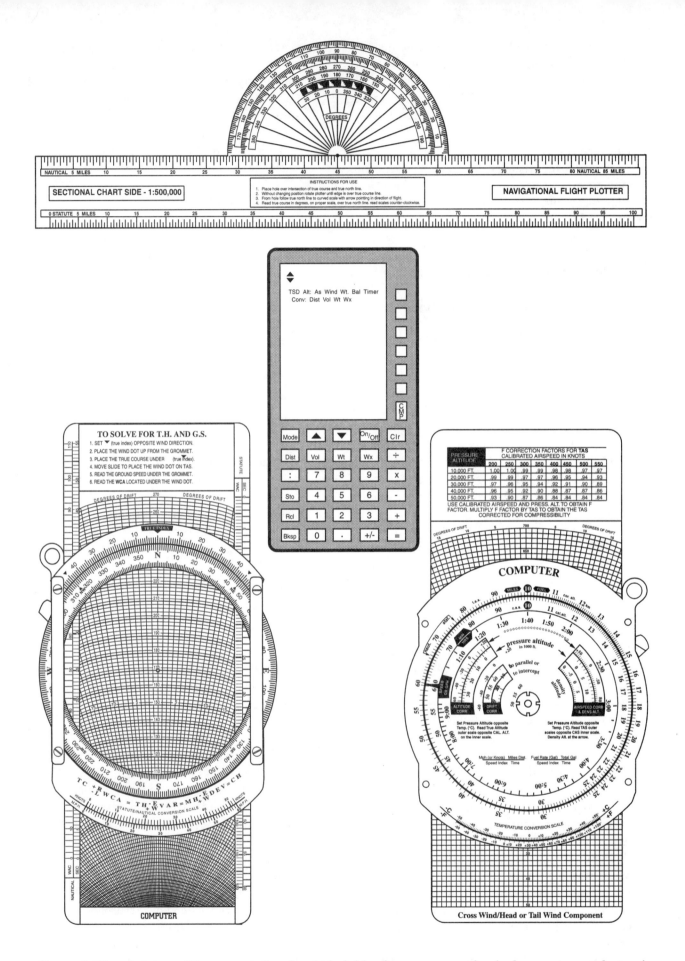

FIGURE 8-16.—A picture of the computational and wind side of a common mechanical computer, an electronic computer, and plotter.

checkpoints, remember that the scale of a sectional chart is 1 inch = 8 statute miles or 6.86 nautical miles. For example, if a checkpoint selected was approximately one-half inch from the course line on the chart, it is 4 statue miles or 3.43 nautical miles from the course on the ground. In the more congested areas, some of the smaller features are not included on the chart. If confused, hold the heading. If a turn is made away from the heading, it will be easy to become lost.

Roads shown on the chart are primarily the well traveled roads or those most apparent when viewed from the air. New roads and structures are constantly being built, and may not be shown on the chart until the next chart is issued. Some structures, such as antennas may be difficult to see. Sometimes TV antennas are grouped together in an area near a town. They are supported by almost invisible guy wires. Never approach an area of antennas less than 500 feet above the tallest one. Most of the taller structures are marked with strobe lights to make them more visible to a pilot. However, some weather conditions or background lighting may make them difficult to see. Aeronautical charts display the best information available at the time of printing, but a pilot should be cautious for new structures or changes that have occurred since the chart was printed.

DEAD RECKONING

Dead reckoning is navigation solely by means of computations based on time, airspeed, distance, and direction. The products derived from these variables, when adjusted by windspeed and velocity, are heading and groundspeed. The predicted heading will guide the airplane along the intended path and the groundspeed will establish the time to arrive at each checkpoint and the destination. The word "dead" in dead reckoning is actually derived from "ded," or deduced reckoning. Except for flights over water, dead reckoning is usually used with pilotage for cross-country flying. The heading and groundspeed as calculated is constantly monitored and corrected by pilotage as observed from checkpoints.

The Wind Triangle or Vector Analysis

If there is no wind, the airplane's ground track will be the same as the heading and the groundspeed will be the same as the true airspeed. Only on rare occasions does this condition exist. A wind triangle, the pilot's version of vector analysis, is the backbone of dead reckoning.

The wind triangle is a graphic explanation of the effect of wind upon flight. Groundspeed, heading, and time for any flight can be determined by using the wind triangle. It can be applied to the simplest kind of cross-country flight as well as the most complicated instrument flight. The experienced pilot becomes so familiar with the fundamental principles that estimates can be made which are adequate for visual flight without actually drawing the diagrams. The beginning student, however, needs to develop skill in constructing these diagrams as an aid to the complete understanding of wind effect. Either consciously or unconsciously, every good pilot thinks of the flight in terms of wind triangle.

If a flight is to be made on a course to the east, with a wind blowing from northeast, the airplane must be headed somewhat to the north of east to counteract drift. This can be represented by a diagram as shown in figure 8-17. Each line represents direction and speed. The long dotted line shows the direction the plane is heading, and its length represents the airspeed for 1 hour. The short dotted line at the right shows the wind direction, and its length represents the wind velocity for 1 hour. The solid line shows the direction of the track, or the path of the airplane as measured over the Earth, and its length represents the distance traveled in 1 hour, or the groundspeed.

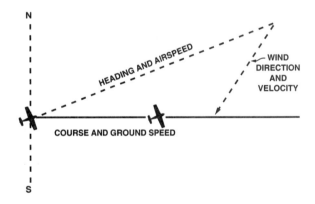

FIGURE 8-17.—Principle of the wind triangle.

In actual practice, the triangle illustrated in figure 8-17 is not drawn; instead, construct a similar triangle as shown by the black lines in figure 8-18, which is explained in the following example.

Suppose a flight is to be flown from E to P. Draw a line on the aeronautical chart connecting these two points, measure its direction with a protractor, or plotter, in reference to a meridian. This is the true course which in this example is assumed to be 090° (east). From the National Weather Service, it is learned that the wind at the altitude of the intended flight is 40 knots from the northeast (045°). Since the National Weather Service reports the windspeed in knots, if the true airspeed of the airplane is 120 knots, there is no need to convert speeds from knots to MPH or vice versa.

Now on a plain sheet of paper draw a vertical line representing north and south. (The various steps are shown in figure 8-19.)

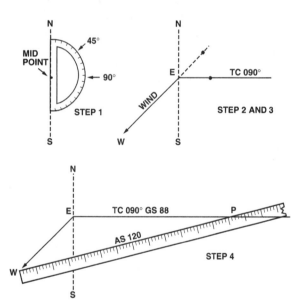

FIGURE 8-18.—*The wind triangle as is drawn in navigation practice. Blue lines show the triangle as drawn in figure 8-17.*

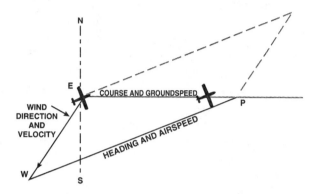

FIGURE 8-19.—*Steps in drawing the wind triangle.*

Place the protractor with the base resting on the vertical line and the curved edge facing east. At the center point of the base, make a dot labeled "E" (point of departure), and at the curved edge, make a dot at 90° (indicating the direction of the true course) and another at 45° (indicating wind direction).

With the ruler, draw the true course line from E, extending it somewhat beyond the dot by 90°, and labeling it "TC 090°."

Next, align the ruler with E and the dot at 45°,

and draw the wind arrow from E, not toward 045°, but downwind in the direction the wind is blowing, making it 40 units long, to correspond with the wind velocity of 40 knots. Identify this line as the wind line by placing the letter "W" at the end to show the wind direction. Finally, measure 120 units on the ruler to represent the airspeed, making a dot on the ruler at this point. The units used may be of any convenient scale or value (such as 1/4 inch = 10 knots), but once selected, the same scale must be used for each of the linear movements involved. Then place the ruler so that the end is on the arrowhead (W) and the 120 knot dot intercepts the true course line. Draw the line and label it "AS 120." The point "P" placed at the intersection, represents the position of the airplane at the end of 1 hour. The diagram is now complete.

The distance flown in 1 hour (groundspeed) is measured as the numbers of units on the true course line (88 nautical miles per hour or 88 knots).

The true heading necessary to offset drift is indicated by the direction of the airspeed line which can be determined in one of two ways:

• By placing the straight side of the protractor along the north-south line, with its center point at the intersection of the airspeed line and north-south line, read the true heading directly in degrees (076°). [Figure 8-20]
• By placing the straight side of the protractor along the true course line, with its center at P, read the angle between the true course and the airspeed line. This is the wind correction angle (WCA) which must be applied to the true course to obtain the true heading. If the wind blows from the right of true course, the angle will be added; if from the left, it will be subtracted. In the example given, the WCA is 14° and the wind is from the left; therefore, subtract 14° from true course of 090°, making the true heading 076°. [Figure 8-21]

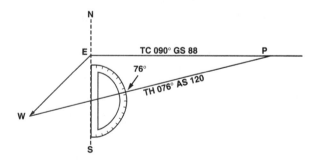

FIGURE 8-20.—*Finding true heading by direct measurement.*

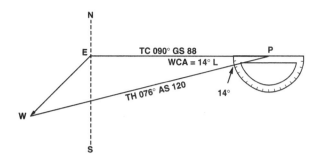

FIGURE 8-21.—Finding true heading by the wind correction angle.

After obtaining the true heading, apply the correction for magnetic variation to obtain magnetic heading, and the correction for compass deviation to obtain a compass heading. The compass heading can be used to fly to the destination by dead reckoning.

To determine the time and fuel required for the flight, first find the distance to destination by measuring the length of the course line drawn on the aeronautical chart (using the appropriate scale at the bottom of the chart). If the distance measures 220 NM, divide by the groundspeed of 88 knots, which gives 2.5 hours or (2:30) as the time required. If fuel consumption is 8 gallons an hour, 8 x 2.5 or about 20 gallons will be used. Briefly summarized, the steps in obtaining flight information are as follows:

- **TRUE COURSE**—Direction of the line connecting two desired points, drawn on the chart and measured clockwise in degrees from true north on the mid-meridian.
- **WIND CORRECTION ANGLE**—Determined from the wind triangle. (Added to TC if the wind is from the right; subtract if wind is from the left.)
- **TRUE HEADING**—The direction measured in degrees clockwise from true north, in which the nose of the plane should point to make good the desired course.
- **VARIATION**—Obtained from the isogonic line on the chart. (Added to TH if west; subtract if east.)
- **MAGNETIC HEADING**—An intermediate step in the conversion. (Obtained by applying variation to true heading.)
- **DEVIATION**—Obtained from the deviation card on the airplane. (Added to MH or subtracted from, as indicated.)
- **COMPASS HEADING**—The reading on the compass (found by applying deviation to MH) which will be followed to make good the desired course.
- **TOTAL DISTANCE**—Obtained by measuring the length of the TC line on the chart (using the scale at the bottom of the chart).
- **GROUNDSPEED**—Obtained by measuring the length of the TC line on the wind triangle (using the scale employed for drawing the diagram).
- **TIME FOR FLIGHT**— Total distance divided by groundspeed.
- **FUEL RATE**—Predetermined gallons per hour used at cruising speed.

NOTE: Additional fuel for adequate reserve should be added as a safety measure.

FLIGHT PLANNING

Title 14 of the Code of Federal Regulations (14 CFR) part 91 states, in part, that before beginning a flight, the pilot in command of an aircraft shall become familiar with all available information concerning that flight. For flights not in the vicinity of an airport, this must include information on available current weather reports and forecasts, fuel requirements, alternatives available if the planned flight cannot be completed, and any known traffic delays reported by air traffic control (ATC).

Careful preflight planning is extremely important. With adequate planning, the pilot can complete the flight with greater confidence, ease, and safety. Statistics show inadequate preflight planning is a significant cause of fatal accidents.

Assembling Necessary Material

The pilot should collect the necessary material well before the flight to be sure nothing is missing. An appropriate current sectional chart and charts for areas adjoining the flight route should be among this material if the route of flight is near the border of a chart.

Additional equipment should include a flight computer or electronic calculator, plotter, and any other item appropriate to the particular flight—for example, if a night flight is to be undertaken, carry a flashlight; if a flight is over desert country, carry a supply of water and other necessities.

Weather Check

It may be wise to check the weather before continuing with other aspects of flight planning to see, first of all, if the flight is feasible and, if it is, which route is best. Chapter 5 on weather discusses obtaining a weather briefing.

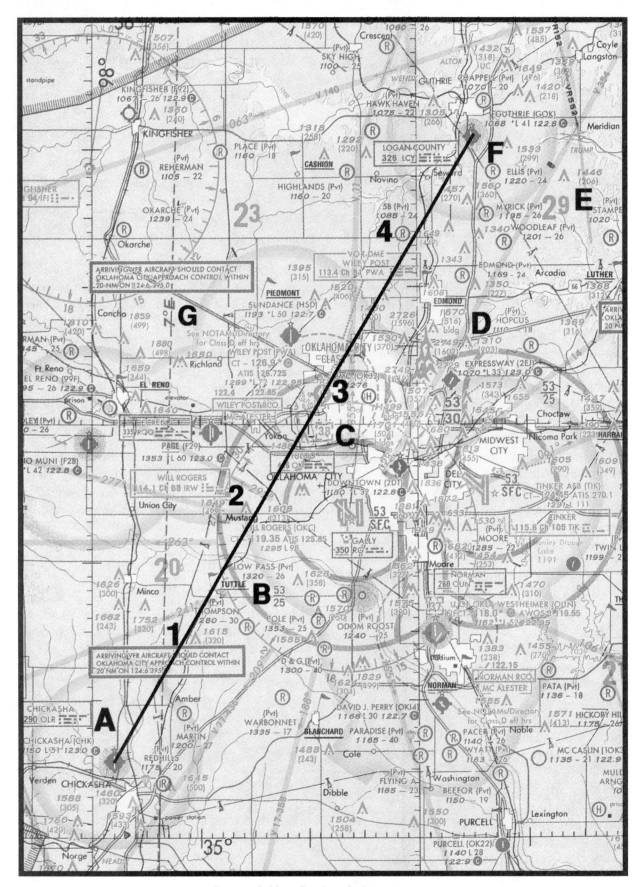

FIGURE 8-22.—Sectional chart excerpt.

Use of the Airport/Facility Directory

Study available information about each airport at which a landing is intended. This should include a study of the Notices to Airmen (NOTAMs) and the Airport/Facility Directory. This includes location, elevation, runway and lighting facilities, available services, availability of aeronautical advisory station frequency (UNICOM), types of fuel available (use to decide on refueling stops), AFSS/FSS located on the airport, control tower and ground control frequencies, traffic information, remarks, and other pertinent information. The NOTAMs, issued every 14 days, should be checked for additional information on hazardous conditions or changes that have been made since issuance of the Airport/Facility Directory.

The sectional chart bulletin subsection should be checked for major changes that have occurred since the last publication date of each sectional chart being used. Remember, the chart may be up to 6 months old. The effective date of the chart appears at the top of the front of the chart.

The Airport/Facility Directory will generally have the latest information pertaining to such matters and should be used in preference to the information on the back of the chart, if there are differences.

Airplane Flight Manual or Pilot's Operating Handbook

The Airplane Flight Manual or Pilot's Operating Handbook should be checked to determine the proper loading of the airplane (weight and balance data). The weight of the usable fuel and drainable oil aboard must be known. Also, check the weight of the passengers, the weight of all baggage to be carried, and the empty weight of the airplane to be sure that the total weight does not exceed the maximum allowable. The distribution of the load must be known to tell if the resulting center of gravity is within limits. Be sure to use the latest weight and balance information in the FAA-approved Airplane Flight Manual or other permanent aircraft records, as appropriate, to obtain empty weight and empty weight center-of-gravity information.

Determine the takeoff and landing distances from the appropriate charts, based on the calculated load, elevation of the airport, and temperature; then compare these distances with the amount of runway available. Remember, the heavier the load and the higher the elevation, temperature, or humidity, the longer the takeoff roll and landing roll and the lower the rate of climb.

Check the fuel consumption charts to determine the rate of fuel consumption at the estimated flight altitude and power settings. Calculate the rate of fuel consumption, then compare it with the estimated time for the flight so that refueling points along the route can be included in the plan.

CHARTING THE COURSE

Once the weather has been checked and some preliminary planning done, it is time to chart the course and determine the data needed to accomplish the flight. The following sections will provide a logical sequence to follow in charting the course, filling out a flight log, and filing a flight plan. In the following example, a trip is planned based on the following data and the sectional chart excerpt in figure 8-22.

Route of flight: Chickasha Airport direct to Guthrie Airport

True Airspeed (TAS)	115 knots
Winds Aloft	360° at 10 knots
Usable fuel	38 gallons
Fuel Rate	8 GPH
Deviation	+2°

Steps in Charting the Course

The following is a suggested sequence for arriving at the pertinent information for the trip. As information is determined, it may be noted as illustrated in the example of a flight log in figure 8-23. Where calculations are required, the pilot may use a mathematical formula or a manual or electronic flight computer. If unfamiliar with how to use a manual or electronic computer competently, it would be advantageous to read the operation manual and work several practice problems at this point.

First draw a line from Chickasha Airport (point A) directly to Guthrie Airport (point F). The course line should begin at the center of the airport of departure and end at the center of the destination airport. If the route is direct, the course line will consist of a single straight line. If the route is not direct, it will consist of two or more straight line segments—for example, a VOR station which is off the direct route, but which will make navigating easier, may be chosen (radio navigation is discussed later in this chapter).

Appropriate checkpoints should be selected along the route and noted in some way. These should be easy-to-locate points such as large towns, large lakes and rivers, or combinations of recognizable points such as towns with an airport, towns with a network of highways and railroads entering and departing, etc. Normally, choose only towns indicated by splashes of yellow on the chart. Do not choose towns represented by a small circle—these may turn out to be only a half-dozen houses. (In isolated areas, however, towns represented by a small circle can be prominent checkpoints.) For this trip, four checkpoints have been selected. Checkpoint 1 consists of a tower located east of the course and can be further identified by the highway and railroad track which almost parallels the course at this point. Checkpoint 2 is the obstruction just to the west of the course and can be further identified by Will Rogers Airport which is directly to the east. Checkpoint 3 is Wiley Post Airport which the aircraft should fly directly over. Checkpoint 4 is a private non-surfaced airport to the west of the course and can be further identified by the railroad track and highway to the east of the course.

The course and areas on either side of the planned route should be checked to determine if there is any type of airspace with which the pilot should be concerned or which has special operational requirements. For this trip, it should be noted that the course will pass through a segment of the Class C airspace surrounding Will Rogers Airport where the floor of the airspace is 2,500 feet mean sea level (MSL) and the ceiling is 5,300 feet MSL (point B). Also, there is Class D airspace from the surface to 3,800 feet MSL surrounding Wiley Post Airport (point C) during the time the control tower is in operation.

Study the terrain and obstructions along the route. This is necessary to determine the highest and lowest elevations as well as the highest obstruction to be encountered so that an appropriate altitude which will conform to part 91 regulations can be selected. If the flight is to be flown at an altitude more than 3,000 feet above the terrain, conformance to the cruising altitude appropriate to the direction of flight is required. Check the route for particularly rugged terrain so it can be avoided. Areas where a takeoff or landing will be made should be carefully checked for tall obstructions. TV transmitting towers may extend to altitudes over 1,500 feet above the surrounding terrain. It is essential that pilots be aware of their presence and location. For this trip, it should be noted

that the tallest obstruction is part of a series of antennas with a height of 2,749 feet MSL (point D). The highest elevation should be located in the northeast quadrant and is 2,900 feet MSL (point E).

Since the wind is no factor and it is desirable and within the airplane's capability to fly above the Class C and D airspace to be encountered, an altitude of 5,500 feet MSL will be chosen. This altitude also gives adequate clearance of all obstructions as well as conforms to the part 91 requirement to fly at an altitude of odd thousand plus 500 feet when on a magnetic course between 0 and 179°.

Next, the pilot may want to measure the total distance of the course as well as the distance between checkpoints. The total distance is 53 NM and the distance between checkpoints is as noted on the flight log in figure 8-23.

After determining the distance, the true course should be measured. If using a plotter, follow the directions on the plotter. The true course is 031°. Once the true heading is established, the pilot can determine the compass heading. This is done by following the formula given earlier in this chapter. The formula is:

$$TC \pm WCA = TH \pm VAR = MH \pm DEV = CH$$

The wind correction angle can be determined by using a manual or electronic flight computer. Using a wind of 360° at 10 knots, it is determined the WCA is 3° left. This is subtracted from the TC making the TH 28°. Next, the pilot should locate the isogonic line closest to the route of the flight to determine variation. Point G in figure 8-22 shows the variation to be 7 °E which means it should be subtracted from the TH giving an MH of 21°. Next, add 2° to the MH for the deviation correction. This gives the pilot the compass heading which is 23°.

Next, the groundspeed should be determined. This can be done using a manual or electronic calculator. It is determined the GS is 106 knots. Based on this information, the total trip time, as well as time between checkpoints, and the fuel burned can be determined. These calculations can be done mathematically or by using a manual or electronic calculator.

For this trip, the GS is 106 knots and the total time is 35 minutes (30 minutes plus 5 minutes for climb) with a fuel burn of 4.7 gallons. Refer to the flight log in figure 8-23 for the time between checkpoints.

As the trip progresses, the pilot can note headings and time and make adjustments in heading, groundspeed, and time.

COURSE	TC	WIND		WCA	TH	VAR	MH	DEV	CH	TOTAL	GS	TOTAL	FUEL	TOTAL
		KNOTS	FROM	R+ L-		W+ E-				MILES		TIME	RATE	FUEL
From:Chickasha	031°	10	360°	3° L	28	7° E	21°	+2°	23	53	106kts	35 mins	8 GPH	38 gal
To: Guthrie														
From:														
To:														

PLANE IDENTIFICATION **N123DB**   DATE

VISUAL FLIGHT LOG

TIME OF DEPARTURE	NAVIGATION AIDS	COURSE		DISTANCE		ELAPSED TIME		GS	CH	REMARKS
POINT OF DEPARTURE Chickasha Airport	NAVAID IDENT. FREQ.	TO	FROM	POINT TO POINT CUMULATIVE		ESTIMATED ACTUAL		ESTIMATED ACTUAL	ESTIMATED ACTUAL	WEATHER AIRSPACE ETC.
CHECKPOINTS #1				11 NM		6 MIN +5		106 kts	023°	
#2				10NM	21 NM	6 MIN		106 kts	023°	
#3				10.5 NM	31.5 NM	6 MIN		106 kts	023°	
#4				13 NM	44.5 NM	7 MIN		106 kts	023°	
DESTINATION Guthrie Airport				8.5 NM	53 NM	5 MIN				

FIGURE 8-23.—*Pilot's planning sheet and visual flight log.*

FILING A VFR FLIGHT PLAN

Filing a flight plan is not required by regulations; however, it is a good operating practice, since the information contained in the flight plan can be used in search and rescue in the event of an emergency.

Flight plans can be filed in the air by radio, but it is best to file a flight plan either in person at the FSS or by phone just before departing. After takeoff, contact the FSS by radio and give them the takeoff time so the flight plan can be activated.

When a VFR flight plan is filed, it will be held by the FSS until 1 hour after the proposed departure time and then canceled unless: the actual departure time is received; or a revised proposed departure time is received; or at the time of filing, the FSS is informed that the proposed departure time will be met, but actual time cannot be given because of inadequate communication. The FSS specialist who accepts the flight plan will not inform the pilot of this procedure, however.

Figure 8-24 shows the flight plan form a pilot files with the Flight Service Station. When filing a flight plan by telephone or radio, give the information in the order of the numbered spaces. This enables the FSS specialist to copy the information more efficiently. Most of the spaces are either self-explanatory or nonapplicable to the VFR flight plan (such as item 13). However, some spaces may need explanation.

Item 3 asks for the aircraft type and special equipment. An example would be C-150/X which means the aircraft has no transponder. A listing of special equipment codes is listed in the Aeronautical Information Manual.

Item 6 asks for the proposed departure time in Universal Coordinated Time (indicated by the "Z").

Item 7 asks for the cruising altitude. Normally "VFR" can be entered in this block, since the pilot will choose a cruising altitude to conform to FAA regulations.

Item 8 asks for the route of flight. If the flight is to be direct, enter the word "direct;" if not, enter the actual route to be followed such as via certain towns or navigation aids.

FLIGHT PLAN

1. TYPE	2. AIRCRAFT IDENTIFICATION	3. AIRCRAFT TYPE/ SPECIAL EQUIPMENT	4. TRUE AIRSPEED	5. DEPARTURE POINT	6. DEPARTURE TIME		7. CRUISING ALTITUDE
X VFR IFR DVFR	N123DB	C150/X	115 KTS	CHICKASHA AIRPORT	PROPOSED (Z) 1400Z	ACTUAL (Z)	5500

8. ROUTE OF FLIGHT
Chickasha direct Guthrie

9. DESTINATION (Name of airport and city)	10. EST. TIME ENROUTE		11. REMARKS
Guthrie Airport Guthrie, OK	HOURS	MINUTES 35	

12. FUEL ON BOARD		13. ALTERNATE AIRPORT(S)	14. PILOT'S NAME, ADDRESS & TELEPHONE NUMBER & AIRCRAFT HOME BASE	15. NUMBER ABOARD
HOURS 4	MINUTES 45		Jane Smith Aero Air Oklahoma City, OK (405) 555-4149	1

16. COLOR OF AIRCRAFT	CLOSE VFR FLIGHT PLAN WITH ___McAlester___ FSS ON ARRIVAL
Red/White	

FIGURE 8-24.—Flight plan form.

Item 10 asks for the estimated time en route. In the sample flight plan, 5 minutes was added to the total time to allow for the climb.

Item 12 asks for the fuel on board in hours and minutes. This is determined by dividing the total usable fuel aboard in gallons by the estimated rate of fuel consumption in gallons.

Remember, there is every advantage in filing a flight plan; but do not forget to close the flight plan on arrival. Do this by telephone with the nearest FSS, if possible, to avoid radio congestion. If there is no FSS near the point of landing, the flight plan may be closed by radio with the nearest FSS upon arrival at the destination airport.

RADIO NAVIGATION

Most airplanes flown in today's environment are equipped with radios that provide a means of navigation and communication with ground stations.

Advances in navigational radio receivers installed in airplanes, the development of aeronautical charts which show the exact location of ground transmitting stations and their frequencies, along with refined cockpit instrumentation make it possible for pilots to navigate with precision to almost any point desired. Although precision in navigation is obtainable through the proper use of this equipment, beginning pilots should use this equipment to supplement navigation by visual reference to the ground (pilotage). If this is done, it provides the pilot with an effective safeguard against disorientation in the event of radio malfunction.

There are four radio navigation systems available for use for VFR navigation. These are:

- VHF Omnidirectional Range (VOR)
- Nondirectional Radiobeacon (NDB)
- Long Range Navigation (LORAN-C)
- Global Positioning System (GPS)

Very High Frequency (VHF) Omnidirectional Range (VOR)

The word "omni" means all, and an omnidirectional range is a VHF radio transmitting ground station that projects straight line courses (radials) from the station in all directions. From a top view, it can be visualized as being similar to the spokes from the hub of a wheel. The distance VOR radials are projected depends upon the power output of the transmitter.

The course or radials projected from the station are referenced to magnetic north. Therefore, a radial is defined as a line of magnetic bearing extending outward from the VOR station. Radials are identified by numbers beginning with 001, which is 1° east of magnetic north, and progress in sequence through all the degrees of a circle until reaching 360. To aid in orientation, a compass rose reference to magnetic north is superimposed on aeronautical charts at the station location.

VOR ground stations transmit within a VHF frequency band of 108.0 - 117.95 MHz. Because the equipment is VHF, the signals transmitted are subjected to line-of-sight restrictions. Therefore, its range varies in direct proportion to the altitude of

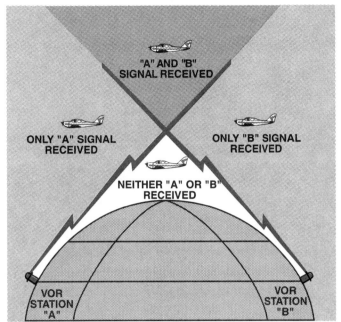

FIGURE 8-25.—VHF transmissions follow a line-of-sight course.

receiving equipment. Generally, the reception range of the signals at an altitude of 1,000 feet above ground level is about 40 to 45 miles. This distance increases with altitude. [Figure 8-25]

For the purpose of this discussion, the term "VOR" will be used to include both VOR and VORTAC. Briefly, a VORTAC station provides, in addition to azimuth information, range information. If the airplane is equipped with distance measuring equipment (DME), the distance from the station in nautical miles is displayed on the instrument.

VORs and VORTACs are classed according to operational use. There are three classes:

- T (Terminal)
- L (Low altitude)
- H (High altitude)

The normal useful range for the various classes is shown in the following table:

VOR/VORTAC NAVAIDS
Normal Usable Altitudes and Radius Distances

Class	Distance Altitudes	(Miles)
T	12,000' and below	25
L	Below 18,000'	40
H	Below 18,000'	40
H	Within the conterminous 48 states only, between 14,500 and 17,999'	100
H	18,000' -FL 450	130
H	Above FL 450	100

The useful range of certain facilities may be less than 50 miles. For further information concerning these restrictions, refer to the Comm/NAVAID Remarks in the Airport/Facility Directory.

The accuracy of course alignment of VOR radials is considered to be excellent. It is generally within plus or minus 1°. However, certain parts of the VOR receiver equipment deteriorate, and this affects its accuracy. This is particularly true at great distances from the VOR station. The best assurance of maintaining an accurate VOR receiver is periodic checks and calibrations. VOR accuracy checks are not a regulatory requirement for VFR flight. However, to assure accuracy of the equipment, these checks should be accomplished quite frequently along with a complete calibration each year. The following means are provided for pilots to check VOR accuracy:

- FAA VOR test facility (VOT);
- certified airborne checkpoints; and
- certified ground checkpoints located on airport surfaces.

A list of these checkpoints is published in the Airport/Facility Directory.

Basically, these checks consist of verifying that the VOR radials the airplane equipment receives are aligned with the radials the station transmits. There are not specific tolerances in VOR checks required for VFR flight. But as a guide to assure acceptable accuracy, the required IFR tolerances can be used which are ±4° for ground checks and ±6° for airborne checks. These checks can be performed by the pilot.

The VOR transmitting station can be positively identified by its Morse code identification or by a recorded voice identification which states the name of the station followed by the word "VOR." Many Flight Service Stations transmit voice messages on the same frequency that the VOR operates. Voice transmissions should not be relied upon to identify stations, because many FSS's remotely transmit over several omniranges which have different names than the transmitting FSS. If the VOR is out of service for maintenance, the coded identification is removed and not transmitted. This serves to alert pilots that this station should not be used for navigation. VOR receivers are designed with an alarm flag to indicate when signal strength is inadequate to operate the navigational equipment. This happens if the airplane is too far from the VOR or the airplane is too low and therefore, is out of the line-of-sight of the transmitting signals.

Using the VOR

Using the VOR is quite simple once the basic concept is understood. The following information, coupled with practice in actually using this equipment, should erase all the mysteries and also provide a real sense of security in navigating with the VOR.

In review, for VOR radio navigation, there are two components required: the ground transmitter and the aircraft receiving equipment. The ground transmitter is located at specific positions on the ground and transmits on an assigned frequency. The aircraft equipment includes a receiver with a tuning device and a VOR or omninavigation instrument. The navigation instrument consists of (1) an omnibearing selector (OBS) sometimes referred to as the course selector, (2) a course deviation indicator needle (Left-Right Needle), and (3) a TO-FROM indicator.

The course selector is an azimuth dial that can be rotated to select a desired radial or to determine the radial over which the aircraft is flying. In addition, the magnetic course "TO" or "FROM" the station can be determined.

When the course selector is rotated, it moves the course deviation indicator or needle to indicate the position of the radial relative to the aircraft. If the course selector is rotated until the deviation needle is centered, the radial (magnetic course "FROM" the station) or its reciprocal (magnetic course "TO" the station) can be determined. The course deviation needle will also move to the right or left if the aircraft is flown or drifting away from the radial which is set in the course selector.

By centering the needle, the course selector will

indicate either the course "FROM" the station or the course "TO" the station. If the flag displays a "TO," the course shown on the course selector must be flown to the station. If "FROM" is displayed and the course shown if followed, the aircraft will be flown away from the station. [Figure 8-26]

FIGURE 8-26.—VOR indicator.

Tracking with Omni

The following describes a step-by-step procedure to use when tracking to and from a VOR station. Figure 8-27 illustrates the discussion:

- First, tune the VOR receiver to the frequency of the selected VOR station. For example: 115.0 to receive Bravo VOR. Next, check the identifiers to verify that the desired VOR is being received. As soon as the VOR is properly tuned, the course deviation needle will deflect either left or right; then rotate the azimuth dial to the course selector until the course deviation needle centers and the TO-FROM indicates "TO." If the needle centers with a "FROM" indication, the azimuth should be rotated 180° because, in this case, it is desired to fly "TO" the station. Now, turn the aircraft to the heading indicated on the omni azimuth dial or course selector. In this example 350°.

- If a heading of 350° is maintained with a wind from the right as shown, the airplane will drift to the left of the intended track. As the airplane drifts off course, the VOR course deviation needle will gradually move to the right of center or indicate the direction of the desired radial or track.

• To return to the desired radial, the aircraft heading must be altered approximately 30° to the right. As the aircraft returns to the desired track, the deviation needle will slowly return to center. When centered, the aircraft will be on the desired radial and a left turn must be made toward, but not to the original heading of 350° because a wind drift correction must be established. The amount of correction depends upon the strength of the wind. If the wind velocity is unknown, a trial and error method can be used to find the correct heading. Assume, for this example a 10° correction or a heading of 360° is maintained.

• While maintaining a heading of 360°, assume that the course deviation begins to move to the left. This means that the wind correction of 10° is too great and the airplane is flying to the right of course. A slight turn to the left should be made to permit the airplane to return to the desired radial.

• When the deviation needle centers, a small wind drift correction of 5° or a heading correction of 355° should be flown. If this correction is adequate, the airplane will remain on the radial. If not, small variation in heading should be made to keep the needle centered, and consequently keep the airplane on the radial.

• As the VOR station is passed, the course deviation needle will fluctuate then settle down, and the "TO" indication will change to "FROM." If the aircraft passes to one side of the station, the needle will deflect in the direction of the station as the indicator changes to "FROM."

• Generally, the same techniques apply when tracking outbound as those used for tracking inbound. If the intent is to fly over the station and track outbound on the reciprocal of the inbound radial, the course selector should not be changed. Corrections are made in the same manner to keep the needle centered. The only difference is that the omni will indicate "FROM."

• If tracking outbound on a course other than the reciprocal of the inbound radial, this new course or radial must be set in the course selector and a turn made to intercept this course. After this course is reached, tracking procedures are the same as previously discussed.

Tips on Using the VOR

• Positively identify the station by its code or voice identification.

• Keep in mind that VOR signals are "line-of-

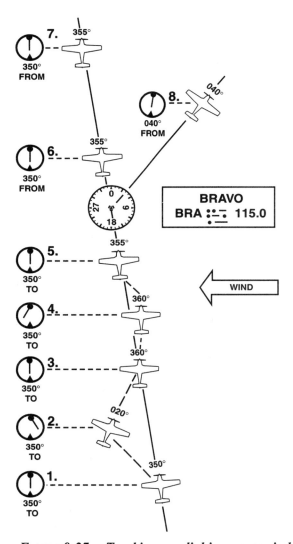

FIGURE 8-27.—*Tracking a radial in a crosswind.*

sight." A weak signal or no signal at all will be received if the aircraft is too low or too far from the station.

• When navigating to a station, determine the inbound radial and use this radial. If the aircraft drifts, do not reset the course selector, but correct for drift and fly a heading that will compensate for wind drift.

• If minor needle fluctuations occur, avoid changing headings immediately. Wait momentarily to see if the needle recenters; if it doesn't, then correct.

• When flying "TO" a station, always fly the selected course with a "TO" indication. When flying "FROM" a station, always fly the selected course with a "FROM" indication. If this is not done, the action of the course deviation needle will be reversed. To further explain this reverse action, if the aircraft is flown toward a station with a "FROM" indication or away from a station with a "TO" indication, the course deviation needle will indicate in an opposite direction to that which it should. For example, if the aircraft drifts to the right of a radial being flown, the needle will move to the right or point away from the radial. If the aircraft drifts to the left of the radial being flown, the needle will move left or in the opposite direction of the radial.

Automatic Direction Finder

Many general aviation-type airplanes are equipped with automatic direction finder (ADF) radio receiving equipment. To navigate using the ADF, the pilot tunes the receiving equipment to a ground station known as a NONDIRECTIONAL RADIOBEACON (NDB). The NDB stations normally operate in a low or medium frequency band of 200 to 415 kHz. The frequencies are readily available on aeronautical charts or in the Airport/Facility Directory.

All radiobeacons except compass locators transmit a continuous three-letter identification in code except during voice transmissions. A compass locator, which is associated with an Instrument Landing System, transmits a two-letter identification.

Standard broadcast stations can also be used in conjunction with ADF. Positive identification of all radio stations is extremely important and this is particularly true when using standard broadcast stations for navigation.

Nondirectional radiobeacons have one advantage over the VOR. This advantage is that low or medium frequencies are not affected by line-of-sight. The signals follow the curvature of the Earth; therefore, if the aircraft is within the range of the station, the signals can be received regardless of altitude.

The following table gives the class of NDB stations, their power, and usable range:

NONDIRECTIONAL RADIOBEACON (NDB)
(Usable Radius Distances for All Altitudes)

Class	Power (Watts)	Distance (Miles)
Compass Locator	Under 25	15
MH	Under 50	25
H	50-1999	*50
HH	2000 or more	75

*Service range of individual facilities may be less than 50 miles.

One of the disadvantages that should be considered when using low frequency for navigation is that low-frequency signals are very susceptible to electrical disturbances, such as lighting. These disturbances create excessive static, needle deviations, and signal fades. There may be interference from distant stations. Pilots should know the conditions under which these disturbances can occur so they can be more alert to possible interference when using the ADF.

Basically, the ADF aircraft equipment consists of a tuner, which is used to set the desired station frequency, and the navigational display.

The navigational display consists of a dial upon which the azimuth is printed, and a needle which rotates around the dial and points to the station to which the receiver is tuned.

Some of the ADF dials can be rotated so as to align the azimuth with the aircraft heading, others are fixed with 0° representing the nose of the aircraft, and 180° representing the tail. Only the fixed azimuth dial will be discussed in this handbook. [Figure 8-28]

FIGURE 8-28.—ADF with fixed azimuth and magnetic compass.

Figure 8-29 illustrates the following terms that are used with the ADF and should be understood by the pilot.

- **Relative Bearing**—is the value to which the indicator (needle) points on the azimuth dial. When using a fixed dial, this number is relative to the nose of the aircraft and is the angle measured clockwise from the nose of the aircraft to a line drawn from the aircraft to the station.

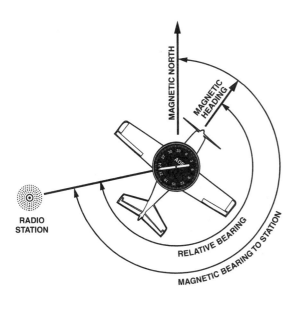

FIGURE 8-29.—ADF terms.

• **Magnetic Bearing** —"TO" the station is the angle formed by a line drawn from the aircraft to the station and a line drawn from the aircraft to magnetic north. The magnetic bearing to the station can be determined by adding the relative bearing to the magnetic heading of the aircraft. For example, if the relative bearing is 060° and the magnetic heading is 130°, the magnetic bearing to the station is 060° plus 130° or 190°. This means that in still air a magnetic heading of approximately 190° would be flown to the station. If the total is greater than 360°, subtract 360° from the total to obtain the magnetic bearing to the station. For example, if the relative bearing is 270° and magnetic heading is 300°, 360° is subtracted from the total, or 570° − 360° = 210°, which is the magnetic bearing to the station.

To determine the magnetic bearing "FROM" the station, 180° is added to or subtracted from the magnetic bearing to the station. This is the reciprocal bearing and is used when plotting position fixes.

Keep in mind that the needle of fixed azimuth points to the station in relation to the nose of the aircraft. If the needle is deflected 30° to the left or a relative bearing of 330°, this means that the station is located 30° left. If the aircraft is turned left 30°, the needle will move to the right 30° and indicate a relative bearing of 0° or the aircraft will be pointing toward the station. If the pilot continues flight toward the station keeping the needle on 0°, the procedure is called homing to the station. If a crosswind exists, the ADF needle will continue to drift away from zero. To keep the needle on zero, the aircraft must be turned slightly resulting in a curved flightpath to the station. Homing to the station is a common procedure, but

results in drifting downwind, thus lengthening the distance to the station.

Tracking to the station requires correcting for wind drift and results in maintaining flight along a straight track or bearing to the station. When the wind drift correction is established, the ADF needle will indicate the amount of correction to the right or left. For instance, if the magnetic bearing to the station is 340°, a correction for a left crosswind would result in a magnetic heading of 330°, and the ADF needle would indicate 10° to the right or a relative bearing of 010°. [Figure 8-30]

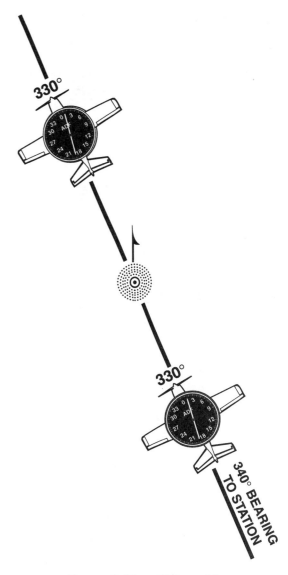

FIGURE 8-30.—ADF tracking.

When tracking away from the station, wind corrections are made similar to tracking to the station but the ADF needle points toward the tail of the aircraft or the 180° position on the azimuth dial. Attempting to keep the ADF needle on the 180Υ position during winds results in the aircraft flying a curved flight leading further and further from the desired track. To correct for wind when tracking outbound, correction should be made in the direction opposite of that in which the needle is pointing.

Although the ADF is not as popular as the VOR for radio navigation, with proper precautions and intelligent use, the ADF can be a valuable aid to navigation.

Other Navigational Systems

There are other navigational systems which are more advanced such as long range navigation (LORAN-C) and global positioning system (GPS).

The long range navigation uses a network of land-based radio transmitters developed to provide an accurate system for long range navigation. The system is based upon the measurement of the difference in time of arrival of pulses of radio-frequency energy radiated by a group or chain of transmitters which are separated by hundreds of miles.

The global positioning system is a satellite-based radio positioning, navigation, and time-transfer system developed by the U.S. Department of Defense. The concept of GPS is based on accurate and continuous knowledge of the spatial position of each satellite in the system. GPS provides accurate information 24 hours a day and is unaffected by the weather.

If more detailed information on these systems is desired, the pilot may reference the Aeronautical Information Manual. Since both LORAN and GPS have various presentations, a pilot should refer to the Aircraft Flight Manual for the individual make and model for proper usage.

CHAPTER 9

AEROMEDICAL INFORMATION

Introduction

A pilot is responsible for maintaining an awareness of the mental and physical standards required for operating an aircraft. This chapter provides information on medical certification and on aeromedical factors with which pilots must be concerned in their flying activities.

Obtaining a Medical Certificate

All pilots except those with a recreational pilot certificate or those flying gliders or free air balloons must possess a valid medical certificate in order to exercise the privileges of their airman certificates. If a medical certificate is not required, then pilots must certify that they have no known medical condition which would prohibit them from exercising the privileges of the certificate.

The periodic medical examinations required for medical certification are conducted by designated aviation medical examiners, who are physicians with a special interest in aviation safety and training in aviation medicine.

The standards for medical certification are contained in 14 CFR part 67. The requirements for obtaining medical certification are contained in 14 CFR part 61.

Prior to beginning flight training, a flight instructor should interview the prospective student about any health conditions and determine the ultimate goal of the student as a pilot. Good advice would be to obtain the class of medical certificate required before beginning flight training. Finding out immediately whether the student is medically qualified could save time and money.

Students who have physical limitations such as impaired vision, loss of a limb, hearing impairment, etc., may possibly be issued a medical certificate valid for "Student Pilot Privileges Only." This kind of medical certificate will allow them to continue flight training and to prepare for the pilot certification practical test. During pilot training, flight instructors should ensure that students can perform all required tasks safely to the required standards. Special devices may be necessary to allow students to manipulate the flight controls. If unable to perform certain tasks, the student may have a limitation placed on his/her pilot certificate. For example, impaired hearing would require the limitation "Not Valid for Flight Requiring the Use of Radio." Another limitation may allow the pilot to only operate a certain make and model airplane such as one without rudder pedals.

When students with a physical limitation meet all of the knowledge, experience, and proficiency requirements, they should write a letter to the FAA Regional Flight Surgeon requesting a special medical flight test. The student's medical file is reviewed and a Letter of Authorization or Denial is issued to the student. If the test is authorized, the student will be instructed to contact the nearest Flight Standards District Office (FSDO) and request a test. After showing that they can operate the airplane with the normal level of safety, they are issued a waiver or statement of demonstrated ability (SODA). This waiver or SODA is valid as long as their physical impairment does not worsen. Additional information can be obtained on this subject at the local FSDO. Unless otherwise limited, medical certificates are valid for a period of time specified in 14 CFR part 61.

The medical certificate for a private pilot is a third class. It is valid for 3 years for those who are under 40 years of age and then it is valid for 2 years.

A commercial pilot certificate requires at least a second class medical certificate which is valid for 1 year.

An airline transport pilot certificate requires a first class medical certificate which is valid for 6 months.

A pilot should note that the class of medical required applies only when exercising the privilege of the certificate for which it was required. This being the case, a first class certificate would be valid for 1 year if exercising the privileges of a commercial certificate and 2 or 3 years, as appropriate for exercising the privileges of a private certificate. The same applies for a second class certificate.

HEALTH FACTORS AFFECTING PILOT PERFORMANCE

Minor illnesses, especially those requiring medications can seriously degrade pilot performance. Even many normal occurrences of everyday living such as fatigue, stress, allergies, etc., can affect pilot performance. The safest decision when feeling a little under par is not to fly. If unsure, consult a Medical Examiner.

Regulations prohibit pilots from performing crewmember duties while using any medication that affects the pilot's ability to operate an aircraft safely. Over-the-counter medications may also have side-effects to the point of causing dangerous reactions. Pain relievers can cover up or mask an illness that could impair one's judgment or cause dizziness, nausea, or hyperventilation. Some medications for colds and flu may cause dizziness, blurred vision, or impairment of coordination. Bowel preparations can cause unexpected bowel activities as well as drowsiness, depression, and blurred vision. Some appetite suppressants cause excessive stimulation, dizziness, and headaches. The result of taking sleeping aids is self-explanatory.

Caffeine may appear to wake a person up, but too much can cause excessive stimulation, tremors, and even palpitations. Mixing some of these can cause unexpected results.

The Aeronautical Information Manual (AIM) also includes a discussion on pilot aeromedical factors.

Alcohol

There is only one safe rule to follow with respect to flying and the consumption of alcohol: **DON'T**. Alcohol is metabolized at a fixed rate by the human body. This rate is not altered by the use of coffee or other popular so called remedies.

Alcohol is a factor in a number of fatal general aviation accidents. In spite of the high fatality rate, some pilots are not impressed and are under the delusion that flying after a few drinks is no more dangerous then driving under the same conditions.

We must accept two simple facts. First, flying an airplane is more complex than the two dimensional demands of driving an automobile. Second, altitude multiplies the effects of alcohol on the body.

For all practical purposes, only the brain gets "drunk." When a person drinks, the alcohol immediately begins to pass from the stomach to the bloodstream. Two ounces of bourbon will be absorbed by the bloodstream in 10 minutes, 4 ounces in 30 minutes. Alcohol is carried to all parts of the body with varying effects, but the brain is most affected. Alcohol numbs the brain in the area where our thinking takes place, then proceeds to the area that controls body movement. Coordination is affected, eyes fail to focus, and hands lose their dexterity.

14 CFR part 91 prohibits pilots from performing crewmember duties within 8 hours after drinking any alcoholic beverage or being under the influence of alcohol. The best rule is to allow at least 12 to 24 hours between "bottle and throttle" depending on the amount of alcohol consumed.

Fatigue

Fatigue is a normal occurrence of everyday living. Fatigue is feeling tired after long periods of physical or mental strain. Some common causes are strong emotional pressure, heavy mental workload, monotony, lack of sleep, etc. Alertness and coordination suffer while performance and judgment become impaired.

Anxiety

Anxiety is a state of uneasiness arising from fear. It slows down the learning process. Reactions vary from a person who reacts to "do something even if it's wrong" to a person who "freezes" and refuses to act. Others may do things without rational thought or reason.

Anxiety can be countered by learning to cope with fear and realizing that fear is a normal reaction. Anxiety for student pilots is often associated with performing certain flight maneuvers. Instructors should introduce flight maneuvers with care, so that students know what to expect, and what their reactions should be. Education is the best way to cope with fear of the unknown.

Stress

Stress is defined as the body's response to demands made upon it by everyday living. In flying, these stresses consist of physical, physiological, and psychological stress. Physical stress consists of such things as cold, noise, or lack of oxygen. Physiological stress consists of fatigue, poor health, lack of food, or sleep. Psychological stress consists of emotional factors such as illness in the family, personal problems, or a high mental workload during an inflight situation.

Anything perceived as a threat causes the body to gather its resources to cope with the situation. The adrenal gland produces hormones which prepare the body to meet the threat. The heart rate quickens, certain blood vessels constrict and divert blood to the organs which will need it, and other changes take place. Normal individuals begin to respond rapidly within the limits of their experience and training. Many responses are automatic, which points to the need for proper training in all situations. The affected individual thinks and acts rapidly, often leading to stress overload. The pilot begins to use poor judgment which often leads to poor decision making. This leads to tunnel vision or concentrating on the perceived threat rather than dealing with all elements of the situation.

In student training, the best way to deal with severe stress is to terminate the flight period, return to the airport, and deal with the problem tomorrow. In other situations, pilots need to recognize the symptoms of stress or stress overload and learn how to manage it. A good physical fitness program, proper rest, and regular meals are a good beginning. The pilot should know his/her capabilities and limitations and operate within them. Avoid stressful situations such as pressing the weather or overflying that planned fuel stop.

Emotion

Being emotionally upset has the same effect on a pilot as extreme stress or fatigue. There are many causes such as divorce, loss of job, death in the family, financial trouble, etc. It causes anger, depression, and anxiety. This emotion affects judgment and alertness to a dangerous degree. Don't fly when emotionally upset.

Tobacco

At ground level, smoking reduces a person's visual acuity and dark adaptation to the extent of that encountered in flight at 8,000 feet MSL. Smoking at 10,000 feet MSL produces hypoxia equivalent to 14,000 feet. The absorption of nicotine into the blood causes a corresponding drop in blood oxygen saturation and will lead to hypoxia. Smoking causes specific physiological debilitation and diseases that are medically disqualifying for pilots. Smoke also damages gyroscopic instruments in those aircraft drawing flight deck air through the instruments, and fouls the outflow valves in pressurized aircraft.

ENVIRONMENTAL FACTORS WHICH AFFECT PILOT PERFORMANCE

Human beings, who are designed for living on Earth, must now learn to survive in a slightly different environment. The effects of a deficiency of oxygen, changing pressures on the ears and sinuses, spatial disorientation, illusions in flight, and visual requirements require procedures and aids not commonly used on the surface.

Hypoxia

Hypoxia is a deficiency of oxygen which impairs the brain functions and other organs. As we gain altitude, the atmosphere decreases in pressure. Although the air still is 21 percent oxygen, the amount of oxygen present also is decreased as the air pressure is decreased.

Night vision begins to deteriorate at about 5,000 feet MSL. From about 12,000 to 15,000 feet MSL, judgment, memory, alertness, coordination, and ability to make calculations are impaired. Some pilots might feel dizzy or drowsy. A sense of well-being (euphoria) or belligerence can occur. A pilot's performance can seriously deteriorate within 15 minutes at 15,000 feet MSL. Above 15,000 feet MSL, the periphery of the visual field grays out to a point where only central vision remains (tunnel vision). Fingernails and lips turn blue. The ability to take corrective and protective action is lost in 20 to 30 minutes at 18, 000 feet and 5 to 12 minutes at 20,000 feet MSL, followed soon thereafter by unconsciousness.

The effect of hypoxia occurs at lower altitudes with the use of some medication, smoking, alcohol, emotional stress, etc. The worst part is the fact that hypoxia is very difficult to recognize because of the gradual dulling of the senses. Since symptoms of hypoxia do not vary in an individual, the ability to recognize hypoxia can be greatly improved by experiencing and witnessing the effects of it during an altitude chamber "flight." The FAA provides this opportunity through aviation physiology training, which is conducted at the FAA Civil Aeromedical Institute (CAMI) and at many military facilities across the United States. To attend the Physiological Training Program at CAMI telephone (405) 954-6212 or write:

Mike Monroney Aeronautical Center
Airman Education Program Branch
AAM- 420 CAMI
P.O. Box 25082
Oklahoma City, OK 73125

Hyperventilation in Flight

Hyperventilation, or an abnormal increase in the volume of air breathed in and out of the lungs, can occur subconsciously when a stressful situation is encountered in flight. As hyperventilation "blows off" excessive carbon dioxide from the body, a pilot can experience symptoms of light-headedness, suffocation, drowsiness, tingling in the extremities, and coolness – and react to them with even greater hyperventilation. Incapacitation can eventually result from incoordination, disorientation, and painful muscle spasms. Finally, unconsciousness can occur.

The symptoms of hyperventilation subside within a few minutes after the rate and depth of breathing are consciously brought back under control. The buildup of carbon dioxide in the body can be hastened by controlled breathing in and out of a paper bag held over the nose and mouth.

Early symptoms of hyperventilation and hypoxia can occur at the same time. Therefore, if a pilot is using an oxygen system when symptoms are experienced, the oxygen regulator should immediately be set to deliver 100 percent oxygen, and then the system checked to assure that it has been functioning effectively before giving attention to rate and depth of breathing.

Middle Ear Discomfort or Pain

This is one environmental phenomenon that pilots and passengers are aware of immediately. Any discomfort can be relieved, and is not harmful if the eustachian tube is periodically opened to equalize pressure on each side of the ear drum. This can be accomplished by swallowing, yawning, tensing muscles in the throat; or if these do not work, by a combination of closing the mouth, pinching the nose closed, and attempting to blow through the nostrils.

Flying with any upper respiratory infection, such as a cold or sore throat, or a nasal allergic condition can produce enough congestion around the eustachian tube to make equalization difficult. An ear block produces severe ear pain and loss of hearing that can last from several hours to several days. Rupture of the ear drum can occur in flight or after landing. Fluid can accumulate in the middle ear and become infected. Adequate protection is usually not provided by decongestant sprays or drops to reduce congestion around the eustachian tubes. Oral decongestants have side effects that can significantly impair pilot performance.

During ascent and descent, air pressure in the sinuses equalizes with the aircraft cabin pressure through small openings that connect the sinuses to the nasal passages. Either an upper respiratory infection, such as a cold or sinusitis, or a nasal allergic condition can produce enough congestion around an opening to slow equalization. The difference in pressure between the sinus and cabin increases, and eventually plugs the opening. As with the ear block, the only solution is not to fly with upper respiratory problems.

Spatial Disorientation and Illusions in Flight

Many different illusions can be experienced in flight. Some can lead to spatial disorientation. Others can lead to landing errors. Illusions rank among the most common factors cited as contributing to fatal aircraft accidents.

Various complex motions and forces and certain visual scenes encountered in flight can create illusions of motion and position. Spatial disorientation from these illusions can be prevented only by visual reference to reliable, fixed points on the ground or to flight instruments.

An abrupt correction of a banked attitude, which has been entered too slowly to stimulate the motion sensing system in the inner ear (the leans) can create the illusion of banking in the opposite direction. The disoriented pilot will roll the aircraft back into its original dangerous attitude or, if level flight is maintained, will feel compelled to lean in the perceived vertical plane until this illusion subsides. Any time an attitude is maintained for an extended period, the ears will try to deceive the pilot into believing that the aircraft is in straight-and-level flight.

An abrupt head movement in a prolonged constant-rate turn that has ceased stimulating the motion sensing system can create the illusion of rotation or movement in an entirely different axis. An abrupt change from climb to straight-and-level flight can create the illusion of tumbling backwards, while an abrupt upward vertical acceleration, usually by an updraft, can create the illusion of being in a climb. The most overwhelming of all illusions in flight may be prevented by not making sudden, extreme head movements, particularly while making prolonged constant-rate turns under instrument flight rule (IFR) conditions.

Sloping cloud formations, an obscured horizon, a dark scene spread with ground lights and stars, and certain geometric patterns of ground light can create illusions of not being aligned correctly with the actual horizon. In the dark, a static light will appear to move about when stared at for a period of time. The disoriented pilot will lose control of the aircraft in attempting to align it with the light.

Various surface features and atmospheric conditions encountered in landing can create illusions of incorrect height above and distance from the runway threshold. Landing errors from these illusions can be prevented by anticipating them during approaches, aerial visual inspection of unfamiliar airports before landing, using electronic glide slope or VASI systems when available, and maintaining proficiency in landing procedures.

A narrower-than-usual runway can create the illusion that the aircraft is at a higher altitude than it actually is. A wider-than-usual runway can have the opposite effect, with the risk of leveling out high and landing hard or overshooting the runway.

An upsloping runway, upsloping terrain, or both, can create the illusion the aircraft is at a higher altitude than it actually is. A downsloping runway, downsloping approach terrain, or both, can have the opposite effect.

An absence of ground features, as when landing over water, darkened areas, and terrain made featureless by snow, can create the illusion that the aircraft is at a higher altitude than it actually is.

Rain on the windscreen can create the illusion of greater height, and atmospheric haze can give the illusion of being at a greater distance from the runway.

Lights along a straight path, such as a road, and even lights on moving trains can be mistaken for runway and approach lights. Bright runway and approach lighting systems, especially where few lights illuminate the surrounding terrain, may create the illusion of less distance to the runway.

Motion Sickness

Anyone who has experienced motion sickness knows how unpleasant it can be. Most important, it can jeopardize the pilots' flying efficiency at critical times when their skills are required the most. Student pilots sometimes experience motion sickness during early flight training. The flight instructor will usually recognize the onset of motion sickness and terminate the flight lesson. With increasing experience, the problem usually goes away.

Motion sickness is caused by continued stimulation of the inner ear which controls the sense of balance. The symptoms are progressive. Pilots may experience loss of appetite, saliva collecting in the mouth, perspiration, nausea, and possible disorientation. The head aches and there may be a tendency to vomit. If allowed to become severe enough, the pilot may become incapacitated.

Pilots who are susceptible to motion sickness should not take the preventive drugs available over the counter or by prescription. These drugs can cause drowsiness, depression of brain function, and loss of motor skills.

When suffering from motion sickness, open the air vents, loosen clothing, and use oxygen if available. Try to keep the eyes focused on a point outside the airplane and avoid unnecessary head movements. Terminate the flight as soon as possible.

Carbon Monoxide Poisoning

Carbon monoxide is a colorless, odorless, and tasteless gas contained in exhaust fumes. When breathed even in minute quantities over a period of time, it can significantly reduce the ability of the blood to carry oxygen. Consequently, effects of hypoxia occur.

Most heaters in light aircraft work by air flowing over the engine exhaust manifold. Use of these heaters while exhaust fumes are escaping though exhaust manifold cracks and seals are responsible every year for several nonfatal and fatal aircraft accidents from carbon monoxide poisoning.

A pilot who detects the odor of exhaust or experiences symptoms of headache, drowsiness, or dizziness while using the heater should suspect carbon monoxide poisoning, and immediately shut off the heater and open air vents. If symptoms are severe, or continue after landing, medical treatment should be sought.

Decompression Sickness After Scuba Diving

A pilot or passenger who intends to fly after scuba diving should allow the body sufficient time to rid itself of excess nitrogen absorbed during diving. If not, decompression sickness due to evolved gas can occur during exposure to altitude and create a serious inflight emergency.

The recommended waiting time before going to flight altitudes up to 8,000 feet MSL is at least 2 hours after diving and at least 24 hours after diving which has required controlled ascent. The waiting time before going to flight altitudes above 8,000 feet MSL should be at least 24 hours after any scuba dive. For more detailed information, contact your Medical Examiner.

Vision in Flight

Of the body senses, vision is the most important for safe flight. Major factors that determine how effectively vision can be used are the level of illumination and the technique of scanning the sky for other aircraft.

Under conditions of dim illumination, small print and colors on aeronautical charts and aircraft instruments become unreadable unless adequate cockpit lighting is available. Moreover, another aircraft must be much closer to be seen unless its navigation lights are on.

In darkness, vision becomes more sensitive to light, a process called dark adaptation. Although exposure to total darkness for at least 30 minutes is required for complete dark adaptation, the pilot can achieve a moderate degree of dark adaptation within 20 minutes under dim red cockpit lighting. Since red light severely distorts colors, especially on aeronautical charts, and can cause serious difficulty in focusing the eyes on objects inside the aircraft, its use is advisable only where optimum outside night vision capability is necessary. Even so, white cockpit lighting must be available when needed for map and instrument reading, especially under IFR conditions. Dark adaptation is impaired by exposure to cabin pressure altitudes above 5,000 feet MSL, carbon monoxide inhaled in smoking, from exhaust fumes, deficiency of Vitamin A in the diet, and by prolonged exposure to bright sunlight. The pilot should close one eye when using a light to preserve some degree of night vision.

Excessive illumination, especially from light reflected off the canopy, surfaces inside the aircraft, clouds, water, snow, and desert terrain, can produce glare, which may cause uncomfortable squinting, watering of the eyes, and even temporary blindness. Sunglasses for protection from glare should absorb at least 85 percent of visible light and all colors equally, with negligible image distortion from refractive and prismatic errors.